# Chinese Policing

Jeffrey Ian Ross
*General Editor*

Vol. 3

PETER LANG
New York • Washington, D.C./Baltimore • Bern
Frankfurt am Main • Berlin • Brussels • Vienna • Oxford

Kam C. Wong

# Chinese Policing

## HISTORY AND REFORM

PETER LANG
New York • Washington, D.C./Baltimore • Bern
Frankfurt am Main • Berlin • Brussels • Vienna • Oxford

**Library of Congress Cataloging-in-Publication Data**

Wong, Kam C.
Chinese policing: history and reform / Kam C. Wong.
p. cm. — (New perspectives in criminology and criminal justice; v. 3)
Includes bibliographical references and index.
1. Criminal justice, Administration of—China—History.
2. Police—China—History. I. Title.
HV9960.C53W66 363.20951—dc22 2008049789
ISBN 978-1-4331-0017-8 (hardcover)
ISBN 978-1-4331-0016-1 (paperback)
ISSN 1555-3418

Bibliographic information published by **Die Deutsche Bibliothek**.
**Die Deutsche Bibliothek** lists this publication in the "Deutsche Nationalbibliografie"; detailed bibliographic data is available on the Internet at http://dnb.ddb.de/.

The cover image is intended to represent the theme of the book: the need to look behind the officer's back to fully understand Chinese policing.

Cover design by Clear Point Designs

The paper in this book meets the guidelines for permanence and durability of the Committee on Production Guidelines for Book Longevity of the Council of Library Resources.

Printed in the United States of America

To my wife, Rainbow,
who makes my life colorful and our family spiritually rich

# CONTENTS

# SERIES EDITOR'S FOREWORD

Comparison, whether done in a qualitative or a quantitative manner, is the hallmark of social science research. Over the past two decades an increasing number of criminologists and criminal justice researchers have been conducting comparative research. Sometimes this work compares an entire country's criminal justice system with that of another country, while at other times it analyzes a process or procedure between two agencies in distant lands.

One area that is rich in description is the comparative analysis of police agencies. Over the past 10 years, a handful of criminologists have performed comparative studies of police agencies and policing, focusing on areas such as patrol, response time, corruption, and violence. This research is not only presented at our national and international conferences, but also published in our professional and scholarly journals and edited books.

Among those comparative studies is a growing number of English-language scholarly articles that look at policing in the People's Republic of China (PRC). These authors have used both quantitative and qualitative methods to examine various aspects of the Chinese police force, including its role and functions, system and organization, reform strategies and tactics, law and procedures, community-policing theory and practice, decision-making strategies, and citizens' attitudes toward the police. Many of these analyses have been conducted by Dr. Kam C. Wong. A recent review of literature on policing in the PRC cites Wong's research extensively; of the 44 works cited, six bore his name. In fact, Wong is recognized as one of the two most often-cited authors in this field.

As the editor of Peter Lang's series "New Perspectives in Criminology and Criminal Justice," I'm happy to introduce you to K.C. Wong's well-researched and thought-out book, *Chinese Policing*. Wong, a former Hong Kong police inspector, American-trained lawyer, and a professor of criminology/criminal justice, analyzes the unique state of policing in China. Few other researchers are willing to take the time to notice, analyze, and comprehend the nuances of police behavior in the PRC. Collecting accurate and reliable information on police conduct and interpreting it in a meaningful fashion is not a simple task, and Wong has done so with grace.

The third installment in Lang's series, *Chinese Policing* is a formidable piece of cutting-edge scholarship that pushes the boundaries of police science as well as the disciplines of comparative criminology and criminal justice.

This book is not a mere translation of Chinese government documents. Rather, Wong analyzes Western myopia when it comes to policing in the PRC. He emphasizes both overlooked and nontraditional factors involved the decisions made by police officers and agencies in the PRC in the process of fulfilling their obligations.

I'm sure that scholars, instructors, practitioners, and students in policing and law enforcement will be intrigued by Wong's book.

*Jeffrey Ian Ross, Ph.D.*

# PREFACE

The comparative study of criminal justice internationally is still in its infancy. There are two ways to do comparative studies, both of which are still rare. First, one can study particular systems in detail. These are called case studies. When this is done globally, it means using countries as the units of comparison. Second, one can compare several cases, applying a common template to each. In other words, the author selects the features to be studied in advance, using them as a lens through which to view each case. There are advantages and disadvantages to each of these approaches. Case studies provide richer detail but may not allow ready comparison. Because the features chosen for study may vary so much between cases, any subsequent comparison may become an apples-to-oranges situation. Structured comparisons of several cases, on the other hand, solve the mixed- fruit problem but may pass over unique and important features of each country. Viewing a limited array of elements also makes it more difficult to understand the causal dynamics between criminal justice and local environments, especially their history and culture.

This book by K.C. Wong is a case study, a unique as well as ambitious one. Wong is one of the few people able to overcome many of the challenges faced by scholars of Chinese criminal justice, both foreign and Chinese. He discusses these problems in detail in his first chapter. Being Chinese, Wong has access to local documentary material, historical and contemporary, not available to most foreign scholars. At the same time, because Wong has lived, studied, and worked in the United States, he is effectively bicultural. This allows him to discuss Chinese culture and history in ways that can be understood by English-speaking Westerners.

Wong has another great advantage in writing about Chinese police. He has been educated at the doctoral level in American criminology and criminal justice. As a result, he brings to bear conceptual and theoretical insights that allow the book to transcend the limitations of a case study written by Chinese scholars raised exclusively in China. Even though this book is a case study, the book facilitates comparison of China with other countries through the implicit lens of contemporary Western criminology.

Wong's study is thorough with respect to the cultural and historical development of Chinese policing. It covers the current state of knowledge about the Chinese police, its role, origins, history, cultural roots, and contemporary attempts at reform. There is one limitation to his study of Chinese policing that even he cannot surmount. The book does not provide the kind of descriptive detail about police operations and behavior that is the hallmark of police studies in the United States, Britain, Canada, and Australia. Nor does he have access to evaluations of either the crime-prevention effectiveness or behavioral rectitude of Chinese policing.

The problem here is not gaining access to material, it is the lack of a tradition of public policy research in China. From Wong's own description of Chinese documents as well as scholarship, it appears that China approaches the study of police largely from a jurisprudential point of view. That is, it treats how the police are organized, authorized, and directed in formal, meaning legal, terms. Not only is the Chinese government reluctant to let any scholar, indigenous Chinese or otherwise, get too close to operations, but it has not seen the need to do so in order to improve the effectiveness of police operations.

This attitude is not surprising. Viewed internationally, it is not China that is out of step. The behavioral or sociological study of criminal justice is still relatively uncommon outside of developed English-speaking countries and Western Europe. Wong understands this, which is another strength of the book. In terms of Western criminology, he knows what can and cannot be said with authority about Chinese policing.

Altogether, *Chinese Policing: History and Reform* is a major contribution to the field of comparative criminology as well as a unique analysis of the connections between Chinese culture and contemporary policing.

*Distinguished Professor David Bayley*
*10 August 2008*
*School of Criminal Justice*
*State University of New York*
*Albany*

# CHAPTER ONE

# The Study of Policing in China

"Everyone is entitled to his own opinions but not his own facts."

Daniel Patrick

## Introduction

Chinese policing is a neglected field of study, especially outside of China. Our knowledge about Chinese policing is sketchy, spotty, and superficial. This dearth of scholarship evidences a lack of research interest[1] and a difficulty in collecting data.[2] Until the 1990s, research into China has been handicapped by unavailability of sources, inaccessibility to places/people, scarcity of bilingual researchers,[3] and incompatibility of scholarship styles.[4] Chinese research in non-Western countries has fared no better; for example, research in Japan and Vietnam has confronted similar problems.[5]

There is a dire need for more understanding of the Chinese criminal justice system in general and policing in particular. As early as June 1909, the American Institute of Criminal Law and Criminology called for the translation of important foreign criminology works into English to facilitate cross-cultural research.[6] As recently as 1997, William Alford lamented the total misreading of Chinese legal history as a result of cultural ignorance.

In the China studies field, there long existed two parallel scholarly worlds, one Chinese, the other Western. Each of these intellectual domains has its own paradigms, traditions, agendas, methods, and findings. For example, the Western notion of police differs from that of the Chinese.[7] The Western practice of problem-oriented policing (POP) is a police outreach program. The Chinese POP is a community self-governance effort.[8] To the American, POP means discovering and eradicating the larger social and communal problem, of which the citizen's individual complaint is but a manifestation. To the Chinese, POP entails understanding and solving the problem of the citizen. Last but not least, the Western formal criminal justice system fails to capture the expansive reach,[9] holistic nature, dialectical relationship, mutual reinforcement, integrated operations and comprehensive scope of the informal social control system in China, from self-cultivation to family discipline to clan rule to social surveillance to communal self-help to government administration.

A review of occidental literature on Chinese social control and policing shows that there is an imbalance in research output. There is much research about the social control system in imperial China, its historical roots, philosophical foundation, structural framework, and operational process. However, there is very little raw information and scientific research on how Chinese police worked in the past[10] or on People's Republic of China (PRC) public security functions at present.

This chapter introduces readers to the study of policing in China, including problems, issues, approaches and methods, ending with a discussion of the contributions and organization of the book.

This chapter contains five sections. Section 1 discusses "Problems with the Western Study of Chinese Policing." It points out that Western study of Chinese law and policing is ill informed factually and overgeneralized theoretically. Section 2, "Policing with Chinese Characteristics: Another Approach," argues for the study of Chinese policing from the inside out and the bottom up, informed by indigenous perspectives and supported with local data. Section 3, "Researching PRC Policing," recommends methods of conducting police research in China, including sources to consult and issues to ponder. Section 4, "Contributions of This Book," observes that in order to contribute to cross-cultural understanding, the study of policing in China must be conducted with an intimate understanding of local history, a deep appreciation of indigenous culture, and a broad knowledge of people's ways and means. Section 5 outlines the "Organization of This Book."

## Section 1—Problems with the Western Study of Chinese Policing

Western studies of Chinese law and policing have been handicapped by ethnocentrism and cultural ignorance.

In law, a generation of Western legal scholars has adopted the view that China has no rational or functional legal system, notwithstanding historical evidence suggesting otherwise. The *Qing* dynasty (1644 to 1911), for example, has a sophisticated legal code and an effective justice administration system.[11]

One of the earliest reviews of Chinese law literature (on studies by Japanese, Western, and Chinese researchers) was compiled by Cyrus H. Peake.[12] The review spans the years from 1880 to 1937. Peake observed contrasting views between the West and the East over the role of law and the functions of punishment. The West condemned the Chinese legal system as being undeveloped, primitive, and barbaric in adopting a collective criminal responsibility principle (e.g., guilt by association) and an inhuman punishment scheme (e.g., torture and inquisition).

Western condemnation of the Chinese criminal justice system is a recent phenomenon. Before the mid-eighteenth century, Western visitors and missionaries, such as Juan Gonzalez de Mendoza (1588),[13] spoke highly of Chinese law. Notwithstanding its harshness, foreign observers admired the Chinese judicial system for its comprehensiveness, meticulousness, and effectiveness.[14] Such favorable attitudes toward the Chinese legal system turned sour with the departure of compassionate missionaries and pragmatic diplomats and the arrival of calculating traders.

In time, the social and political conditions in Europe changed. European justice administration became less arbitrary and punishment more humane. Ideas and ideal of humanism started to take root and spread all over the world. The Chinese criminal justice system—especially when applied to foreigners, for example, the miscarriage of justice in the Lady Hughes (1748) and Francis Terranova (1821) cases—was found to be objectionable and unacceptable. Extraterritoriality resulted.

Serious study of China, beyond anecdotal accounts of missionaries and routine reports of officials, began in the late 1800s, when foreign powers imposed extraterritoriality on China. Sir George Staunton (1737-1801) who wrote *Ta Tsing Leu Lee* (1810)[15] found Chinese legal codes to be "copious and consistent" and free of "bigotry."[16] Ernest Alabaster (1872-1959) observed that the *Qing* Code was infinitely more exact and satisfactory than English law.[17]

Peake noted two major problems with Chinese legal studies during this time. The first was a lack of comparative methodology, an issue anticipated by Jean Escarra (1885–1955) who spent much time and effort in elucidating and correcting this oversight.[18]

The second was a lack of language facility, a problem still plagues researchers today: "In the future the fullest significance can be derived from the study of Chinese Law only by those scholars trained both in Chinese language and in the field of law in general."[19]

Peake also pointed out the need to study Chinese philosophy and culture in order to fully comprehend and appreciate Chinese law.[20] In this respect, Professor J.J.L. Duyvendak, the father of Dutch sinology, set the precedent in translating *The Book of Lord Shang: A Classic of the Chinese School of Law*[21] into English.

Peake closed with the following observations. First, Chinese law research was just beginning and had a long way to go; for example, there was neither investigation into procedure laws nor study of the influence of Buddhism on legal development. Second, legal scholars needed to look beyond classical text or historical materials to inform their research.[22] Chinese literary work of the time, such as novels, fairly describes the real operations of the system and true attitudes of the people. Court cases also tell how the law was applied in practice and need to be explored.

In policing, Michael R. Dutton wrote the seminal book on Chinese policing.[23] The book addressed the question: How does the traditional technology of policing fuse with the present social control framework?

Dutton began with the observation that the PRC's household registration system is a reproduction and sublimation of past practices rather than a new invention. Specifically, China's present control method is a "remnant" of past feudal practices, for example, the old imperial *Baojia* (保甲) system (akin to Anglo-Saxon England frankpledge) was conveniently borrowed to serve new communist governance needs.

In terms of method, Dutton employed Foucault's "genealogical method" to reconstruct "histories of the present." In the main, Dutton relied on secondary English materials to complete his study.

In terms of theory, Dutton adopted Foucault's theoretical insights [24] to analyze China's household ("hukou") registration regime. He observed that Chinese state control has moved away from inflicting pain on the body to marking files of the person. As evidence, Dutton pointed to Chinese communist use of statistical records to effectively track and keep people in place, for example, the *hukou* system.

In terms of thesis, Dutton postulated that in imperial China the state controlled a person's behavior by anchoring the person within an intricate web of relationships, starting with the family. Individuals were kept in place by critical self-introspection, stern family discipline, and ubiquitous community surveillance. In contemporary China, the state replaces communal supervision with state administration in the guise of a comprehensive household registration system: "[W]e may now see a regime which centers on work and production rather than on family and Confucian ethics, but the form of its policing, the modes of its regulation and the way it constitutes its disciplinary subjects all have resonance in the past."[25]

As a critique, Dutton's book tells more about social control than law enforcement and focuses more on administrative regulation than police supervision. In seeing China through Foucault's lens, Dutton tells us more about what Western people *think* of effective social control in

China, forcefully imposed, than what Chinese people *feel* about necessary official supervision, naturally embraced.

Radcliffe-Brown has cautioned against such Western cultural imposition, sold as sociological imagination[26]: "In the primitive societies that are studied by social anthropology there are no historical records. ... Anthropologists, thinking of their study as a kind of historical study, fall back on conjecture and imagination, and invent 'pseudo-historical' or 'pseudo-casual' explanations."[27]

In essence, where Dutton discovered clear and convincing archeological evidence of historical continuity in a disciplinary state, the Chinese experienced accidental and coincidental confluence of people, events, and circumstances vying for influence over the individual.[28] Essentially, Dutton tried to replace the micro experiences of many with the macro imagination of a few. Where Dutton reached out for a grand design in explaining state governance, the Chinese people settled on human nature ("rensheng")[29] and heavenly providence ("tianming")[30] as reasons for personal discipline and collective obedience.

Finally, whereas Dutton sought to make sense of Chinese social phenomena abstractly and from afar, the Chinese people give meaning to their life circumstances concretely and intimately. Thus observed, Dutton's "theory of policing" is irrelevant to the Chinese people's conception of and feelings toward their police.

The existence of two divergent and competing views of Chinese life raises a larger issue of scientific paradigm in scholarship style and research methodology, from what counts as a sound theory and what is being accepted as good evidence, to whose perspective counts and what issues matters in reconstructing social reality in and of China. Accordingly, the Chinese way of understanding the world is being ignored because it is not deemed as "scientific" to Western observers. The shift in paradigm further implicates issues of positivism vs. post-modernism, or absolute vs. relative ways to see the world. Viewed in this light, the struggle to understand China by Dutton and others becomes a cultural, not scientific, war.

On a still higher intellectual level, Westerners such as Dutton go about reconstructing the Chinese experience out of whole cloth and in accordance with a grand scheme of things, while the Chinese people continue to weave their life course stitch by stitch corresponding with the dynamic "way" ("dao") of the universe. The debate of universal human rights vs. particularistic Asian values is a manifestation of such a disagreement.

This line of critique about the West finds empirical support in recent Chinese law and societal research. Theoretically, law in action is mediated by powerful social actors as driven by a convergence of economic, social, and cultural forces. In "The Practice of Law as an Obstacle to Justice: Chinese Lawyers at Work,"[31] Ethan Michelson found that legal justice in China was subjected to and subverted by the lawyers who acted as gatekeepers to law and justice. Accessibility to the legal system was dictated by professional interests (i.e., who could pay) and circumscribed by cultural values (i.e., who was deserving of help). Empirically, He Xin found in "Why Do They Not Comply with the Law? Illegality and Semi-Legality among Rural-Urban Migrant Entrepreneurs in Beijing"[32] that in practice the *hukou* system did not comport with the administrators' design nor live up to the legislators' expectations. Ultimately, the *hukou* system did not serve to discipline the migrants (as intimated by Dutton) but was negotiated by all those who were affected by it (police, migrants, business) to serve their respective institutional or personal interests. The lesson to be learned is that a grand theory of law in a book seldom, if ever, explains the behavior of law on the streets of China.

If we find Dutton's approach to studying policing in China wanting— sterile and irrelevant—how might we improve? To this central issue we now turn.

## Section 2—Policing with Chinese Characteristics: Another Approach

The Western study of Chinese policing suffers from both cultural and linguistic difficulties.[33]

Harry Harding once observed that the misperception of reform in China has more to do with observers' dispositions toward China than true conditions in China. Our views on China changed with intellectual assumptions of the time; sentiments toward China ran from unrestrained romanticism over Mao's egalitarianism and utopianism in the 1970s to bitter resentment over China's oppressive policy and repressive practices in the 1980s.

By far the most established assumption shared by many China-bound researchers is the idea that there is a connection between economic development and demands for political liberation,[34] in that economic reform would inevitably lead to political liberation.[35]

Taking this admonition to heart, we find that few if any existing Western social or police theories fit well with China's particularistic cultural pattern and complex social conditions. Many of them suffer from various minor inaccuracies[36] if not overall distortions. More significantly, there is not enough valid and reliable empirical data[37] to support any comprehensive theory building on and about China.[38] This has led a minority of scholars in China to caution against uncritical and wholesale importation and transplanting of foreign ideas on reform in China. Zhu Xudong from Chinese People's Public Security University (PSU) observed that *bentuhua* or domestication of foreign ideas and practices, caused Western ideas and ideals to be privileged over domestic ones, starting with the importation of science in the late nineteenth century. Because policing research is basically local knowledge, police studies must reflect Chinese historical, social, and cultural characteristics. Police research must focus on Chinese problems and issues and must purge itself of foreign influences.

Three observations may help improve China police studies.

First, geographically and culturally, China is made up of many distinctive parts of an ill-fitting whole.[39] There is a tendency, however, to reference PRC police as a monolithic entity or treat Chinese policing as a uniform activity. This is a misconception. Confucian culture is not ubiquitous.[40] Communist ideology is not all consuming.[41] Simply put, Chinese people do not think and act alike. The public reception of and reaction to government policy in China vary, depending on locale,[42] are contingent on issues,[43] and change with people.[44] In like manner and for the same reasons, police in China perform their duties differently from region to region.

China is a big country with diverse conditions in geography, ethnicity, and culture. In as much as policing is a grassroots activity and public order is a local concern, we can expect national policy and priorities are not equally shared locally.[45] Similarly, social problems and political dynamics affect different communities differently.[46] When devising legislative solutions, national law must be made to fit local conditions. Local government, especially the police, must be afforded the flexibility to apply national law creatively and experiment boldly with local regulations.[47]

Thus, as one might expect, CPC directives and policies were interpreted and applied differently in local context. For example, when national police leadership called for police reform in 2001, provincial police bureau chiefs reported different focus and achievements in 2002:

(1) The Shanghai Public Security Bureau reported focusing on modernization of the police department, that is, systemization (*zhiduhua*), regularization (*guifanhua*), and legalization (*fazhi hua*);

(2) The Henan Public Security Bureau reported focusing on improving political ideology and professional accountability of the police when engaging in "strike hard" (*yanda*) campaigns. The major focus was on purging the police of corruption and abuse, for example, the existence of a "protective umbrella" (*baohu san*).
(3) The Anhui Public Security Bureau reported focusing on eradicating organized gangs and secret societies (*heshehui*). The other focus was in reforming the police work style with the conduct of three education campaigns. Four police reform projects were at hand: establishment and perfection of the education and training system (*jiaoyu peixun*); management and appraisal process (*guanli kaohe*); command and control structure (*jiandu zhiyue*); protection for police work (*jingwu baozheng*).
(4) The Jingsu Public Security Bureau reported focusing on improving police service through enhancing police law enforcement standards, introducing police management review, and adopting technology upgrades (i.e., "Golden Shield" (*Jindun*) project).
(5) The Sichuan Public Security Bureau reported focusing on making police work more efficient, transparent, and accountable to the public. The police reformed the household registration system to make it more rational and efficient. They also tried to address recurring and persistent police service problems (e.g., impolite and unresponsive police attitudes).
(6) The Xianxi Public Security Bureau reported focusing on *yanda* over serious crimes. The major focus was on building a comprehensive public security prevention and control system (*zhian fangkong xitung*). They recommended that the police reform process should be further strengthened to lay a foundation for the future economic development of the western region.
(7) The Helungjian Public Security reported focusing on breakthrough in six reform areas: (1) maintaining public order; (2) "striking hard" at criminal offenders; (3) promoting social order; (4) serving the nation's open door and economic reform needs; (5) using technology to enhance police performance (*kexue qiangjing*); (5) facilitating police troop construction (*duiwu jianshe*).
(8) The Guangzhou Public Security reported focusing on six objectives to improve public security and social order within two years and to deal with anticipated public order problems associated with WTO. The six objectives were: liberating ideas, promoting economic reform, stepping up with public security and social order campaigns,

speeding up public security reform, and enhancing public security quality and standards.[48]

The implication of this observation for police scholars bound for China is clear: any attempt to theorize about Chinese policing in universal and essentialist terms, without indigenous perspective and grounded research, is likely to fail. In Gary G. Hamilton's words, "I suggest that western typology of traditional, charismatic, and legal domination needs revisions if it is to help and not hinder understanding of non-Western societies."[49]

Second, we need reliable data more than critical opinions. Most, if not all, China-bound police researchers have relied heavily on government data. Information supplied by the Chinese government (official statistics, policy papers, legislative documents, court cases, journal articles, media accounts) deserves careful reading, with attention to possible incompleteness, omission, distortion, misrepresentation and bias.[50]

In terms of public security journal articles, they are written, selected, and edited to promote ideological correctness and follow Party policy lines. Critical examination of issues is not welcome. Open challenge of official policy is discouraged. Free discussion of different and divergent ideas is frowned upon.[51]

In terms of public security media, Public Security Legal News has been relied upon by many police researchers, inside and outside of China, to provide empirical data for research. Such media reports, however, have little guarantee of validity and reliability. Specifically, the quality and reliability of Public Security Legal News has been called into question, with accusations of pandering to the public through reports of violence and sex, with little supervision and still less accountability.[52]

In terms of official crime data, Chinese crime rates cannot be meaningfully compared with those from the West because of "dark figures" of crime resulting from the following: (1) PRC Criminal Laws have fewer kinds of crime than the U.S.; (2) PRC official crime rate—the "Criminal Case Recording Rate" ("xingshi anjian faan shu")—only reports/records cases from public security, not other branches of law enforcement within Ministry of Public Security (MPS), such as customs, courts, and procuratorates; (3) China reports minor public order cases ("zhian guanli chufa tiaoli") while Western countries do not count misdemeanors as crimes; (4) Western countries record all property crimes. China only records crime when minimum requirements ("lian biaozhun") are met; (5) In the U.S. about 35% of crimes happened in supermarkets. In China most businesses do not report such crimes, preferring to take care of them in house; (6) Urbanization has a direct relationship to crime rates. In the U.S. 80–90% of the country is urbanized. In China only 30% is.[53]

In terms of official reports, police reports and legal documents might not have been prepared properly. First, officers have a tendency to substitute common terms for legal ones. Second, officers might choose to use non-recognized police terms. Third, officials might use vague and confusing terminologies.

In terms of research reports, data analysis provided by elites is more likely to be driven by theory than practice. As to official reports, they are colored by ideology at the expense of facts. Both information sources are unlikely to have been informed by grassroots experience and bottom up perspective. All this should remind China-bound researchers that it is difficult to ascertain the truth about policing in China once we get away from official pronouncements and expert analysis. It is appropriate to end this observation with the often-quoted statement, "Everyone is entitled to his own opinions but not his own facts."

The implication for Chinese policing research is clear—we need to look at China from inside out and from the bottom up.

Third, China must be understood on her own terms, in the context of Chinese history and culture, and, more recently, ideology and personalities. If we were to make an effort to understand Chinese policing in China's own terms, we should start by investigating local communal, familial, and self control. That is to say, we should take a bottom up, rather than a top down, approach, seeking rich empirical observations instead of imposing essentialistic theoretical postulates, that is, seeing the forest before examining the trees, or pursuing a deductive instead of a inductive approach.

If we should look at China from the bottom up and empirically, we will find that policing as a function starts with self and ends with the family/community, that is, self-governance.

In imperial China, Confucianism was promoted as a state-sponsored moral code and state craft. Confucian ("Rújia") taught that all social control starts with self and realized through the family. To understand Chinese social control we must look at how the family functions as a self-governing unit. The Kongfu (Confucius) household in imperial China is such an ideal type of self-governance and informal social control. More significant for purposes of our illustration, the Kongfu household enjoyed delegated rights of self-government and autonomous powers of social control. Kongfu enjoyed hereditary nobility. Kongfu was given property to manage. Kongfu has a right to appoint officials, to levy taxes, and to select local magistrates. The head of Kongfu has a right to govern its household members exclusively and discipline its charges summarily. The Kongfu household has full authority to establish conduct norms within its household and over the disposition of its property in the community. It could discipline and punish its household members, charges, and intruders, summarily and without recourse. Kongfu has a right to make enforceable rules to protect its communal welfare and seek help of the officials to promote its collective interests. At all times, Kongfu mediated between its members and the outside world. Officials could only approach, communicate, and deal with Kongfu members with the special permission of the emperor, by and through the head of the Kongfu household.

The conclusion from this brief excursion is as unmistakable as it is revealing: the Kongfu household played a significant role in social control matters in imperial China through independent moral leadership and by virtue of delegated governmental social control powers from the emperor. As a result it shared in social control responsibilities with local officials, as co-equals. It was a "private government" unto itself.

Thus to observe that China has no institution of formal police might be technically correct. But to imply that there is no informal "policing" in China before 1898 is a gross misunderstanding that results from the Westerner's idea of police.[54] The idea of police as we know it today is beholden to Western conception, ideology, organization, style, and means.

In summation, the most productive method in Chinese police studies is to take a different approach, one that is informed by indigenous perspective and based on empirical data, or simply a more context-anchored, fact-driven approach.

The remainder of this chapter details difficulties and ways to go about conducting research into PRC policing—what sources to consult, which journals to read, and what Chinese and English literature exists.

## Section 3—Researching PRC Policing

### Research Difficulties

A brief discussion on problems and methods of research into PRC police is in order. As a general observation, research problems confronted by police scholars bound for China are the same as those faced in other academic fields, except more so due to the security consciousness of communist regimes and the secretive culture of police everywhere.

Prior to World War II, American study of China was limited to a handful of experts trained in the French sinology tradition, which stressed linguistic, biographical, and philosophical preparation.[55] Scholars of China have always suffered from linguistic and social barriers, and after the establishment of the PRC, political obstacles were added to the list.

Before the 1960s, China was virtually inaccessible to outsiders. First, studying China requires substantial investment of time and effort to master her difficult language, long history, and rich culture. Second, statistical data was not available from China before and well into the reform era. Third, McCarthyism in the United States in the 1950s deterred students from entering the field for fear of retribution.

In the early 1960s, most research was based on translated secondary sources—mostly newspapers and government documents furnished by the U.S. Consulate in Hong Kong. In the mid to late 1960s, this was supplemented by exit interviews in Hong Kong. In the 1970s, illegally obtained documents bearing on the Cultural Revolution were smuggled out of China. Since 1979, mainland libraries and national archives have been increasingly open to public inspection on site. Discreet visits and personal observations have provided the bulk of the research materials. Since the 1980s, researchers from China have been allowed to study in the West. They have brought with them valuable data, rich personal experience, and wide family connections. In the 1990s, the Internet provided armchair researchers with direct access to many library sources and databases that a decade before were inaccessible.[56]

In 1979 a great change came about in Chinese research, in terms of attitude, facility, opportunities, and output. Since that time, PRC political leaders have wanted more scientific research to help reform. Businesspeople have wanted more research to help with modernization. The scholarly community has wanted to revive the dysfunctional educational system.

Researching public security and policing in China is a difficult task. Cohen's observation about the difficulties of researching into China, while dated, remains relevant.[57] The Communists are not given to open government. The PRC police are not keen on sharing state secrets and operational details with outsiders, much less foreigners.[58] There is no right to public information in China. Publicly available data are often "sanitized" to serve the State's propaganda, education, and socialization needs.[59] Field survey research is officially prohibited. Document 598 circulated by the State Education Commission in December of 1990 states: "Notice of Issues Relating to Cooperation with Foreigners: Doing Social Investigation in our Country" (prohibits) "all higher education institutions from conducting sociological survey in the form of public opinion poll or written questionnaire with foreign academic institutions and research institutes. This includes cooperative research based on questionnaire." Of late the tight grip on social survey on crime has been relaxed somewhat as reported by Lening Zhang and others in "Criminological Research in Contemporary China Challenges and Lessons Learned From a Large-Scale Criminal Victimization Survey." (2007)

On a more optimistic note, researching in the PRC is getting easier. Consistent with PRC overall policy to open up government agencies, including the police,[60] for citizens' inspection and public scrutiny is that more and more information is being made available to the people, for example, books, journals and papers designated for internal circulation are increasingly being placed in public circulation and for private subscription. For instance, *Gongan Yanjiu* (Public Security Research) is now freely circulated, and *Renmin Gongan Bao* (Public Security Press) is available on the web.

Although the PRC government still does not welcome outside scholars to study the PRC police system and process, PRC scholars themselves have been allowed to conduct research and publish their findings based on open source and informal interviews much more than before.

It goes without saying the MPS reserves the right to approve the content of any published materials requiring their assistance, endorsement or attention, e.g., publication with *Renmin Gongan Daxue Chubanshe* (Chinese People's Public Security Press) or *Qunzhong Chubanshe* (Masses Press) both publishing outlets for the Ministry. More often than not, sensitive issues, e.g., Falun Gong (法輪功), or improper ideas, e.g., ("Taiwan" not "Republic of China") would be edited out as a matter of course, though not without lengthy consultation with the author.

## Emergence of Police Studies in China

Until recently, there was no formal police studies program in China, nor were there any independent research enterprises on policing in China. This has changed with the appearance of Ministry of Public Security "think tanks" in the body of Chinese Police Studies Association ("Zhongguo Jincha Xuehui") and various research institutes, e.g., MPS Fourth Research Institute which published such studies as *Quntixing Shi-*

*jian Yanjiu Lunweiji* (Compilation of research essays on mass incidents) (2001).

Little research is deemed necessary because police role and functions are accepted as an act of faith and based on ideological dogma; that is, police are an instrumentality of the ruling class. Due to China's unique history, experience, and culture, policing methods and practices are never questioned.

To be published in official journals, police research must accept editing to achieve political correctness in terms of topic, theme, and content.[61]

Problems with police studies and research in China are best captured in the General Administrative Office of Ministry of Public Security (MPS), "The Notice about Enhancing Research Work into Public Security Theories and on Improving further Public Security Studies," Gonban [2000] 82 Hao:

> However, it must be observed that currently public security research is not well developed, particularly with respect to theoretical development. This is demonstrated by pre-occupation with stylistic research; lack of theoretical support; absence of insightful (*jiandi*) findings ...[62]

There are encouraging signs. Police studies and research are increasingly being recognized. In 1993, the Minster of Education first approved the study of public security–related subjects in universities as degrees, including criminal investigation, public security, police administration, risk management, and police physical education. In July 1998, the Ministry of Education recognized Public Security Studies (*Gongan Xueke*) as a subdiscipline to Jurisprudence (*Faxue*) in the "Putong gaodeng yuanxiao benke zhuanye mulu" (General higher education school undergraduate course professional catalogue). The newly minted discipline has eleven primary study fields (*kexue menlei*) and seventy-two subfields (*erdang lei*). Primary subjects of study include: police theory (*lilun gongan xue*), police history (*lishi gongan xue*), and public security studies (*gongan xue*). Secondary fields include public order studies (*zhian xue*) and investigative studies (*zhencha xue*). Thus, police study has now developed to a stage of maturity with its own theory, concepts, research methods, and findings. The first master degree program in criminal procedure was approved in December 1993. By 2002, there were nine masters programs in the nation, five at PSU and four at Criminal Investigation College.[63]

Notwithstanding the gradual improvement in the stature and reputation of police studies as a discipline in China, substantial issues remain concerning its mission, boundary, methods, focus, and contribution. In essence, there is little consensus and much contention as to what the discipline is all about and where it is going. For example, while a majority of scholars are of the opinion that police studies is an independent discipline with well-defined subject matter, educational objectives, and course content, a sizable minority argue that police studies is a multiple disciplinary field, requiring the integration of theories and practices from natural science and social science, arts and humanities, law and politics. As such, there is much disagreement over the research focus and methods. Some scholars are of the opinion that police studies should be devoted to the study of police origin, development, and regulations in a search for patterns and theory. This school argues against pairing researchers with applied police work, for example, criminal investigation or police administration. Others insist on a broad, interdisciplinary approach to police studies as a scientific field. According to this vision, scholars should apply scientific methods to the study of police work in theory and practice. Still others think that the investigation of police in China should link up with police researchers worldwide.

Police theoretical research is necessary to improve on applied police work.[64] The way to improve on public security research in China is with more scientific studies and empirical research, which requires the dedication of resources and the training of people to conduct police research.[65]

Currently, there is an overall tendency to ignore the relevancy, importance, and utility of academic research in daily police work. There is now a common saying within police circles that "police studies and theory sounds important when proposed, appears to be necessary when applied, not being used when in urgency." In essence Chinese police officers at the operational level do not think that police theory, research, and findings are useful in their day-to-day work.[66]

To jump-start police research, police leadership wants to: (1) Provide an incentive structure for people to conduct research; (2) speed up the processing and distribution of research findings; and (3) develop police scholars by inviting outside researchers to share insights and viewpoints.

## How to conduct police research in China

In terms of research materials, there are original data in the form of legislation and regulations, National People's Congress (NPC) reports and communications, crime statistics, and police documents. There is an abundance of Chinese published materials, mostly by scholars and teachers associated with one of the public security universities or some other center of higher education.

Inside China, public security literature includes public security books, journals, newspapers, meeting records, scientific data/technical reports, government publications, student dissertations, public security files, and press releases. In terms of academic journals, every one of the twenty-four public security colleges and universities publishes one or more law or police journals. According to the public security integrated index, a typical public security college library carries about 341 foreign police journals/magazines and 228 domestic ones. Since 1998, libraries have collected about 1,800 public security and law books, increasing at a rate of 300 per year. Public security literature is being used for three purposes: policy making, operational direction, and teaching and research, [67]

## Legislations

One of the more common types of research materials is legislative and regulatory materials.

Under the PRC Constitution, there is one national law uniformly enforced in China. "The Legislation Law of the People's Republic of China" (2000) (LL) makes provisions for how national, local, and administrative laws and regulations are made and interpreted.

The highest authority to make and interpret law in China is vested with the NPC and in its absence the NPC Standing Committee. Article 7 of LL provides that: "The National People's Congress and Standing Committee thereof shall exercise state legislative power," and Article 42 of LL provides that: "The power to interpret a national law shall vest in the Standing Committee of National People's Congress."

The other national rule-making authority is the State Council. Article 56 of LL provides that: "The State Council enacts administrative regulations in accordance with the Constitution and national law," that is, they can promulgate regulations as empowered by the NPC.

Finally, legislators at various local levels—province, autonomous region, municipality directly under the central government—are allowed to make laws and central administrative regulations. Article 63 of LL provides that: "In light of the specific situations and actual needs of the jurisdiction, the People's Congress of a province, autonomous region, municipality directly under the central government and the Standing Committee thereof may enact local decrees provided that they shall not contravene any provision of the Constitution, national law and administrative regulations."

As an illustration of how police legislation—national, administrative, or local—can contribute to an understanding of PRC police work, we may address a common police research question: Is a warrant of arrest or summons for appearance always necessary to effect an arrest or appearance?

We start with the observation that when processing crimes and handling criminals, PRC police officials are governed by the Criminal Procedure Law of the People's Republic of China ("Zhonghua renmin gongheguo xingshi susong fa") (CPL) and People's Police Law of the People's Republic of China ("Zhonghua renmin gongheguo jingcha fa")(PL), both national laws, as implemented by "Procedure regulations of Public Security organs in handling criminal cases" ("Gongan jiguan banli xingshi anjian chengxu guiding") (PSR), an administrative regulation.

Specifically, the issuance of a warrant or summon is provided for in "Chapter VI Compulsory Measures" of CPL, being Articles 50 to 78, Articles 61 to 154 of PSR, and "Chapter II Functions and Powers" of PL, being Articles 7 to 9.

Article 50 of CPL provides that: "The People's Courts, the People's Procuratorates and the public security organs *may*, according to the circumstances of a case, issue a warrant to compel the appearance of the criminal suspect or defendant, order him to obtain a guarantor pending trial or subject him to residential surveillance" (italics added). This suggests that the Courts or Procuratorates have the authority, but are not required, to issue a warrant on application of the police.

Article 59 of CPL provides that: "Arrests of criminal suspects or defendants *shall be subject to approval* by a People's Procuratorate or decision by a People's Court and shall be executed by a public security organ" (italics added). This suggests the police must apply for a warrant before an arrest. This is consistent with the doctrine of "mutual coordination" and "mutual check and balance" between the procuratorate and police.

Police are allowed to make arrests without warrant in very limited and clearly defined circumstances.

First, Article 61 of CPL provides that: "Public security organs may initially detain an active criminal or a major suspect under any of the following conditions:

(1) if he is preparing to commit a crime, is in the process of committing a crime or is discovered immediately after committing a crime;
(2) if he is identified as having committed a crime by a victim or an eyewitness;
(3) if criminal evidence is found on his body or at his residence;

(4) if he attempts to commit suicide or escape after committing a crime, or he is a fugitive;
(5) if there is likelihood of his destroying or falsifying evidence or tallying confessions;
(6) if he does not tell his true name and address and his identity is unknown; and
(7) if he is strongly suspected of committing crimes from one place to another, repeatedly, or in a gang."

Secondly, Article 62 provides: "The persons listed below may be seized outright by any citizen and delivered to a public security organ, a People's Procuratorate or a People's Court for handling:

(1) any person who is committing a crime or is discovered immediately after committing a crime;
(2) any person who is wanted for arrest;
(3) any person who has escaped from prison; and
(4) any person who is being pursued for arrest."

In both instances, the police must follow up with a detention warrant. Article 64 of CPL provides that: "When detaining a person, a public security organ *must* produce a detention warrant."

There is little doubt, from this brief legislative law and administrative regulation analysis that arrest or detention without a warrant is not allowed, as Article 71 of CPL makes clear: "When making an arrest, a public security organ must produce an arrest warrant."

The research into the legislative/regulatory framework for police arrest powers only begins the research exercise. The next issue is how such laws and regulations are being interpreted and applied across the nation and in different location; that is, do arrest procedures in practice vary from locale to locale in China, or are they uniformly implemented across the country?

In this we learn that the implementation of CPL has always been a major concern.[68] The PRC government has taken drastic, and increasingly effective, steps to make sure that police follow CPL. It has not always been successful.

In principle, CPL and PL on arrests are supposed to be uniformly and strictly applied nationwide, since violation of CPL and PL is subject to Party discipline, organizational sanction, administrative appeal, legal challenges, media supervision, and legislative (NPC) oversight.[69] In terms of actual practice, however, arrest procedures differ from locale to locale, having to conform to local customs reflecting indigenous circumstances.[70]

More pertinently, under the current command and control structure, police in China are subject to dual command and control. Professionally and administratively, local police are commanded by the central government through province police bureaus and county police offices. Financially and operationally, police at the county, township, and village level are provided for and directed by local Party and government institutions and personalities.

The above dual command and control structure has resulted in great disparity and wide variation in police operational practices. In reality, central command and control of police has existed in name only.

There are a number of reasons accounting for such local disparities: First, public security leaders, particularly those at the rural, village, and township level, are ignorant of the legal responsibility and authority of the police. They have overemphasized the necessity to coordinate local police work with central Party policy directives at the expense of enforcing national laws uniformly and implementing administrative regulations dutifully, that is, allowing Party policy to trump the rule of law.[71] Second, public security officials in the local areas routinely fail to follow established laws and regulations. They are consistently unable to resist illegal orders from local Party leaders who control their appointment, employment, and promotion. They are also afraid of spoiling the "good" or "established" relationship with the local village and township leaders, thereby making their work difficult, if not impossible. Third, there is a lack of checks and balances guarding against abuses of police authority. Fourth, local public security has inadequate funding to carry out national law and The MPS directives.

Normally, public security is funded by local governments, that is, village and township. According to historical data, the county and township are only able to fund one-fifth to three-fifths of public security expenditures. The public security officials are expected to raise their own operational funding by means of fines and other efforts. In some cases, the village and township leaders even go so far as requiring the line officers to come up with sufficient funds to finance police operations or risk having their salaries reduced. In other cases, the county and township would pay only for salaries, leaving daily expenses, such as office rent, room and board, phone, water, and electric power, to the village or township government. In such cases, the local police must obey the instructions and follow the directions of the local village or township officials or risk having their office closed or their electricity or water turned off. Oftentimes, this means abuse of laws and neglect of procedures, resulting in central control giving way to local misconduct.

In conclusion, arrest procedure is governed by national law and central procedures in theory, but subject to different interpretations and divergent application in practice by local Party and government officials.

The Party is keenly aware of the problem and has taken big steps to remedy the situation, for example, by rationalizing the budget process, so that police managers do not need to look to local Party and government officials for financial support.

The lesson from Chinese police arrest law is that we must not only look at national laws and police regulations but also seek to understand how such laws and regulations are being interpreted and applied.

## Administrative documents

China is an administrative state. The Communist Party prides itself on central planning and control. Investigation into Chinese policing is a study of administrative structure and process. This begins with reading police administrative documents, or *gongan* "xingzheng gongwen."

Public security scholars define *gongan* "xingzheng gongwen" as "documents compiled during the administrative process that are with legal and prescriptive effect" ("falu xiaoli de guifan ti weshu").[72] The State Council further elaborated upon the purposes and functions of such documents as follows:

> Administrative agency documents ("xingzheng jiguan gongwen") … are an important tool for the communication and implementation of the Party and State's principles, policies, rules, regulations, and measures, and in requesting instructions, answering questions, providing guidelines, planning work, reporting activities, and exchanging views.[73]

All public security administrative documents have the following intrinsic and defining functional characteristics: political ("shengzhi sheng"), legal ("fa dings sheng"), authoritative ("quanwei sheng"), and restrictive ("guifan sheng"). In terms of classification, official documents are of three kinds:

(1) directive document ("zhiling sheng gongwen"), that is, an order or instruction from the Party, State, or government officials to subordinates, such as "mingling" (order), "jueding" (decision), "pifu" (written reply), or "yijian" (opinion);
(2) informational document ("zhaohui sheng gongwen"), that is, communication between public security organs, such as "tongzi" (in-

form) "tongbao" (release), "tonggao" (notice), "hanjian" (correspondence) or "huyi jilu" (records of meeting);

(3) reporting (for approval) document ("baoqing sheng gongwen"), that is, reports or requests filed by subordinate to superiors.

The State Council has provided for set methods in dealing with a variety of administrative documents.[74] There are twelve kinds of administrative documents a researcher might likely encounter. The following four illustrate such a diverse administrative framework:

(1) "Mingling"[75] or "ling" (order or instruction).[76] This can be used to issue administrative rules and regulations; take disciplinary measures; or void government actions.
(2) "Yian"[77] (proposal or motion).[78] "Yian" are legislative proposals submitted by government units at various levels to the People's Congress or its Standing Committee at a corresponding level, as required or permitted by law.
(3) "Jueding"[79] (resolution or decision).[80] "Jueding" are major legal, policy, operations, or personnel decisions.[81]
(4) "Zhishi"[82] (direct or instruct). These are directives to subordinate agencies to coordinate actions.

These documents, to the extent they are available, are indispensable for conducting police research. Such documents, if properly analyzed, tell us what is going on inside the public security agency by providing context, revealing mindsets, describing problems,[83] registering concerns, interpreting laws, analyzing issues, articulating policy, outlining strategies, explaining methods, and documenting results. The limitations of using such documents are many; for example, many of the documents are not made available, and those that are available hide more than they reveal. Finally, there is always a common concern of politics, that is, to what extent reports reflect reality and administrative utility or political correctness.

### Books

There are a number of tool books one can use to begin his/her research into Chinese policing:

(1) If one wants to obtain an overview of public security work in China, he or she should consult *Dangdai Zhongguo gongan gongzuo* (Contemporary public security work in China, 1992).
(2) If one wants to understand the characteristics of PRC policing in the 1990s—socialist policing with Chinese characteristics—one is well

advised to consult *Zhongguo teshe gongan zhi yanjiu* (*Research into public security with distinctive Chinese characteristics*, Chinese Police Studies Association, 1996).

(3) If one wants to trace the development of PRC policing, he or she should take a look at *Jiangguo yilai gongan gongzuo dashi yaolan* (An Outline of Major Events of Public Security Work Since Liberation, 2003). The companion volume on law and criminal justice is *Zhonghua renmin gongheguo fazhi dashiji* (1949-1990)(Major events about PRC legal system, 1990).

(4) If one wants to trace PRC legal development from 1949–1988 he or she should consult *Xin Zhongguo fazhi jianshe: Shisi nian yao lan: 1949–1988* (*New China legal system construction: Forty year overview of significant events, 1949–1988*, 1990).

(5) If one wants to learn about the techniques, skills, and procedures of PRC police investigation, he or she should consult *Zhonghua renmin gongheguo zhencha yewu quanshu* (*Comprehensive manual for PRC investigation work*, 1990).

(6) If one wants to read up on laws, rules, and regulations affecting public security work, the works to consult are *Gongan fagui huibian (1950–1979)* (*Compilation of public security rules and regulations*, 1980) and *Gongan fagui huibian (1980–1986)* (1987).

(7) If one is interested in finding out official interpretations and notices pertaining to laws, rules, and regulations affecting public security work, one should consult *Zhonghua renmin gongheguo falu guifanxing jieshi jicheng* (*A Compilation of PRC law and regulatory explanations*, 1990).

(8) If scholars are interested in police laws, regulations, policies, and interpretations they should consult the *Zhonghua renmin gongheguo gongan falu quanshu* (*Compendium of PRC Public Security Laws*, 1995).

(9) Xian Dang's *Police work implicating foreign concerns (Zhongguo shewai jingwu)* (1991) tells everything a researcher might want to know about how PRC police deal with crime implicating foreign persons and interests.

(10) Yan Li wrote a comprehensive working manual for working in police posts—*Gongan paichusuo yewu quanshu* (*A comprehensive manual for public security post*, 1994).

(11) If researchers are interested in private security, they should consult Liu Jiarei's *Baoan yuan bibei* (The essentials for private security personnel, 2006).

(12) Finally, there are two source books that are necessary companions to every China-bound police researcher. The *Zhongguo gongan baike quanshu (Chinese Public Security Encyclopedia)* (Zhongguo gongan baike quanshu editorial committee, 1989) is a handy reference to everything you want to know about PRC policing. It is especially useful in defining terms and finding important documents. One problem, however, is that it is a dated work in a fast-changing field. The other source book is an annual series. The *Law Yearbook of China*, published annually, contains much information on legal activities in China, on police strengths, crime statistics, and important events affecting PRC police that are more pertinent for our purposes.

## Journals

To keep professionally current and conduct scholarly research into specific issues on PRC policing, one cannot do away with reading public security journals. These are journals sponsored by the MPS but managed editorially by the respective public security universities.[84] It is commonly recognized in the PRC and by China-bound police scholars that public security higher education journals in China suffer from a lack of scholarship, stemming from incompetent editors and low standards of scholarship. The editors are neither specialists nor scholarly.

The journals also suffer from having to be politically correct in abiding by Marxist principles and following Party lines. Articles must also be of practical value and of a suitable subject, which means they must deal with concrete and relevant issues of the day. They are not allowed to be critical of PRC political authority or police administration.

The MPS and respective police universities/colleges are making serious efforts to improving the content of the submissions and upgrade the quality of the journals. An in-depth 15 years review (1993 – 2008) of the content of Chinese People's Public Security Journals by this author shows that the publications have improved in scholarship in the following dimensions: focus (more defined), scope (more expansive), diversity (more variegated), methods (more and better design) and authority (more citations).

The three most prominent and often-consulted public security journals of official standing are:

*Gongan Yanjiu* (*Public Security Studies*) is the official journal of the Chinese Police Studies Association (Zhongguo Jingcha Xuehui). It is managed and edited by the MPS, Public Security Research Bureau. The journal is a bimonthly scholarly publication devoted to theoretical police studies. It is designated as an international journal, freely subscribed to by police scholars and practitioners all over the world. Being an official publication, it insists on political correctness. At a recent editorial board meeting, the board made this observation: "There is no forbidden zone to research, but there should be discipline in promotion of ideas." For example, confidential data should not be published. The Journal started to publish monthly in 2001.

*The Gongan Daxue Xuebao* (*Journal of Chinese People Public Security University*) is the official publication of the PSU. The journal is a bi-monthly professional publication devoted to applied police studies. The contributors are either professors from PSU or field police leaders from all over the nation. It is managed and edited by the PSU. It is considered one of the most authoritative, prestigious, and influential journals in the PRC policing community. It is one of the "core" police academic journals in the nation. The journal, now in its fifteenth year, was first available in 1988 as an internal publication. Beginning in 1996, the internal circulation restriction was lifted. In 1998, a number of high quality internally circulated public security journals were publicly released. Since 2000, police university journals are free to spread police research in order to strengthen police operations and services through the exchange of ideas and findings by way of research and publication. The Journal retains its format throughout, though the substance and quality of the articles have improved through the years in terms of rigorousness of research and sophistication of argument. At present, it is a much more academic and less ideological journal, though it still promotes "ideological zealousness" and political correctness with uncommon candor. Public security higher education journals are required to adhere to "dangxin yuanzhe" ("Principle of Party spirit"). This means that articles selected for publication should be informed by Marxist basic principles and follow the Party line, guiding principles, and policies. Articles are grouped under different headings for ease of reference; for example, public security management, public security management research, jurisprudence research, and crime research. Such headings change from issue to issue, but remain thematically the same.

*Gongan Lilun Yu Sijian* (*Theory and Practice of Public Security*). The journal is published under the auspices of the Shanghai Public Security Bureau and edited by Shanghai Public Security Academy. It is reported here as an example of one of the more famous regional/local journals. The journal was first published in 1987, originally as a quarterly. Beginning with the first issue of 1999, the journal was also published under the joint title of (Shanghai Gongan Gaodeng Zhuanke Xuexiao Xuebao), in English (*Journal of Shanghai Public Security Academic*). From this date, the journal has been available for public circulation by subscription, domestically as well as abroad. This is a deliberate and concerted move to make the journal more academic, professional, and relevant.

## Newspapers

Currently, the most accessible data about Chinese policing comes mainly from the *Renmin gongan bao* and related public security publications.

*Renmin gongan bao* is the official newspaper published by the PRC MPS. It was first published in October 1984, and was originally restricted to internal circulation. The paper provides public security officers with up-to-date information on public security happenings. The content of the paper includes guidelines, policies, and directives of the administration; legal and public security information; and crime reports, police stories, and personalities. On July 1, 1988 the paper was released for public and foreign distribution.

When consulting newspapers, the most common strategy for uncovering and discerning what is happening with the PRC police is to follow these four steps:

*Note important announcements.* One should analyze the public pronouncements of PRC public security officials reported as "zhongyao yanlun" ("important opinions") in public security media. Such policy initiatives often surface when national political leaders or public security executives make speeches at important events.

*Follow policy debates.* One should investigate the policy debate and initiatives during national or provincial public security meetings.

*Trace implementation of initiatives.* An effective research technique is examining the application of such policy initiatives at the grassroots and operational levels. This is best achieved through reading on how local police managers seek to realize national policy initiative in concrete terms and material ways. Real case studies of successful implementation of such policy initiatives are most illuminating.

*Read police discussions.* The researcher should read police discussions on the merit and/or problems of various policies and practices.

## Local gazetteers ("Difanzhi")[85]

China began publishing local gazetteers (or history) again in the 1980s.[86] Local gazetteers are a rich research data source of what goes on in a province, city, or county, politically, economically, and socially. *Difang-*

*zhi* compiled locally allow researchers to look at China from the bottom up and with diverse points of view on crime and policing issues. Most *defangzhi* have a section on police development and happenstance dating back to the 1900s and include most major events, such as the first establishment of police posts in the area, and important statistics, such as arrests during *yanda* of 1987. Beginning in 2000, *difangzhi* have been increasingly accessible on the web. *Difangzi* compiled by local history committees can suffer from bureaucratic group thinking, for example, secrecy over accuracy and political correctness over truthfulness, and thus should be read with care, not as recorded history but as an official account of what matters.

### Web blogs

Web blog entries allow researchers to gauge the public's reaction to police programs and conduct. For example, opinions and comments posed to the "sohu.com web-friends discussion forum" (wangyou pinglun) often deal with police misconduct, corruption, and abuses. The forum allows sohu web users to react to a certain posed news item. The news items originated from other printed or e-news outlets, for example, China Daily or People's Daily. Comments on topics are of various sizes and lengths. Some topics collected hundreds of comments, others a few. The length of the comments varies but most of them are from one to three lines. One liner (in actuality ten words or less) is the norm and one or two words are not uncommon. The longer ones, about 10%, are from four to eight lines. Few went beyond twelve lines. The style of comments ranges from emotional outburst to cynical rebuke to enthusiastic support to rational discussion. Most of them are negative and critical.

The most popular police blog is the "jingcha tiandi"[87] with 21,364 comments and 333,457 responses, with an average of 50 comments posted daily (as of September 3, 2008). The topics discussed range from police relationship with the public to work conditions of criminal investigator vs. patrol officers to problems with gun use policy.[88]

## Section 4—Contributions of This Book

There are very few scholarly works on contemporary Chinese policing in academic libraries or in general circulation to help researchers, students, and policymakers on PRC police and policing. Academic researchers, graduate students, intellectuals, policy experts, and media professionals now have to rely on occasional journal articles and mundane newspaper accounts to get a glimpse of the inside world of PRC police. The former, while accurate, are too narrowly focused and selective in approach to provide a full picture and comprehensive understanding of an academic field. The latter, while informative, pander to the public. They are otherwise not well informed of the long history, broad context, and deep current shaping policing in China. The dearth of information is more acute when we consider the import of the subject matter on the national policy and research community. The lapse in scholarship on accessible data and usable knowledge on Chinese policing is particularly perplexing when we consider the output of publications on Chinese law, business, and political science since 1979. Currently, there is only one PRC policing book in the library, *Policing and Punishment in China: From Patriarchy to 'the People'* by Michael R. Dutton, a learned Chinese political scientist from Australia. The book has little to do with policing as a political institution and social practice. Rather the book is about household registration and control, with a Foucault theoretical framework imposed. The more recent edited book *Crime, Punishment, and Policing in China*, by Borge Bakken contains two chapters on Chinese policing. Both articles are more discursive than empirical, descriptive than theoretical.

The latest book on transformation of Chinese police power in the reform era is that of *Legal Reform and Administrative Detention Powers in China* by Sarah Biddulph published by Cambridge University Press, 2007. Although informative on police legal reform, Biddulph has little to say about the idea, history, theory, and practice of policing in China, which is at the heart of this book.

This book is the only volume that provides for a systematic and comprehensive treatment of various aspects of Chinese policing, including: study, idea, origin, history, education, culture, reform, and theory.

This book can best be used as a textbook for a course such as "Introduction to Chinese Policing" or a companion book for a course on "Comparative Policing: China vs. United States" for undergraduate seniors or graduate students. In both cases, it is best to supplement this primary text with supportive source materials for more detailed discussion and broader context.

This book should also serve as a desk reference for policy staffers and academic researchers who want to study Chinese policing and as a research guide in every library.

It is hoped that this book will encourage other researchers and provide the necessary foundation for further and more specialized investigation into various unexplored aspects of Chinese policing, such as use of deadly force. In this regard, the most logical place to start is to study problems and issues with Chinese police reform, with an eye toward operational issues and concerns, such as how to fight cybercrime or deal with mass incidents.[89]

Finally, as to scholarly contributions, the theory proposed at the end of the book promises to explain scientifically and predict empirically what police and policing is all about in China, past and present. In so proposing, I hope that Chinese policing philosophy and theory can earn her place in the world stage and be taken seriously, as a one of a kind police strategy that looks at crime as problems to people and police as resources to individuals.

It is time to study and understand China on her own terms.

The above discussion suggests that there is a dire need to study policing in China with an open mind. Particularly, there is a need to trace, analyze, and discuss recent developments—ideology, philosophy, organization, law, and operations—in Chinese policing within a broader context of Chinese history of social control and PRC political reform since 1979. This kind of study will help to discern historical legacy, discover emerging patterns, and speculate upon future trends. The hope is that this kind of scholarship can contribute to our understanding of PRC police as an evolving entity and pragmatic enterprise caught between past dreams and future hopes, traditionalism and liberalism, ideological dogma and practical necessities.[90]

This book should contribute to scholarship on five levels.

First, police institutions—organization, process, and practices—are not the same everywhere.[91] Police agencies differ in institutional mandate. But they also share much commonality in terms of goals and means. In order to study police cross-culturally, we need to understand similarities and discern differences in policing between nations and across cultures. This requires building up a database of police organizations and practices in many countries as a first step.

Second, to improve upon policing in China, it is necessary to gather empirical data about the performances of police reform programs, processes, and outcomes for analysis and assessment purposes.

Third, to build up a Chinese policing study field outside of China, domestic literature, indigenous perspectives, local data, and inside-out, bottom-up views must be recorded.[92] One proposal is to have bicultural researchers who are at ease in both cultures.[93] Intimate knowledge of culture and good facility with language allow a researcher to reach back into forgotten historical memory, dig deep into obscured cultural meaning, and access latent emotional feelings to provide a more complete and holistic picture of matters under investigation and materials to be interpreted. Although Huang made clear that his preference for bicultural researchers is not meant to exclude "foreign" researchers, it is also clear that Huang thought that researchers locally born and bred had a natural advantage over and above those who just learned about China by education and through immersion.

Fourth, there is a dire need to supplement foreign views of Chinese reform in general and police reform in particular, counterbalancing them with internal perspectives, domestic voices, and grassroots understanding.

Finally, such a study contributes to the growing understanding of PRC police as an evolving institution caught between past legacy and future vision while struggling to maintain a semblance of continuity amidst fast-paced political, economic, social, and cultural change that *are* China in the last thirty-eight years.[94]

China must be studied and engaged on its own terms with a mixture of domestic and domesticated viewpoints in order to gain a fuller understanding of the yet-to-be-explored policing system of the PRC.[95]

## Section 5—Organization of This Book

This book is thematically organized into eight chapters. Chapter 1 provides an overview of the problems and issues, approaches and methods to the study of Chinese policing. It argues for the study of Chinese policing from inside out and bottom up, as informed by indigenous theory and empirical data. Chapter 2 introduces the readers to "The Idea of Police" in China. It explains how the idea of police originated and developed in China. It observes that Western concept of police entered China at a very late day, i.e., late 1800s. The functions of social control were performed at the grassroots level by family, clan and community in imperial China. Chapter 3 ("Origin of Communist Policing") and 4 ("History of Communist Policing") investigates into CCP's first encounters with policing, and their relevancy today. Chapter 5 explores the history, philosophy and organization of "Police Education" in modern China, in comparison to the United States. It ends with a survey of how PRC police college students view their education, in content, process and outcome. Chapter 6 explains why there is a lack of rule of law and constitutionalism in PRC. Chapter 7 is a discussion of "Police Reform" in PRC as a result of Deng's "four modernization." It variously looks into the philosophy, direction, policy, process, impact and implications of police reform in the earlier years, i.e., 1979 to 1999. The final chapter is on "Chinese Theory of Community Policing" (Chapter 8). The theory as proposed, Police Power as a Social Resource Theory, looks at crime and police from the people's, not the state's, perspective, i.e., as personal problems and social resource, not legal violation and law enforcement.

# CHAPTER TWO

# The Idea of Police

"In traditional China and for a long time, there was no distinction between military and administration (*junzheng bufen*), there was no distinction between police and administration (*jingzheng bufen*), there was no distinction between judicial and penal administration (*sifa xingzheng bufen*), in reality there was no independent ... public order system in China."
*History of Traditional Public Order System in China* (1998)[1]

"Police is a historical phenomenon. It originates with the state and disappears with the state. The basic characteristic (*benzhi teshi*) of police is an important instrumentality of the state to effectuate dictatorship (*guojia zhuanzheng gongju*) ..."
"Definition of *jingcha*," *Chinese Public Security Encyclopedia* (1989)

## Introduction

Police are not the same everywhere. The mandate and legitimacy, vision and mission, role and function, structure and process, operations and style of the police are variously determined by history and tradition, philosophy and ideology, and culture and custom. David Bayley investigated forty-seven police forces in five developed countries worldwide and discovered discernible differences in police structure and process as reflecting disparate historical development and cultural influences.[2] James Q. Wilson examined eight communities across the United States and found varieties of policing style, as determined by communal structure and local politics.[3]

Differences aside, the actual practice[4] of policing worldwide share much in common in terms of goals, such as crime prevention and order maintenance, and means, such as use of force. Such similarities register basic human instincts, for example, striving for safety and justice, and reflect durable collective aspirations, like a yearning for order and security.

In the case of China, since antiquity, policing functions, from political control to social ordering, have been achieved informally, by way of family and with the help of the community. In imperial China, family and, by extension, clan, were the most basic units of economic production and social control. Parents had powers to make and enforce family rules with delegated authority from the state. The situation was similar in Japan and other Asian countries that assimilated Chinese culture.[5]

In modern time and under Communist rule, the clan/family as a social control site has been replaced by the work units (*danwei*).[6] The work units controlled individuals ideologically, economically, and socially.

The myth that China had no formalized and organized social control arrangements before the *Qin* dynasty (秦朝) (221 to 207 B.C.) should be discarded. As described in *Shang Shu* (*Book of History*, 尚書) beginning with the *Xia* dynasty (夏朝), (21 to 16 B.C.), there were functional police operatives within the government and social control agents (parents and gentries) dispersed in the community.[7]

Specialized and professional police came to China around 1889 by way of Japan.[8] Western policing, in the guise of bureaucratic, scientific, technocratic, and legalistic policing, began to spread and take root in the People's Republic of China (PRC) after 1979.[9] Given China's lack of exposure to Western policing, it is interesting and useful to investigate how China came to police herself through the ages and, more pointedly, whether China has her own indigenous conception of police. In the words of Deng, what does policing "with Chinese characteristics" look like, conceptually, organizationally, and operationally?

This chapter is an investigation into the origin of "police" as a conceptual entity and the development of "policing" as a social practice in early imperial China. It addresses two related issues: What is the cultural meaning of police (*jingcha* or *jing cha*, 警察) in China? How were policing functions organized and performed in imperial China?

The difficulty with conceptualizing police in China is that the term is a transplanted idea with no indigenous roots. Starting at the translation level, there is a poor correlation between policing or *jing cha* (as a verb) versus police or *jingcha* (as a noun). More significantly, police or *jingcha* as a specialized state control agency is not an important, still less an exclusive, social and political institution to secure political obedience, maintain social order, and provide personal services in China. That is to say, up through the centuries, political control, social regulations, and public order were achieved in other, more informal, organic, integrated and dispersed ways.

This chapter is organized into the following sections. After this brief introduction, Section 2 covers the "Research Focus, Method, and Contributions." Section 3 as a "Literature Review," provides overall coverage of various research projects in Chinese police and policing. Section 4, "Problems with Historical Police Research," discusses reasons for the lack of historical police research in China. Section 5, "Conceptualizing Police and Policing," explores how police and policing have been conceptualized or defined in China. Section 6, "The Concept of Police in

China," investigates the linguistic roots and cultural meaning of "jing cha" (police) in imperial China and, more recently, "baowei" (security-defense) and "gong-an" (public security) in the PRC. Section 7, "The Origin and Development of Chinese Policing," traces the first recorded undertaking of policing functions by the state to the time of *Xia* dynasty, and the first centrally organized police bureaucracy to the *Qin* dynasty. Section 8, "Conclusion," summarizes the findings and articulates the lessons learned.

## Section 2—Research Focus, Method, and Contributions

In the understanding of Chinese policing, history matters,[10] which is so for the following reasons.

First, Chinese people in general and Confucian scholars in particular are extremely historically conscious. They look to history for mistakes made and lessons learned.[11] The first emperor of the *Han* dynasty (漢朝) (206 B.C. to 220 A.D.), Han Gaozu (漢高祖) (256 to 195 B.C.), after defeating the *Qin* empire, wanted to learn about the mistakes of the *Qin*'s rule, as historical lessons. Later, the Emperor Gaozu of Táng (566 to June 25, 635 B.C.), Li Yuan (李淵) observed, "Examination of winning and losing, investigation of ebb and flow of events … know more about history, leave something behind for the future." The avowed purpose for Sima Qian compiling *Shi Ji* (*Records of the Grand Historian*, 史記) was to: "Relate the past, prospect the future."[12] Emperors used history to leave a legacy, as captured by this admonition: "qian gu liu ming" ("leave a good name for a thousand years") vs. "wei chou wan nian" ("leave a bad name for ten thousand years").

Second, doctrinally Karl Marx preached historical materialism as the science of politics. According to Marx, the material base and production relationship and, in turn, the superstructure of the society and social consciousness of the people moves through predictable and inevitable historical stages–from tribalism to feudalism to capitalism to communism. Thus, in order to prepare for the future, one must know the past. More importantly, in order to liberate oneself from the domination of the exploitative capitalistic class, one must study history, as Friedrich Engels did with his *Manifesto of the Communist Party* (1888).

Third, Mao was a librarian. He was an avid reader of Chinese classics and political history. Many of Mao's thoughts were rejuvenations and extensions of traditional Chinese thought.

This cursory review of Chinese culture, ideology, and personality shows that to understand China is to intimately engage with Chinese history. The Chinese police professionals take this to heart. For example, a review of Chinese police texts finds many obligatory references to the past.

As observed below, there is a lack of Western research into the origin of police and the history of policing in China. This research is a first attempt to fill this research lapse. It is based predominantly on Chinese historical materials, supplemented by and illuminated with occasional English literature.

## Section 3—Literature Review

Focused study on policing in China before the 1870s did not exist. Thus, it is best to consult general historical treatises on political, for example, *Zhongguo zhengzhi zhidu shi* (1987),[13] administrative, for example, *Zhongguo gudai xingzheng lifa* (1990),[14] or legal, for example, *Zhongguo falu zhidu shi tonglan* (1989)[15] development to understand social control, public administration, and political governance in China. These treatises, while illuminating different aspects—philosophy, structure, methods, practices—of governance in imperial China, are not very informative on police as a distinctive intellectual concept or policing as a normative social/political control function.

The earliest discussion of Chinese police history was by Huang Zunxian (黃遵憲) (1848–1905), a *Qing* diplomat turned police reformer,[16] known as the "contemporary Chinese police foundation-layer" ("Zhongguo jindai jingcha dianji ren"). He was instrumental in establishing the short-lived but trend-setting *Hunan Baowei Ju* (Hunan security defense office) in China modeled on Western policing.

Huang traced the first discussion of police origin in China to two classical treatises *Zhou Li* (*Rites of Zhou*, 周禮) and *Guan Zi* (*Master Guan*, 管子). *Zhou li* detailed the titles, roles, and responsibilities of various central officials responsible for law and order functions, and *Guan Zi* described how government administrative practices such as *baoji* were carried out.[17]

*Zhonguo Baojia Zhidu* (Chinese Baojia Systeme, 中國保甲制度) (1936)[18] was the first book on policing in China. It described traditionally how Chinese communal social control was organized—specifically, how communities that were tied to farmland, lived in close proximity, and were connected by blood relationships were organized into a self-help, mutual aid, and communal responsibility system known as *boajia*. However, it has little to say about the police as a centrally organized, bureaucratically administered, functionally specialized, professionally trained agency in China.

*Contemporary Police History* (1999) is the most authoritative and comprehensive study on Chinese police history in recent years.[19] It provides detailed description and meticulous documentation of how the Chinese dysfunctional police system was reformed, organized, and operated during the late *Qing* dynasty and early Republic of China periods. The book began with the establishment of the *Hunan Baowei Ju* in 1887.[20]

According to *Contemporary Police History*, Ge Yuanxi, a long-time Shanghai resident, wrote a book *Huyou zaji* (*Miscellanies on Shanghai sojourn*) in 1876 about the people, customs, and happenings in Shanghai during that time. Ge provided a vivid first-person account of foreign police operating in China.[21] Ge observed that according to the "Shanghai zudi zhangcheng" (Charter for Shanghai Settlement) (1851), Shanghai Municipal Council was responsible for providing law and order in the international settlements. Accordingly, it established "xunbu fang" (patrol police stations, 巡捕房) staffed by half Western and half Chinese officers. They were identified with numbers on their uniforms and worked in various British, French, and American concessions in Shanghai.[22] Patrol officers were assigned to beats and patrolled the streets on foot at night. The Western police officers were equipped with knives and the Chinese with batons. Their duties were to deter crime, track criminals, maintain order, and handle emergencies.[23] The chief of police was appointed by the Municipal Council Board, its members elected by Western commercial leaders.

He Qi and Hu Liheng wrote the book *Zhongguo yi gailiang xinzheng lun* (*Discussion on how China ought to introduce new administration reform*), which made a number of far-reaching and radical reform proposals to save the *Qing* regime, including the establishment of "xunbu" (police) in China, modeled on the West.

In 1895 Cheng Guanying wrote the book *Shengzhi weiyan* (*Warning during prosperous time*) with a chapter on police ("Xunbu"). In the chapter, Cheng detailed the operations of police in New York City and the Shanghai concession, with growing admiration and sobering observation:

> In the old time, people's culture was simple and sincere, natural and unsophisticated, doors were not locked at night and lost properties were not picked up. Nowadays there are differences of opinion and varieties of characters. If there are no effective laws to eradicate the wicked and good regulations to arrest the criminals, there is no way to remove the evil and promote the good. This is why

> the West set up the police (*xunbu*). In examining Western legal systems, (we find that) there are police stations (*xunbu fang*) in big cities and major urban centers. They are divided into morning and night shifts. Police officers are on duty in the street and supervised by beats. When they observe suspicious activities and come upon assaults, kidnaps and robberies, they immediately make arrest and present the offenders to (justice) officials. Thus the rascals dare not cause trouble and lay people are not fearful at night. If there are small disputes between neighbors, they will quiet down and stop arguing, thus avoiding personal injuries. Their ability to prevent crime and protect residents contributed much to the local welfare. This is what Western style governance can offer.[24]

In 1999, Hon Yanlung and Su Yigong (*Contemporary Police History*) observed that there was a lack police historical research. The observation is a valid one. A comprehensive survey of articles published in *Gongan daxue xuebao* (*Journal of Chinese People's Public Security University*) (*PSUJ*) between 1994 and 2007 uncovers only thirteen articles discussing aspects of the history of policing in China. A review of another leading provincial police journal, the *Journal of Jiangsu Police Officer College* ("Jiangsu jingguan xueyuan xuebao"), for one year, 2003, shows only one article on police history, that being Xia Min, "Establishment of Modern Chinese Police System in Late Qing Dynasty" ("Wan Qing shiqi zhongguo jingdai jingcha zhidu jianshe"), *Journal of Jiangsu Police Officer College* Vol. 18(1), 142–147.

On public security historical research, Liu and Kuang's work offered one of the more systematic and comprehensive assessments.[25] According to the authors, the interest in Chinese public security historical research started in the early 1980s with the formation of a special research group at MPS ("Gongan shigao jiliao zhengji yanjiu lingdao xiaozu" — Public security historical data collection and research leadership core group") ("PS Research Leadership Group") with the dedicated resources, offices and staff. This was followed by provincial efforts in establishing local public security annals research organizations. Other researchers from a variety of academic disciplines and perspectives (Party history, social history) soon joined hands. As to activities, the PS Research Leadership Group held a number of workshops in 1982, 1983, and 1984 to plan, coordinate, and direct research work.

Into the 1990s, the MPS changed its research direction and disbanded the PS Research Leadership Group. The Fourth Research Institute at MPS has since taken up the leadership role in coordinating and directing public security research nationally. It continue to compile oral history, trained researchers, and solicited manuscripts from provinces and local public security organs around the country. There was, however, a noted decline of interest and reduction of efforts in Chinese police historical research. This has led the Chinese Police Association in 1999 to sound the alarm about the lapse of leadership and demise of such research. This prompted the PSU to redouble the effort in launching Chinese police history as a teaching research area in 1999.

Overall, public security research initiatives in the 1980s and 1990s boasted the following achievements. In terms of publications, there are: *History of Public Security* (*Zhongguo renmin gongan shigao*) (Beijing: Jingguan jiaoyu Chubanshe, 1997); *Contemporary public security work* (*Dangdai gongan gongzuo*) (Beijing: Dangdai Zhongguo chubanshe, 1993); *Mao Zedong public security work theory* (*Mao Zedong gongan gongzuo lilun*) (Beijing: Qunzhong chubanshe, 1993); *Luo Ruqing discussing people public security work* (*Luo Ruqing lun renmin gongan gongzuo*) (Beijing: Qunzhong chubanshe, 1994); *First Minister of Public Security — Luo Ruiqing* (*Xing zhongguo diyi ren gonganbu chang—Luo Ruiqing*) (Beijing: Qunzhong chubanshe, 1993). These are all essential police literature in understanding public security thinking and development, particularly before Deng's reform.

In terms of local efforts, the most valuable ones are the public security annals ("Difang Gongan zhi") of different regions or areas. This set of data promises to be a gold mine of research into public security history and development from different parts of the country.

In terms of data collection, the most comprehensive and authoritative publication is the *Overview of major public security events since the establishment of the nation* (*Jianguo yilai Gongan gongzuo dashi yaolan*) (Beijing: Qunzhong chubanshe, 2002), which documented public security development from October 1949 to 2002.

Finally, substantial amounts of internal historical materials are reported in the internal publication *Public Security Historical Research Materials* (*Gongan shi yanjiu ziliao*) as representative and validation of PS Research Leadership Group's work in the 1980s and 1990s. Such internal data is essential in reconstructing and understanding police development from an inside-out perspective.

As a critique of public security historical research, Liu and Kuang observed uneven development and lack of systematic, in-depth, and well grounded research. The first resulted from poor coordination, and the latter is caused by a lack of well-trained and experienced researchers.

In terms of future historical research, Liu and Kuang suggested a number of areas and issues of interest: First, the Party's theory, direction, policy, and strategy for public security construction during the reform period, especially their evolution and development, pattern and trend, and problems and issues; second, the thinking of third (now fourth) generation leadership and their historical significance and future implications on police development and operations; third; the evolution—continuity and change—of public security organs as a political and social institution; fourth, the conduct, process, and outcome of various public security campaigns, events and activities (e.g., strike hard campaign and anti-corruption drive); fifth, the ebb and flow of people's support and participation in public security work; finally, the change in public security operational environment. In terms of methods, the research should adopt the viewpoint of historicism and materialism, with a focus on the relationship between public security and history, the Party and the people.

As intimated, the scarcity of police historical research in the PRC reform era resulted from deliberate government policy. MPS was more interested in applied research, policy analysis, and case studies. As an example, a standard *PSUJ* "applied research" article usually starts with an introduction that contextualizes the study. This involves a focus and scope statement that articulates its objectives and delineates its reach. The article then discusses key concepts that set forth the nature of the problem being studied. This is followed by a presentation on incidence and prevalence, distribution and pattern, development and trend, causation and impact of the problem under discussion. The article ends with a rendering of solutions and remedies for the problem. Such articles are long on description and short on analysis; firm on policy and short on critique; detailed with prescription and short on data.

These kinds of research share one thing in common—they help the police to deal with recurring problems and controversial issues brought about by the reform process[26] along Party/government policy lines.

The struggle of public security historical research to establish itself as a respected field of study is also a struggle for the disciplinary identity of police studies as a whole. Should police studies be an academic or a professional field? Increasingly, the professional study and applied research school is gaining the upper hand. Academic police studies, including historical research, are in eclipse. The latest death knell came from changing the education mission at the PSU. Beginning in the fall of 2008, the PSU is no longer accepting undergraduate police cadets. PSU will be devoted entirely to professional training for in-service officers and graduate studies of the applied kind.[27]

Unlike Western police scholarship, which treasures diversity of approaches and rewards originality in findings, Chinese police research promotes uniformity in theory and consensus of interpretation.

This is not difficult to explain. Western social science scholarship in general, and police studies in particular, are built upon an interdisciplinary research tradition and are informed by a constructionist approach. The other tendency is to make the study of police a "science" for the purpose of earning disciplinary legitimacy. This has led to standardization of methods and uniformity of findings. Interpretation gives way to measurements, and understanding to prediction.

Chinese research, on the other hand, has long been devoted to finding eternal and universal truth through the use of historical data. This scholarship orientation is exacerbated by the Communist Party's ideology of historical materialism that is deemed scientific in nature and not to be disputed. This dampens inquisitive spirit and fosters a conformist mentality in Chinese police researchers, who are not independent scholars but state-sponsored researchers.

However, the search for eternal truth has never been easy or successful. It runs against strong currents of individual interpretation and subjective understanding of what historical events mean. Thus, beneath the appearance of shared agreement hide many contentious schools of thought and still more individual renditions of facts. Not being able to challenge orthodoxy, from Confucianism to Communism, Chinese scholars pour their inventiveness and creativity into writing poetry that speaks from the subliminal mind and caters to the yearning spirit.[28]

Zheng Zhongwu's four-part series, "Exploring the Historical Origins and Development of Police I, II, III, IV" in *PSUJ* published in 1998, exemplifies contemporary police historical research scholarship in orientation and style, limitations and shortcomngs.[29]

In this series of articles, the Police Chief of Shangxi province, Xiongdong county public security bureau, traced the origin and development of Chinese policing with historical materials. He started by affirming the importance of and need for historical research to maintain historical continuity in Chinese culture and police work.

Zheng analyzed Chinese historical materials *Hanshu* (*Book of Han*, 漢書) with a Marxist theoretical framework and found that there were no police in prehistoric times and with primitive tribal hunting communities.[30] Social order was maintained by custom and taboo, enforced by spiritual leaders such as "wushi" (wizard) or "jishi" (ceremonial officer), acting in the name of gods.

According to *Shangshu: Yaodian* (*Book of History—The Cannon of Yao*), during Yao Di rule (2357 to 2255 B.C.) there was evidence of the maintenance of public orde, e.g., a guard room for people who moved in the cities. Furthermore, by Yu Shun's time (2255 to 2205 B.C.) there were already many kinds of punishment and a penal officer (*xingguan*), which suggested the emergence of a rudimentary criminal justice system.

*Xia* (ca. 2100 to 1600 B.C.) offered China's first organized government structure. According to "Historical records—Xia Imperial Biographies" (*Shiji. Xia ben ji,* 夏本紀) *Xia* constructed the first prison (*yuan*) to stop people from challenging the emperor's authority.

At this time, there was, however, no separation between the military and the police in securing the state from all kinds of challenges; the military was an extension of the police. Beginning with the *Shang* (1783 to 1134 B.C.) and *Zhou* (1134 to 221 B.C.) dynasties and as reported in "Rites of Zhou" (*Zhouli*), specialized criminal justice officers were established.[31]

Although Zheng's treatment of police development is well supported by classical Chinese historical text, his interpretation was built upon a Marxist theoretical—ideological foundation, that is, police resulted from the discovery of private property, emergence of an exploitative class, and formation of a repressive state.

As a whole, Zheng's work is objectionable on conceptual, theoretical, and historical grounds:

First, conceptually, Zheng never defined the concept of "police." Still, Zheng was able to find police in the *Shun* period and associated police with a variety of law enforcement officials in the *Zhou* dynasty. Many questions need to be answered. Why were these officials considered as police within the Marx-Engels theoretical framework? Is it because they protected class interests with coercive state power? If so, which aspects of their work allow the author to draw such a conclusion?

Second, without a theoretical definition, how can police be properly identified: By the functions they performed, that is, order maintenance, crime fighting, law enforcement? By the legitimacy they possessed, that is, a political mandate? By the means they use to carry out their duties, for example, the use of coercive force?

The meaning of police is a cultural product. It is not a materialistic phenomenon capable of objective validation. Zheng in simplifying complex history to fit essentialist ideological claims overlooked contrary evidence and ignored competing claims.

Third, Zheng's observation is not supported by historical evidence.

Third, Zheng's observation is not supported by historical evidence.

(1) Chinese historical records, although comprehensive and detailed, are selective and constructive official history. Many of the grassroots experiences and local conditions were neglected or ignored. For example, Zheng relied on *Shang Shu*, which was known to be incomplete and unreliable for purposes of ascertaining the application of penal measures of the time.[32]

(2) Instructed by Marx, Zheng found no police agency before the emergence of class interests (slave vs. master) and the discovery of structured conflicts (haves vs. have-nots). The world then was a utopia, with no crime and few conflicts. In so assuming, Zheng, as did Engels, suffered from a bad case of utopianism and idealism.[33] In the natural world, survival of the fittest is the norm (Darwinism) and ruthless competition is the rule (Hobbes). Given this understanding of human nature and social conditions, the existence of a world without individual conflicts and collective warfare is most unlikely. This is evidenced by the constant admonition of the emperors and people to lead a virtuous life and not to give in to expediency and temptation. Also, conflicts between people and crime against society result from many sources, of which competition of interests and differences in values are the two most prominent. Such conflicts and differences must be resolved. It is thus unsound to presume that *all* conflicts are structural in nature and political in kind, existing only in a capitalistic society. It is also not true that only the state has an interest in resolving disputes and suppressing dissents. In China from antiquity, many disputes have been controlled by the family and community. No state police were necessary.

## Section 4—Problems with Historical Police Research

The research literature on Chinese police is meager[34] but adequate to sustain an emerging field.[35] The lack of historical police research and the challenges for researchers are best summed up by Hon Yanlung and Su Yigong:

> Part of the reason is ... the investigation into police history of successive dynasties in our nation's academic community started relatively late. There are no specialized treatises in the area. There are only very few articles ... there is a need for the collection and analysis of data anew. This presents much difficulties ... how to define the concept of police ... though the functions of police in maintaining social security (*shehui zhian*) already existed ...[36]

The lack of police research, especially before the 1990s, is due to several factors. As an emerging discipline, police studies are confronted with many problems and afflicted with boundaries issues. As a professional field, police studies are preoccupied with contemporary problems and focused on emergency issues at the expense of historical research.[37]

Currently, all police journals publish similar subject matter articles, namely: public security education, public security management, public security research, criminological research, public order management, criminal investigation, public security technology, law enforcement research, theoretical learning—political theory, case analysis, jurisprudential research—legal system forum, police culture, anti-drugs research and strategy, preliminary examination strategy and tactics, trace analysis, traffic management, and personnel administration. The editors are admonished to set journals apart from one another in orientation, perspective, and academic standards. Editors are repeatedly and emphatically admonished to publish materials supportive of public security education mission and research findings helpful to police operations. Little mention is made of police historical work.

Everything about police journal publication is politically controlled, ideologically determined, and policy driven.[38] The Party is less interested in historical research and more attuned to applied study.[39] Traditionally, police journals are not academic forums to exchange ideas and debate issues as in the West but are another tool to transmit Party doctrine in China.

Given this historical propaganda role[40] and traditional polemic style, police scholarship in the reform era was torn between political correctness and academic excellence, ideology purity, and scientific integrity.[41]

The poverty of historical research into policing should also be viewed in a larger intellectual, social, cultural and historical context.

Traditional Chinese intellectual discourse, in orientation, style, and substance, did not make room for the idea of police to grow.[42]

*Intellectually*, Chinese sage scholars were humanists.[43] Confucius preferred the rule of man over the rule of law.[44] As observed by Thomas Metzger, Chinese officials and scholars perceived "a kind of ideal, saintly, cosmologically grounded moral order or *gemeinschaft* according to which ... Chinese utopianism' is a peculiar phenomenon ... [and] describes the pursuit of an impracticable goal of political perfection by people insisting it is practicable....The Chinese have often been well aware that contemporaneous evils could not be conveniently overcome, but they still saw this recalcitrance as an eradicable condition, not as a reflection of permanent human frailties."[45]

The sage scholars were not interested in a discussion of how to actualize their ideals in organizational and practical terms, still less in a scientific way. Thus unlike the legalist Hon Feizi, Confucian scholars offered no systematic treatment on law enforcement and criminal punishment.

In addition, Chinese sage scholars were holistic thinkers.[46] They offered comprehensive and integrated solutions to governance problems in exhortative terms and with general principles. Thus, Confucian scholars were much less interested in offering particularistic answers and concrete solutions to day-to-day government problems and issues, such as a theory of and best practice in policing.

Also, Chinese intellectuals were not supposed to engage in "base people's" ways of thinking and behavior.[47] Specifically, according to Confucianism, the personal disposition and moral compass of scholars and the masses are different. Scholars are motivated by moral duty, and the masses by materialistic utility, the former moved by shame, and the latter by punishment. Thus it is inappropriate to use common thinking to understand the scholars' mentality. Therefore many basic tenets and fundamental propositions of the Chinese sage scholars mitigated against effective intellectual engagement with police and punishment issues, for example, prevention obviates punishment and education trumps supervision.

Chinese sage scholars adopted a governing philosophy that aimed at creating an orderly society through the development of a wholesome person functioning in a harmonious world. More specifically, people are to be internally driven, not externally regulated, starting with self-cultivation:

Self-cultivation holds the key to the betterment of mankind, and personal discipline leads to orderly society.[48] Perhaps the most famous of all Confucian admonitions in this regard is "Direct the people with moral force and regulate them with ritual, and they will possess shame, and moreover, they will be righteous" (*Analects*: 2.3). As a result, Confucius' ideas of "self-cultivation, discipline the family, govern the country and pacify the world" are well integrated into China's cultural beliefs, social practices,[49] and political program.[50] Thus there is no need to discuss law enforcement and policing.

*Socially*, the Chinese people shun involvement with the police. Police are considered as a necessary evil and a last resort. In the past, external policing was deemed unnecessary in an intimately related, tightly bonded, and closely watched community that was China.[51] Self-discipline, family surveillance, and social pressure were considered sufficient to induce conformity and regulate conduct. Also, officials and police are considered outsiders. Community disputes and personal problems can be best resolved within the tightly knit group.

*Culturally*, Chinese are taught to avoid confrontation and absorb affronts.[52] They are expected to seek accommodation through tolerance and resolve disputes by way of mediation,[53] at all costs. Additionally, involvement with officials and association with the police spell trouble for all concerned.[54] Finally, petty law enforcement agents held low socioeconomic status in Chinese society. They were uneducated and came from the underclass. They were mostly corrupted,[55] exploitative, and oppressive.[56] There is no need to record their activities, much less study them. This attitude still prevails today; young people are discouraged from joining the police.

*Historically*, Chinese historiography is constituted of writings by court historians (official history) and supplemented by the work of retired officials and scholars (unofficial history). Inasmuch as official and unofficial historical accounts tend to document events and report matters from the authors' perspective, and because police and policing were not a conceptual category, they were rarely attended to. There is no special provision made for police or policing in historical texts. The mentions of police are merely incidental. In the private arena, documentation of police matters can be extracted from biographies of scholars and officials. Again, as a result of their station in life, police and policing were hardly the kind of subject matter the scholars or officials indulged in when writing their biographies.

## Section 5—Conceptualizing Police and Policing

### Introduction

Inasmuch as this research is about the origin of the idea of police and development of practices of policing in China, it is appropriate to start with a discussion of how police vs. policing are defined; in what way they are the same and to what extent they are different.

### Conceptual Definitions

*Police* is defined as a formal institution of social control of and by the state.[57] *Policing* is defined as formal or informal functions of social control.

Whereas all society needs some form of policing, not every society has a police agency that is state sanctioned and centrally organized. In fact for a long time, policing functions of maintaining control, preserving order, and providing services have been achieved informally and voluntarily, through community self-help such as China's *Song* dynasty's *baojia* or Mao's mass campaign.

## Theory of more or less government

In theoretical terms, Kam C. Wong has challenged the basic assumption of a monolithic and monopolizing governmental control scheme—one state-organized police. He observed that historically and empirically there are many kinds of police agencies and policing agents sponsored and supported by the state in society, from family discipline to private security. These "lesser" police agencies partake in policing functions with a well-defined scope of control (e.g., corporate security works within a company's premises) and clear delegation of power (e.g., the father in a family can physically punish the children).

Table 1: Wong's more vs. less government authority: Varieties of police agencies as a function of relative governmental (police) authority

| | **Crime** | **Order** | **Service** |
|---|---|---|---|
| **More governmental (police) authority** | State police over criminal acts | State police on patrol | State police responding to 911 calls |
| **Less governmental (policing) authority** | Family discipline over violation of family rules | Community surveillance over public area | Clan social and economic support while away from home |

Non-state or private policing, depending on its relative association with, and degree of support by, the state, exhibits more or less state characteristics; that is, the more policing is sponsored by the government, the more it pursues state goals and acts in government's image. Thus, in the case of China, clan and family are in reality state-sponsored police units conducting policing on behalf of the state.

Chinese police scholars have independently come to the same conclusions. For example, in an article "The Definition for Police—Starting Point for the Study of Cop Subculture," the authors Zhang Zhaoduan and Wang Linsong observed the need to redefine *jingcha* or police away from a normative model. The authors suggested that police should not be defined by the purpose or objective of what a police agency should do, such as suppression of crime or maintenance of order. Instead, police should be defined functionally, by the policing activities in which a person engages.

The authors rightly pointed out that while the formal and legal police purpose and objectives cannot be readily assumed by "non-police" private citizens or community group, still those groups can engage in police-related activities.[58]

In arguing for an activities-driven model, the authors recognized all those who perform police functions or activities as de facto police agents. In so doing, the authors have created two issues. First, if all who perform policing activities are police agents of one kind or another, how can we separate formal/public police from informal/private police agents? Second, if police-related activities are used as a litmus test of being a police agent, analytically what kind of functions and activities are designated or considered as policing activities?

### Toward a normative definition of police

Marx postulated that the law (by extension the police) is the instrumentality of the state to dominate the people. Particularly, the police are established to fortify the capitalistic class interests at the expense of the proletarians.[59] Thus observed, police are not morally neutral but ideologically biased in favor of the ruling class.

Informed by this ideological tradition, PRC police scholars define police as "professional militant personnel for the maintenance of state regulation and social order, it is an important instrumentality of the state class oppression."[60]

Similarly, though less politically, Chapman observed that "the police power, as an extension of sovereignty, is the basis of the practical authority of the state."[61] In the United States police power is defined as:

> An authority conferred by the American constitutional system in the Tenth Amendment, U.S. Const., upon the individual states, and in turn delegated to local governments, through which they are enabled to establish a special department of police, adopt such laws and regulations as tend to prevent the commission of fraud and crime, and secure generally the comfort, safety, morals, health, and prosperity of its citizens by conserving the public order, preventing a conflict of rights in the common intercourse of the citizens, and insuring to each an uninterrupted enjoyment of all the privileges conferred upon him or her by the general laws.[62]

In this image the police conduct the state's business, from securing order to promoting welfare, with the endorsement and support of the sovereign state.

More democratically, Reith observed that the police are agents of the community to secure law and order.[63] In the same vein, Bayley defined police as "people authorized by a group to regulate interpersonal relations within the group through the application of physical force."[64]

All these police scholars and commentators envisioned the police as a coercive force in the bringing about of political (Marx), social (Bayley), or communal (Reith) normative order. Thus, the study of police and policing is the study of maintenance of collective normative order by the use of organized force. Four fundamental concepts inform this definition:

First, policing is a collectively *sponsored* activity by and for a group, sometimes political (state) other times social (communal). The studying of modern police is the study of politically (state) *sponsored* policing.

Second, police are there to promote and maintain collective *normative* order of all kinds—political, social, economic, and so on, directly (fighting riots) or indirectly (suppressing dissent).

Third, the collective (political authority or social community) endorses the use of force to maintain order.

Fourth, the use of police as a force must be *organized*; that is, the use of force is subject to larger organizational principles of when, how, and to what extent force should be used. More significantly, the organized use of force means that such use of force is to be held strictly accountable—monitored, supervised, and reviewed.

## Section 6—The Concept of Police in China

### Introduction

The concept of police as conventionally understood and contemporarily practiced in the West, did not exist in China.[65] According to *Ci Yuan* (*Sources of Words* 辭源), the term *jing cha* was not used in imperial China with reference to police.[66] The closest reference is to *jing xun*, which refers to a military internal security patrol[67] during the *Song* dynasty (宋朝) (960 to 1279).

As to why a military security patrol is considered as policing, it is important to point out that in imperial China, physical force—from beating to killing—was used against all kinds of people who offended the emperor or challenged the state authority. There was no artificial distinction drawn between military use of arms to repel foreign aggressors and the police resort to punishment of domestic offenders. Thus both enemies and offenders were subject of coercive sanctions for challenging the emperor's rule or disturbing public order. Within this context, it is easy to understand why, in imperial China, soldiers assumed internal security police patrol and local magistrates took part in purging bandits.

The idea of *jingcha* is an imported idea and an alien institution. The *Qing* dynasty (清朝) (1644 to 1912) reformers imported the idea and practice from Japan,[68] which first borrowed the term from the West,[69] that is, France and Germany.[70]

The *Qing* government looked toward Japan for advice and assistance in reforming its police. Particularly, on April 14, 1901, the *Qing* government signed a contract with Japan to set up a police academy in China at the capital. The contract provided that Japan was solely responsible for management of the academy, including designing academic programs, setting up recruitment standards, and assessing police work. Finally, a transplanted Western police organization was first established in China in 1889 with the *Hunan Baowei Ju*.[71]

Besides *jing cha* there are other policing-related terms, such as *gongna* (public security), *baowei* (protect and guard against), *baoan* (protect and secure), and *zhian* (public order). We now turn to these varieties of police ideas in China.

## Imperial China conception of *jing cha*

In classical Chinese the term *police* consisted of two Chinese characters, "jing" (警) and "cha" (察). The term literally means to warn ("jing") and be subjected to supervision ("cha").[72] More tellingly, the character "jing" is made up of two radicals (top "respect" and bottom "words" ) that mean a person has to keep to his own pledge to heaven and likewise "cha" is made up of two radicals (top "roof' and bottom "sacrificial ceremony") that mean heaven above is asked to keep check of pledges made by people. In this way, the responsibility to keep order is made a personal undertaking and ethical duty and policing activities are considered universal and moral obligations. Policing is about bringing about heavenly order on earth.

Together *jing cha* means to keep a watchful eye over unpredictable and undesirable events or guard against untoward conduct and unbecoming persons, with an eye toward self-defense and preservation.

Conceptualizing "jing" and "cha" this way has grave implications on Chinese social control and justice administration. People are expected to honor his words to act as a good citizen. Consequently, a violator is expected to owe up to his transgression by asking for forgiveness from haven through confession and with contrition. Conversely, everyone in the community has an affirmative obligation to keep the heaven's peace and on the look out for violators of pledge to heaven. In essence, self-discipline and collective surveillance are necessary to create good order.

Although no one disputes the linguistic roots of *jing* and *cha*, there is a perennial debate as to when and how *jingcha* as we come to use the term today, that is, for police or policing, originated.

### *Qing* conception of *jingcha*

The term *jingcha* as a foreign concept was first imported into China in late *Qing* times, ca.1876. Huang Zunxian, the putative father of modern Chinese policing, introduced foreign police theory and practice to China in establishing the *Hunan Baowei Ju*.[73] Years of living and traveling overseas afforded him the rare opportunity to observe foreign police systems up close and around the world. Upon his return, Huang was committed to bringing his foreign experience on Western policing to reform and strengthen the Chinese government. Huang put his ideas of foreign police ideas to work in establishing the *Hunan Baowei Ju*.

Huang envisioned the police role and function to be protecting the people. Specifically, police should be responsible for arresting criminals, tracking wanted people, rendering emergency assistance, escorting drunk and insane people home, and protecting seniors, youngsters, females, and foreigners.

Finally, if one were to draw a distinction between the imported concept of police (*jingcha*) in *Qing* and the indigenous idea of policing (*jing cha*) from China's imperial past, it can be observed that:

*Jingcha* refers to police as an enforcing agency or agent and *jing cha* to policing as rule/norm supervision or surveillance practice;

*Jingcha* is always a state agency or agent, and *jing cha* can be performed by anyone and by groups.

*Jingcha* are state agencies or agents who enforce state laws and maintain public order, and *jing cha* involves anyone providing supervision, surveillance, or monitoring of state law, public order, communal norms, social customs, moral order, or even natural disasters. That is to say, *jing cha* provides surveillance over anything that should not have happened ("bu gai").

*Jingcha* derives its power from state authority and with the use of coercion; *jing cha* gathers its influence from moral legitimacy derived from state endorsement, community support, and social pressure.

### Communist conception of *jingcha*

One of the salient features of PRC police are their overtly political and ideological nature. Above all else, police in a communist state are considered as a coercive instrumentality of the state. *Zhongguo gongan baike quanshu* defines *jingcha* as follows: "Administrative power of the state that is of an armed nature (*wuzhuang xingzhi*) for the maintenance of social order (*weichi shehui diexu*) and protecting of national security (*baohu guojia anquan*). Police is a historical phenomenon. It originated with the state, and disappears with the state. The basic characteristic (*benzhi teshi*) of police is that it is an important instrumentality of the dictatorship of the state (*guojia zhuanzheng gongju*)..."[74]

The political nature and ideological orientation of communist policing are best captured by the official duties of political officers attached to police units. According to "Regulations on People's police basic unit political instructor work" (1984),[75] political officers are supposed to carry out Party ideology and thought work (*zhengzhi xixiang gongzuo*).

Table 2: Three concepts of *jingcha* compared:

| | ***jingcha* (*Qing*)** | ***jing cha* (Historical)** | ***jingcha* (PRC)** |
|---|---|---|---|
| **Time introduced** | 1889 | 960 | 1921 |
| **Linguistic roots** | Imported from France (Paris), Germany[76] by way of Japan | First used together as one term during the *Song* dynasty | Communist ideology espoused by Engels as interpreted by Lenin and applied by Mao to China[77] |
| **Cultural meaning** | Police agency or police officer. | Supervision, surveillance, and guarding activities | Instrument of state (ruling class) to secure people's dictatorship |
| **Source of authority** | Political legitimacy | Mandate from heaven | Revolutionary jusice |
| **Forms of sanction** | Legal punishment | Moral shame | Political violence |
| **Organization** | Formal. organized, centralized, specialized, and differentiated | Informal, unorganized, diffused, and comprehensive | Comprehensive administration, surveillance, and control |
| **Process** | Rule of law | Rule of man | Rule of Party |
| **Comparative paradigm** | Institutionalization, professionalization, legalization and bureaucratization of police | Communalization, socialization, privatization of policing | Politicization of police |

### *Baowei* in contemporary China

Turning to contemporary China, the indigenous term that is closest in meaning to ancient *jing cha* or foreign policing is the concept of *baowei* (保卫). In Chinese the character *bao* means to stand guard (*shou,* 守), and the character *wei* means to defend against (*fangshou,* 防守) or protect from (*weihu* 维护). Together *baowei* means to stand guard over an object/person/place and/or to protect an object/person/place from harm. Thus construed, *baowei* suggests a reactionary self-defense force to keep one from harm against external threats of all kinds. In recent Chinese history, there were many forms of local *baowei* or *baoan* (保安) units performing various kinds of security preservation, order maintenance, and self-defense activities. For example,

(1) In June of 1897, the Hunan province *anchasi* (Minister of Justice), Huang Junxian, advocated for the establishment of *Hunan Baowei Ju* at Changsha.[78]
(2) In August 1930 the Nanjing government set up a *baowei tuan* under the Civil Affairs Department at the provincial level to provide for local security.
(3) In May 26, 1914 the generalissimo, Yuan Shikai (袁世凯), to consolidate his power and extend his control over whole of China, issued the "Difang baoweituan tiaoli" (Regulations on local self-defense association), which consolidated all local militia-defense units in China into one centrally controlled policing force. The role of the *baowei tuan* was to organize local self-defense to aid the police in maintaining law and order. Under Yuan Shikai, the *baowei tuan* served as a mutual aid-security pack or a modern form of *baojia*.
(4) From the beginning, CCP was very concerned about survival and obsessed with security[79] from internal traitors to external spies.[80] The CCP adopted elaborate measures to protect itself, in the form of *baowei gongzuo* (security work) and *baowei bumen* (public security bodies). There were many kinds of *baowei gongzuo* associated with various Party and state agencies. The earliest form of CCP internal security organ was the "Zhongguo Gongchandang Zhongyang Teke" (CCP Central Special Branch) set up in December 1927 in Shanghai.[81] It was placed under the leadership of Zhou Enlai, a member of the CCP Central Special Branch Committee.[82] In subsequent years, during the Second Revolutionary Civil War, the CCP established "sufan weiyuanhui" (Committee for Eliminating Coun-

terrevolution) in the revolutionary bases to conduct "political policing."

In November 1931, the CCP–Soviet People's Delegates established its first formal government structure at Ruijin, that of the China Soviet Republic provisional government and with it the *Minjing guanli ju* (Civil Police Administrative Bureau) and *Guojia zhengzhi baowei ju* (State Political Security-Defense Bureau). Their major functions were to collect intelligence and to defend the Party from KMT spies, infiltrators, and security agents. Later, in February 1939, the CCP integrated and streamlined its intelligence gathering and counterespionage functions in the *Zhonggong zhongyang shehuibu* (Central Department of Social Affairs).[83] *Shehui bu* was responsible for public security. *Baowei weiyuanhui* was responsible for weeding out traitors and spies.[84] After 1949, it was replaced by the Central Investigation Department. In June 1983, the National People's Congress established the Ministry of State Security under the State Council to provide for the security of the state through effective measures against enemy agents, spies, and counterrevolutionary activities designed to sabotage or overthrow China's socialist system.

### *Baoan* in reformed China

In Deng's reform era (1979), the nation's priority shifted from fighting a class war to that of economic reform. In Mao's way of thinking, the struggle was no longer one of contradiction with the enemy but between the people, that is, from an antagonistic to non-antagonistic struggle. As a result, national security became a lesser concern and social stability and public order a more important problem. *Baowei* as a protective function changed its focus from safeguarding political targets, Party organs, government buildings, and military secrets to securing financial assets and commercial buildings. In the reform era, it took up quasi-public, communal, or private security duties and responsibilities. When used in this context, *baowei* takes on a different name, that is, that of *baoan* or "security guard" services.

### *Gongan* in modern China

PRC established the MPS (*Gonganbu*) in November 1949. Before 1949, the CCP briefly set up a *Nan Chang Gongan Ju* on August 1, 1927, after the Nan Chang revolution.[85] On October 2, 1927, the Ministry of Interior promulgated "Geji gonganbu bianzhi daigan" (Outline of Public Security Office at All Levels), which required the naming of all provincial level police agencies as *Gonganbu* (Public Security Departments).[86]

*Gongan* was defined in the *China Public Security Encyclopedia*[87] as: "Actions that are sanctioned by the state ... to maintain social order, protect public safety, public and private property and citizens' personal rights in accordance with the law."

*Gongan* is literally translated as "public" (*gong*) and "security" (*an*).[88] The idea was traceable to the Committee of Public Safety of the French Revolution of April 6, 1793.[89]

## Section 7—The Origin and Development of Chinese Policing

### Introduction

Charles Reith, the pre-eminent police scholar, has defined police as a "necessary force for securing sustained observance of laws in human communities."[90] Since antiquity, there have been two kinds of police forces: kin police and ruler-appointed police. The first corresponds to informal social control, and the latter identifies with bureaucratic policing.

Historically, China has experimented with both kinds of policing. For historical and cultural[91] reasons, community social control was the more dominant kind.[92] Control started from self-cultivation and was followed by family discipline, community surveillance, and finally state sanction, each reinforcing the previous one.

In imperial China, community social controls (e.g., family discipline and community surveillance) were complemented and supplemented by bureaucratic policing.

Traditionally, the Chinese emperors ruled by delegation of authority and with proxy agents. The emperor governed the state by and through his officials,[93] who in turn delegated the responsibility of social control to the local community and indigenous agents, such as family, clan, and village. In theory and practice, the whole nation was organized as one big family.

Social control started with the family and clan, and only as a last resort was it referred to local officials. State law (*guofa*), family admonitions (*jia xun*), and clan rules (*zugui*) reflected and reinforced each other in giving substance to Confucius' ideas and ideals.[94] As described by Dutton: "In classical China, an intricate web of relations, based ultimately upon the family and policed by a labyrinth of mutually self-checking units augmented by an advanced system of documentation, succeeded in maintaining social harmony for most of the dynastic period."[95]

## Origin and development

The following section traces the early development of policing and organization of police in China from the *Xia* to the *Qin* dynasties, 21st century B.C. to 207 B.C.

Table 3: Historical development of policing from *Xia* to *Qin* Dynasty

| | Official—Institution | Implications for Policing | Historical Significance |
|---|---|---|---|
| *Xia* (21st to 16th century B.C.) | "Situ" official: Educate people to avoid disputes.<br><br>Prison: In ground round hole ("huan tu")[96] for the holding of offenders. It is also called "jun tai" or "xia tai": Confinement of rebellious persons. | Experimentation with social control:<br><br>First, proactive social control over reactive punishment.<br><br>Second, incapacity in addition to surveillance as a form of social control. | First appearance of organized social control:<br><br>First appointment of social control agent.<br><br>First appearance of confinement as a social control measure. |

| | Official—Institution | Implications for Policing | Historical Significance |
|---|---|---|---|
| *Shang* (16th to 11th century B.C.) | Emperor as the source of law on earth, justice from heaven, and head of nation (family).<br><br>"Zhen bo" officers in charge of fortune telling before all important decisions being made by emperor. | Principles of law making and enforcement:<br><br>First, mandate of heaven must be followed.<br><br>Second, personal pledge to heaven must be enforced. | Establishment of normative order:<br><br>Principle of "mandate of heaven" as normative order.<br><br>Personal pledge as basic of rule enforcement. |

| | Official—Institution | Implica-tions for | Historical Significance |
|---|---|---|---|
| Western *Zhou* (11th century to 771 B.C.) | Three Constitutional principles:<br>First, emperor ruled supreme.<br>Second, legitimacy of rule from benevolent governance corresponding to mandate from heaven ("yi de pei tian" or "aligning the earth with the heaven").<br>Third, clan ruled absolute.<br>Eight Administrative principles:<br>(1) On staffing ("guan shu")<br>(2) On role and responsibilities ("guan zhi")<br>(3) On collaboration and coordination ("guan lien")<br>(4) On routine duties ("guan chang")<br>(5) On rules and regulations ("guan cheng")<br>(6) On protocol ("guan fa");<br>(7) On rules for five punishment ("guan xing")<br>(8) On supervision of officials ("guan ji").<br>National justice officials:<br>National crime and justice policy was set by "zhun ren."<br>Justice administration is executed by "tai shi."<br>Day to day public order ("an bang") was performed by:<br>"Situ" who looked after the welfare and education of the people.<br>"Sikong" who was in charge of god of the land ("sheji"), temples, imperial clothing, transports, complements.<br>"Sikong" also served as "dai sikou" in charge of justice and punishment.<br>Nation's capital security and justice:<br>"Shi shi" was in charge of the security and crime control and justice administration.<br>Local justice administration:<br>"Xian shilou" was in charge of local justice in criminal ("yu" or imprisonment) and civil cases ("susong" or civil litigations")<br>"Xiang shi" was in charge of litigations, justice and penal measures within 100 *li* (mile) and "zui shi" was in charge of areas beyond 100 *li*<br>Community order<br>Community order was achieved by household registration.<br>"Si min" was in charge of household registration. | Articulation of "Constitutional" principles:<br>First, police powers came from heaven, exercised by the emperor alone.<br>Second, police power subject to mandate from heaven, as natural principles.<br>Third, policing subject to detail and exacting administrative rules.<br>Maturation of grassroots social control doctrine:<br>First, family and clan acted as all purpose grassroots social control—policing agents.<br>Second, administrative and justice officials part take in policing of matters in their jurisdiction and under their charge. | Western *Zhou* provided prototypical model of penal administration and social control working in tandem:<br>(1) Established constitutional government:<br>Mandate, authority, accountability, and control.<br>(2) Develop a system of government—social control based on blood ties.<br>(3) Formulation of administrative principles to organize, guides,<br>and supervise policing activities.<br>(4) No need for separate police agency/ officials, policing as part and partial of justice and social administration.<br>(5) Integrated system of penal -social control: at capital, national, local, communal, family level. |

| | Official—Institution | Implications for Policing | Historical Significance |
|---|---|---|---|
| Spring and Autumn Period (770 to 476 B.C.) and Warring States (475 to 221 B.C.) | National justice officials:<br>(1) "Simin" was in charge of household registration.<br>(2) "Sishi" was responsible for keeping order in the market.<br>(3) "Sibao" was responsible for maintaining social order.<br>(4) "Siji" was responsible for the arrest and punishment of robbers and thieves.<br>(5) "Siwushi" was responsible for enforcement of curfew.<br>(6) "Jinbaoshi" was responsible for the suppressing civil disturbance, prohibition violation, fraud, and disorderly conduct.<br>(7) "Jinshalu" was responsible for maintaining public order and control of criminals.<br>(8) "Sixuanshi" was responsible for fire prevention and fire fighting.<br>(9) "Siluhi" was responsible for the direction and control of traffic.<br>(10) "Sili" was in charge of confiscation of weapons, contrabands, and assignment of slaves.<br>(11) "Sili" was responsible for management of slaves, captives, and arrest of criminals.<br>(12) "Sihuan" was responsible for prison management and punishment.<br>(13) "Simen" was in charge of guarding the capital gates and providing for custom inspection.[100] | Establishment of comprehensive and integrated social control system<br><br>First, broad "police power" of the state for public good<br><br>Second, varieties of administrative officials performing policing functions covering different aspects of social and economic life, including household registration; law enforcement, criminal investigation, emergency services, economic/social ordering; traffic regulation; punishment dispensation.<br><br>Third, conspicuously absent is policing as a service functions that was supplied by family and communities. | Clear delineation/assignment of police functions:<br><br>Providing the clearest evidence that all Western police functions—law enforcement, crime control, order maintenance, internal security, emergency services—were provided for. |

| | Official—Institution | Implications for Policing | Historical Significance |
|---|---|---|---|
| *Qin* dynasty (221 to 207 B.C.) | Imperial rule:<br>"Weiwei" in matters of imperial security.<br>Organized policing with bureaucracy and law. Responsible for guarding the emperor and patrolling the palace grounds.<br>"Zhongwei" in matters of capial security.<br>Responsible for public order and security within the capital grounds.<br>"Tingwei" in matters of justice administration. Responsible for criminal investigation, arrest, adjudication, sentencing, and execution.<br>Local public security administration:<br>Prefecture: "Jun shou"<br>Responsible for all the welfare and security of the local residences, including maintaining law and order within the *jun*.<br>County: "xian ling" (over 10,000 residents) and "xian chang" (under 10,000 residents)<br>Responsible for keeping law and order and administration of justice within his jurisdiction.[101]<br>Rural area: "Xiang" (rural area): "San Lao" (three officials)<br>One was responsible for internal administration and other public health, order and safety—prevention of crime (*qiudao*), arrest of criminals (*buzei*), and maintenance of public health (*wei sheng*).<br>"Ting" (police post)<br>"Tingchang" (chief of the post)<br>Maintain order, suppress crime and enforce the law<br>"Tingzu" (soldier of the post)<br>Community policing:<br>"Baojia" system.<br>A community policing system performing mutual defense, informal surveillance, and collective accountability functions. | First centrally administered military - criminal justice — police system.<br>First, central administration of all government functions.<br>Second, the discovery of rational bureaucracy.<br>Third, justice administration based on rule by law.<br>v<br>Varieties of police innovations:<br>First, federation of police services.<br>Second, legalization of policing.<br>Third, bureaucratization of police organization.<br>Fourth, invention of police post and patrol.<br>Fifth, institutionalization of community policing. | Institutionalization of police. |

### *Shun* (2255 to 2205 B.C.)

The earliest record of policing activities in China was traceable to the legendary sage monarch *Shun*. China then was not a united kingdom but a coalition of tribes, led by a charismatic, respected, and powerful leader. During *Shun* rule, the tribal coalition committee established nine kinds of officials. Two of them carried out modern-day policing functions. *Situ* was responsible for resolving people's disputes and maintaining social order. *Shi* was responsible for policing the border, investigating crime, and maintaining prisons.

### *Xia* (21st to 16th century B.C.)

The *Xia* dynasty[102] inherited the *Shun* order maintenance scheme. *Situ* were central officials. Grassroots order maintenance functions were handled by local officials. Furthermore, from inscriptions on bones and tortoise shells unearthed, historians confirmed the existence of a system of in-ground confinement areas, or prisons being maintained in the *Xia* dynasty.[103] This suggested institutionalized law enforcement activities of some kind.

### *Shang* (16th to 11th century B.C.)

The *Shang* dynasty followed the *Xia* dynasty. In the *Xia* dynasty there was no record of police apparatus or policing officials. However, there were officials in charge of conquered people and captured slaves. Occasionally, the military were mobilized to suppressed rebellion or civil disturbance and to chase after offenders.[104]

### Western *Zhou* dynasty (11th century to 771 B.C.)

The Western *Zhou* dynasty conquered the *Shang* dynasty in the 11th century B.C.[105] The first task at hand was to consolidate its power and perfect its control over an alien nation spread over the vast Central Plain of China. This led to the establishment of a centralized political and social control system denominated in legal and administrative terms.

During the *Zhou* dynasty, the *Shikou* (Minister of Justice) was responsible for justice administration.[106] The *Shikou* assisted the emperor in handling all criminal matters within the realm. In so doing, the *Shikou* followed the well-defined justice philosophy and established penal policy of the emperor.[107]

The Minster of Justice assumed many modern day police functions (e.g., maintaining state authority, national security, and social order. His duties included promulgating laws, running prisons, and adjudicating criminal and civil cases. The Ministry of Justice was the first public, specialized, and professional policing institution in China.[108]

The Minister of Justice was assisted by a number of subordinate officials and local (*difang*) officers.

## Spring and Autumn Period (770 to 476 B.C.) and Warring States (475 to 221 B.C.)

During the Spring and Autumn and Warring States periods, China was politically divided between many factions contending for power. In the end, the Eastern *Zhou* emperor was no longer able to control various rebellious vassal lords.[109]

The vassal lords, free from central control, experimented with and established a variety of policing officials, some of which have counterparts in the PRC today.

## *Qin* dynasty (221 to 207 B.C.)

The *Qin* dynasty made three durable contributions to the development of policing in China. It institutionalized bureaucratic policing, regularized community policing, and provided for the policing of officials.

In bureaucratic policing, the *Qin* dynasty united China by central administration[110] and with uniform law.[111] Centralized and bureaucratic policing came into prominence during the *Qin* dynasty due to five reasons:

First, the First Emperor of *Qin*(*Qin Shihuangdi*) wanted to create a central bureaucratic state out of the loosely organized feudal system of *Zhou*. To do so, he introduced the principle of vertical rule.[112]

Second, in order to unite China, *Qin Shihuangdi* needed unfailing execution of his instructions and total obedience to his orders. This required the establishment of a centrally controlled law enforcement agency to supervise the officials and check on the people.[113]

Third, a central administrative state means an impersonal, rational, and rule-bound bureaucracy to maximize efficiency. This led to the development of specialized and professional police.

Fourth, the *Qin* dynasty introduced the rule by law to China. For the first time, law and punishment were used to control the state and regulate the people. Laws were to be obeyed and achieved by consistently applied reward and punishment. This required the establishment of professional law enforcement agents who executed the law and were restricted by it.

Fifth, the *Qin* dynasty introduced and promoted the use of force to secure people's obedience. This became the responsibility of the policing agents.

With the introduction of vertical rule, legal control, central administration, and coercive rule, law enforcement functions became institutionalized as a state craft and bureaucratic practice. Thus we can argue that the *Qin* dynasty, and particularly Shang Yang, introduced institutionalized policing to China.

The *Qin* dynasty established a comprehensive and integrated criminal justice system with the emperor serving as the ultimate authority; being the fountain of virtue and bestowed with the mandate from heaven.[114] The emperor was assisted by the *tingwei* in matters of justice administration, including the investigation, arrest, adjudication, sentencing, and execution of criminals. The *weiwei* was responsible for guarding the emperor and patrolling the palace grounds. The *zhongwei* was responsible for public order and security within the capital grounds.

Beyond the capital, justice administration was in the hands of local officials. Administratively, *Qin* divided the state into 36 *jun* (prefectures) that were further subdivided into many *xian* (counties) and below the *xian* were yet smaller subdivisions.[115]

In community policing, the smallest and lowest political/social administrative unit was the *li*. The day-to-day administration of justice and the policing of the local population was relegated to a *li dian* who was responsible for keeping the peace and order in the local community. He was assisted in his work with the help of two institutionalized community policing mechanisms:

First, the household registration system monitored the whereabouts and status of every person in the state.[116] Shang Yang established the *baojia* system—a community policing system performing mutual defense, informal surveillance, and collective accountability functions. In this earliest form of *baojia* system, five families were organized into one *wu* and ten families were organized into one *ji*. The other durable contribution of the *Qin* dynasty was the introduction of accountability in government (to the emperor) with the establishment of a formal and rule-bound supervision system (*jiancha zhidu*) or control of officials (*zhi li*).[117]

Emperor *Qin Shi Huang* (259—210 B.C.) set up one of the most complex and elaborate administrative systems up to that point in imperial China.[118] According to the legalist school, which was the dominant philosophy of the time, officials were not to be trusted because they were motivated by self-interest and driven by utility to abuse their position and authority for personal gain. Specifically, if unchecked and given the opportunity, officials would lie and keep the emperor in the dark and lead him to act wisely, as well as causing other serious damage to the society and government. The remedy for all these official indiscretions was establishing a system to secure more systematic and effective supervision and control in testing, appointment, reporting, and promotion of government officials.

The office of the *yushi* (imperial envoy) was established to monitor the conduct of officials and report on their performance. The ultimate goal was to establish responsible government and hold officials accountable.

## Section 8—Conclusion

This chapter attempts to discover the origin of ideas concerning police in imperial China and traces the practice of policing through time.

### General framework

Since antiquity in China, policing functions, including political control and social ordering, have been achieved informally and provided for by way of family and with the help of the community. Western ideas of policing came to China in the late nineteenth century. Professional and technocratic policing began to spread and take root in the People's Republic of China after 1979.

### Communal policing

The earliest record of policing activities appeared with the legendary sage monarch *Shun* (2255–2205 B.C.). The tribal coalition committee established nine kinds of officials, some of whose responsibilities included. resolving people's disputes, maintaining social order, policing the border, investigating crime, and maintaining prisons.

### Bureaucratic policing

The *Qin* dynasty (221 to 207 B.C.) united China with vertical rule, legal control, central administration, and coercive governance, that is, a criminal justice bureaucracy with the emperor serving as the fountain of virtue under heaven.

### Western policing

China's first experience with foreign policing was in 1876 with foreign policing arrangements in the international settlement port of Shanghai. Under the Charter for Shanghai Settlement, police stations were established in various foreign concessions and staffed by Western and Chinese officers in equal numbers. The chief of police was appointed by the Municipal Council Board, with members elected by Western commercial leaders.

Huang Zunxian, putative father of China's modern policing, experimented with foreign police ideas in establishing the *Hunan Baowei Ju*.

## Communist policing

*Gongan* literally means "public peace" (later translated as "public security"). In China the police have been referred to as *gongan* and more recently as *jingcha*. There are two types of police in China: *minjing* or people's police, and *renmin wuzhuang jingcha budui* or People's Armed Police (PAP).

CHAPTER THREE

# Origin of Communist Policing

"Should not only understand China today. Should also understand China's historical development."
Mao Zhedong [1]

## Introduction

It is now common to attribute the origin of Communist policing to the establishment of the People's Republic of China (PRC), and particularly to the formation of the Ministry of Public Security (MPS) in November 1949.[2] There are many, however, who contend that the Communists experimented with policing before 1949. For example, PRC police historians have traced the development of PRC police to the formation of the first Chinese Soviet government in Shan-Gan-Ning in November 1931. In November 1931, as a first act of government, the central executive committee passed the "Provisional organic law for the Soviet local government," which provided for the establishment of the State Political Security Department. The State Political Security Department was responsible for the investigation, arrest, and prosecution of all political crimes. The Organic Law could be considered the first police organizational law in China.

The choice of 1949 as the birth date of PRC policing is supported by two facts: (1) Legally speaking, the PRC existed as a sovereign state only after 1949. (2) Historically, the PRC had no institutionalized police force before 1949.

It is most unfortunate that the investigation of PRC policing should start with 1949 because many of the ideas behind PRC policing—security policing (*baowei*), political policing (*zhengzhi baowei*), and people's policing (*qunzong baoan*)—have a historical root, intellectual origin, and ontological being stretching back to the earliest days of communism in China in 1921.

There are two reasons to investigate the origin of Communist policing:

First, the subject matter has not been thoroughly investigated before.

Second, a thorough understanding of the current PRC police theory and practices must start with its origin. The Communist police exhibit strong continuity with the past in the midst of constant changes. The

PRC leadership learned from past experience[3] in building a Communist police with Chinese characteristics. As aptly observed by Griffin:

> Important members of the pre-1949 leadership group, especially Mao Tse-Tung and Chou En-lai have institutionalized many pre-1949 problem solving techniques, thereby passing them on to subsequent generations. Consequently a detailed study of the 1924 to 1949 period, in which these techniques evolved, leads to a clearer understanding of the governmental methods and leadership styles of modern China.[4]

The PRC public security today, though not a duplicate of the pre-1949 police in role and functions, shows fairly strong resemblance in forms and substances and displays much continuity in theory and practices.

This chapter investigates the origin of Communist policing in China. The research question posed is: How did the Communists enforce law and maintain order under their sphere of political influence in 1925 and 1926? The central thesis is that the Chinese Communist Party had its first experience with organized social control (i.e., policing) during the Canton-Hong Kong Strike of 1925–1926.

This chapter is divided into the following parts: Section 1 "Research Data and Method"; Section 2 "Theoretical Framework: Delegation and Sponsorship of Social Control"; Section 3 "The Historical Context of the Canton-Hong Kong Strike *Jiucha dui*"; Section 4 "The Redistribution of Governmental Social Control—A Case Study of the Canton-Hong Kong Strike Committee"; and Section 5 "*Jiucha dui* as Governmental Social Control."

## Section 1—Research Data and Method

### The research data

This research is based on PRC historical records and archive materials.

Some of the more important historical sources are: Wang Haixing, *Zhongguo gongren yundong shi* on Communist labor movement history,[5] *Zhonggong dangshi ziliao* on CCP party history,[6] Zhang Xipo & Han Yanlong, *Zhongguo geming fazhi shi* (shang) on Communist revolutionary history,[7] *Zhongguo renmin jingcha jianshi* on PRC police history,[8] Frederic Wakeman, Jr., *Policing Shanghai 1927–1937* on KMT police history,[9] Han Yanlong, *Zhongguo jindai jingcha zhidu* on recent Chinese police history,[10] Jean Chesneayx et al., *China: From 1911 Revolution to Liberation* on Communist China political history.[11]

I use six sets of archival materials to ascertain how the Communists maintained law and order in their sphere of influence (i.e., labor organization and strike areas) in the 1920s:

(1) Beijing geming bowuguan (Beijing revolution museum) (ed.), *Beifang diqu gongren yundong ziliao xuanbian* ("Collection of materials on Northern area labor movement") (Beijing chubanshe, 1981) on the "Kai luan" five mine strike.

(2) *Liu Shaoqi yu Anyuan gongren yundong* ("Liu Shaoqi and the Anyuan labor movement") (Zhongguo shehui kexue chubanshe, 1981) on the Anyuan strike by the strike leadership.

(3) *Guangdong danshi yanjiu wenji* ("Collected works on Guangdong party history research") Vol. 1, 2 (Zhonggong dangshi chubanshe, 1993), an oral historical account of Canton labor movement by various contemporary labor leaders.

(4) *Wu-San-Shi yundong he Sheng-Gang bagong* ("The May 30th movement and Canton-Hong Kong Strike") (Jiangsu guji chubanshe, 1985) on Canton-Hong Kong strike from public records.

(5) *Minguo shiqi Guangdong sheng zhengfu, dangan shiliao xuanbian* ("Collection of archive historical materials of Guangdong provincial government during the Nationalist period") (Guangdong sheng danganguan, 1928) Vol. 1 on legislative history and debates during 1925–1926 from official Canton provincial government council meeting minutes.

(6) *Sheng-Gang dabagong ziliao* ("Materials on Canton-Hong Kong Strike") (Guangdong renmin chubanshe, 1980) on the Canton-Hong Kong strike of 1925 from CCP records.

## Research strategy

This research takes a functional approach to investigating the origin of Communist policing. A functional approach discovers alternate organization and process of policing by investigating how essential police functions were performed in the investigated period. The functional approach starts by ascertaining the essential functions of the police (i.e., law enforcement, crime control, order maintenance and social service) and then investigates how such police functions were being performed in China under Communist rule.

The functional approach is most appropriate in investigating emerging police institutions when the exact idea of social control has not yet taken shape and become firmly settled. It is also useful in the study of unconventional police practices when unfamiliarity with the new police, preoccupation with the established police, commitment to the dominant political ideological, and habituation with settled mass culture of the past block our vision and imagination in understanding the nature and role of a novel police institution: the Communist-militant-political policing under investigation.

A functional approach is also more scientific. A functional definition of police is more generic and occupies a higher order in the conceptualization scheme. It opens the eyes of police researchers to other forms and methods of policing that otherwise might be overlooked due to their unfamiliarity.

On the negative side, a functional definition of police is particularly vulnerable to overreaching and, if not applied in a conscientious and disciplined manner, is susceptible to abuse. Although it allows us to look beyond traditional, conventional, and classical policing to search for alternate police forms and functions, it runs the risk of blurring any meaningful distinction between the state organized police force and any number of policing organizations serving incidental policing functions if not carefully implemented.

## Section 2—Theoretical Framework:

### Delegation and Sponsorship of Social Control

In this section I argue that the more the government delegates its social control authority and sponsors non-state actors' social control activities, the more the non-state actors behave like government police agents.

Delegation of social control powers is a redistribution of the constitutional mandate to govern. Delegation is an affirmative granting of powers or acknowledgment of rights to non-state actors by the state, allowing those actors to take part in governmental social control, for example, family discipline or clan rule in traditional China or private policing in modern America.

Depending on the scope of delegated control, the extent of delegated authority, and the degree of supervision over such delegations, the delegated party acts more or less like an autonomous government.

In theoretical terms, the greater the delegation, the more a non-state agent behaves like an autonomous government. The narrower the delegation, the less a non-state actor behaves like an autonomous government.

Social control authority is of three kinds. In decreasing order of authority, they are authority to define social norms, authority to establish social norms, and authority to enforce social norms—corresponding to legal policy setting, lawmaking, and law execution.

More power to exert social control means more power sharing with the dominant political authority and, in turn, power domination over subordinate social subjects. Power sharing is manifested in negotiation for control. Lesser power allows for the negotiation over legal outcomes. Greater power allows for the negotiation over legal content. Power parity allows for the negotiation over legal process. Power domination (from more to less) is manifested in the imposition of the decision-making process, norm, and result.

Table 1: Governmental delegation of public social control (policing) authority—an analytical framework

| Theoretical concepts | Operational definitions | Example |
|---|---|---|
| Government delegation of police powers | *Delegation of social control authority*—the redistribution of government's constitutional power to use force to enforce the law and maintain (political or social) order | Constitutional provisions<br>Enabling legislation |
| | *Delegation of norm defining authority*—the extent to which the government delegates the authority to define general normative expectation | Government social control philosophy<br>Jurisprudential thought<br>Law enforcement policy |
| | *Delegation of norm setting authority*—the extent to which the government delegates the authority to set specific normative expectations. | Police legislation<br>Police rules and regulations |
| | *Delegation of norm enforcing authority*—the extent to which the government delegates the authority to seek compliance with the normative expectations | Licensing<br>Inspecting<br>Policing |

### The concept of sponsorship of private social control

The more the state sponsors non-state policing activities, the more the non-state social control takes on the color of the state or becomes, in effect, government social control. State *sponsorship* of non-state social control functions amounts to state *participation* in non-state social control functions, for all practical purposes. State sponsorship can be in the form of passive endorsement or active involvement.

Passive endorsement includes countenance, approval, or endorsement. Countenance is implied acceptance. Approval is expressed acceptance. It is demonstrated by a formal acknowledgment of non-state social control. Endorsement is positive acceptance. It is an acceptance plus recommendation.

Active involvement includes promotion, sanction, or enforcement.

Promotion is active development. It takes steps to facilitate the establishment, maintenance, growth, expansion, and improvement of social control, including enabling legislation but short of making available legal sanctions for private control enforcement. It is measured by efforts contributing to the development and maintenance of private control, for example, making available material resources or lending needed advisers.

Sanction is making available legal punishment through private social control.

Enforcement is directly participating in social control activities through the exercise of state social control powers and institutional authorities.

## Section 3—The Historical Context of the Canton-Hong Kong Strike *Jiucha dui*[12]

The Canton[13]-Hong Kong strike is one of the longest large-scale strikes in international labor movement history. It lasted eighteen months from June 23, 1925 to October 10, 1926. The strike was precipitated by the indiscriminate shooting of peaceful demonstrators by foreign soldiers stationed in Shamian, Canton, China. It was one of the most organized and well-financed strikes to take place since the workers gained class-consciousness in China.

The strike was directed by the CCP, Guangdong District Committee (*Guangdong quwei*). It was organized by the General Chinese national workers' union (*Zhonghua quanguo zong gonghui*). Deng Zhongxia, who led the strike, was experienced in labor movement and strike affairs.[14] The strike was coordinated by the Canton-Hong Kong Strike Committee (*Sheng-Gang bagong weiyuanhui*) (hereinafter, Strike Committee).

The Strike Committee was formed on June 26, 1925, and adopted the "Sheng-Gang bagong weiyuanhui zhangcheng" ("Charter of the Canton-Hong Kong strike committee") (hereinafter, "Charter"). Article 5 of the Charter provided that the Strike Committee was the highest deliberative body, and Article 6 stipulated that the Committee was to be made up of two representatives from the China workers' union, seven from the Hong Kong workers association and four from the Canton *yangwei gongtun* (foreign business workers' association).

In the course of events, the Strike Committee acted and functioned more like a mini-government than a traditional union. The Strike Committee was publicly referred to as "Guangdong dier zhengfu" ("Canton shadow government") by the people in China and government authority in Hong Kong. Internally, it had departments such as administration, propaganda, recreation, communications, finance, *jiucha* and so on. Externally, it provided education, recreation, welfare, and news services to its members and the public.

In the course of preparing for the strike, the Strike Committee set up a five-regiment (540 men each) *jiucha dui* to direct the strike, supervise the strike members, and enforce the strike laws and union orders. It is clear from archival materials that the *jiucha dui* was not the only voluntary "policing" unit for the strike. For example, "Dispatch from the Guanxi Federation of National Salvation Organizations Enumerating the Evil Deeds of the Nanning General Chamber of Commerce" ("Guangxi jiuguo tuanti lianhe jielu Nanning zonghui zuizhuang daidian") (November 25, 1925) observed that there were a total of six different inspection teams, one of which was the Nanning General Chamber of Commerce inspection team.[15] Other strike inspection teams included:

(1) The Xiamen (Fujian) Student Corps;
(2) The Middle School Student Corps;
(3) The Nanning (Guangxi) Youth Volunteers' Corps for National Salvation.

The Canton province-Hong Kong Strike *jiucha dui* (hereinafter, "Canton-Hong Kong picket") was established on July 5, 1925 by the Strike Committee. The original Canton-Hong Kong picket was organized on November 4, 1925 under the command of Huang Jinyu and was trained by chief instructor Xu Chengzhang. The Canton-Hong Hong picket reported to the newly formed Picket Committee under the Strike Committee.

When the *jiucha dui* was first organized, it had an establishment of 2,000 men. This was later increased to 3,000 men. It had ten armed-patrol boats and 400 guns. Its major role was to enforce the Strike Committee's orders and rules[16] and maintain strike discipline.

There were three kinds of orders and rules to be enforced:

(1) Rules regarding the punishment of enemies of the workers and counterrevolutionaries.
(2) Rules regarding the punishment of corruption and bribery.
(3) Rules regarding dereliction of duties.[17]

The *Jiucha dui*, as provided for in Section 2 of the "Jiucha dui zuzhi fa" (Organic law of the strike pickets), had the following duties: "maintain strike order, intercept grains and provisions, strict apprehension of running dogs, arrest enemies of workers, investigate and confiscate enemy goods, blockade of Hong Kong, Macau, and Sha Mian's transportation network."[18]

The Strike Committee had a training ground for the *jiucha dui* and a prison for the violators (with 300 prisoners in December 1925). The *jiucha dui* dressed in blue uniforms with red armbands. They inspected all goods and persons entering and leaving Hong Kong and Guangdong. They were authorized to arrest anyone who violated the strike order of the Strike Committee and send them to the joint hearing committee and special court for "judicial" disposition. Strike leaders who were accused of corruption and collusion with local troops were subjected to arrest.[19]

The Strike Committee promulgated organizational rules that defined the role, functions, duties, powers, and accountability of the *jiucha dui*. On July 5, 1925, the Strike Committee promulgated the "Discipline which should be observed by the pickets," which defined the role and functions of the *jiucha dui* as: "... to suppress all forms of counter-revolutionary activities" (*zhenya yiqie fan-geming xingwei*) and particularly, "The team member upon the discovery of any enemy spy ... should immediately arrest him and turn him over to this department for examination and discipline."

In time, Chinese scholars have come to refer to the Canton-Hong Kong picket as the earliest form of "revolutionary law enforcement."

## Section 4—The Redistribution of Governmental Social Control: A Case Study of Canton-Hong Kong Strike Committee

> "In order to persist in the strike, the *baweihui* published a newspaper —"The Workers' Road"— organized canteens, housing quarters, hospitals, schools, and established law enforcement agencies, such as a joint-hearing office, a prison, and the *jiucha dui*. It was in reality a workers' government."
>
> *Zhongguo gongren yundong jianshi* (1987)

### Introduction

This part of the chapter concerns itself with two questions: (1) What role did the respective parties (KMT government and Strike Committee) play in the Canton-Hong Kong strike? (2) Did the Strike Committee function as a state-sponsored policing agent with the grant of authority and support from the KMT government?

It has been suggested earlier in Section 2 that a useful theoretical framework for analyzing whether the Strike Committee was a governmental social control agent is to determine whether the Guangzhou National government (hereinafter, the "KMT government" or "National government") had legally delegated state policing powers to the *jiucha dui*, and whether the KMT government had affirmatively sponsored the *jiucha dui* activities through promotion, sanction, or enforcement.

Applying these two analytical conceptual frameworks—delegation of state powers and sponsorship of private activities—it is apparent that the Strike Committee was a governmental strike law enforcement agency. First, the KMT government delegated to the *jiucha dui* substantial powers to enforce the strike laws and maintain strike order. Second, the KMT government sponsored the *jiucha dui* through active support of the Strike Committee and various *jiucha* activities. The delegation of state authority and lending of government support by the KMT government made the Strike Committee a de facto government with quasi-state authority. In this regard, Jean Chesneaux has aptly described the nature of the Strike Committee:

> The responsibilities of the Strike Committee went far beyond the normal field of activities of a union organization dealing with a work stoppage. *During the summer of 1925 the committee became, in fact, a kind of workers' government—and indeed the name commonly applied to it at that time by both its friends and its enemies was "Government No. 2."* This quasi-government status of the Strike Committee was even more evident in its handling of the boycott against Hong Kong and the sanctions it imposed against its infringement.... Anyone infringing the regulations was brought before a court set up by the Strike Committee

> which had appointed the judges; and this court imposed either fines or prison sentences that were served out in jails belonging to the committee.[20] (Italics supplied)

## Co-production of law and order

On July 1, 1925, the Canton provincial government was formally inaugurated[21] (hereinafter, "Canton government"). No sooner had the Canton government been established, when it was confronted with a crisis—the "Shamian massacre" (*Shamian canan*) —of international proportions. The newly formed Canton government was ill-prepared for the incident. At this point in time, it had no established infrastructure,[22] process, resources, or plan to respond to a crisis of such magnitude. The police suffered from inadequate manpower due to reorganization and consolidation. They had not yet formulated a law and order blueprint, much less a crisis management plan. The Canton government relied heavily on the army to carry out its orders. The military was used to supplement the regular police force and even supplant the regular police in the performance of law enforcement duties. The Canton government also relied heavily on volunteerism to implement critical government programs. The Chinese preference for local rule, as manifested in the existence of multiple, indigenous, "natural" social control organizations also played an important part in determining the government's social control policy.[23] Criminal justice and social order were popularized and communized. Local groups were used to maintain law and order. The professional corporate bodies and functional collective organizations were made natural allies. They were considered ideal candidates for self-governance. The Strike Committee was a prime example of such public and private joint-governance and central and local cooperative rule. The only differences were that the Strike Committee had a well-defined mandate, high degree of autonomy, broad police powers, and the discretionary authority to use force with few oversights.

The Strike Committee was also different from other workers' organizations coming before it (e.g., workers' strike organizations of the Chang Shen dian railroad strike, Anyaun lu miners' strike, Shanghai Japanese cotton mill strike, and Jinghan railroad strike). Unlike those earlier organizations, the Strike Committee was a democratic institution; it was a self-governing political body; it was a significant policymaker; and it had legal authority and coercive power. It could make and enforce law.

In short, the Strike Committee came close to being a mini-government with elected lawmaking bodies that could set public policy, enforce law, and maintain order by the use of force.

It is clear that in the early days of the KMT government, it allowed many state law and order functions to be performed locally and privately as a result both of the government's political vulnerability and the nation's cultural legacy. This opened a unique opportunity for the CCP, an increasingly powerful workers' association, to wrest control from the KMT government during the Canton-Hong Kong Strike. This poses an interesting question as to the roles the KMT government and the Strike Committee played in the Canton-Hong Kong Strike.

## The role of the KMT government and the Strike Committee in strike law enforcement

The Canton-Hong Kong Strike was a spontaneous, indigenous, and above all voluntary affair. The Strike Committee, as a duly elected representative of the workers, naturally played a dominant role in the strike. The Strike Committee assumed, by default and without being challenged, the overall responsibility of planning, organizing, coordinating, directing, and executing the strike. This role included the promulgation of strike rules, the enforcement of strike orders, the maintenance of strike discipline, and the adjudication and punishment of internal as well as external strike offenders. The KMT government supported the strikers for ideological and political reasons. However, it chose not to be involved directly.

Ideologically, the KMT had been shifting to the left of the political spectrum ever since the second KMT Congress in January 1924. Domestically, the Guangzhou government had to rely upon the support of workers and peasants to counterbalance the political and military threats posed by the various warring factions. Internationally, the Guangzhou government depended on strikers to rein in foreigners.

Privately the KMT government was supportive of the Strike Committee. It agreed to play a secondary and passive role. Publicly, the KMT government tried to disassociate itself from the strikers. The strikers were allowed to vent their anger and frustration at the imperialists and foreigners with minimal government intervention. The Strike Committee was given a free hand to direct the strike and organize the strikers with very little government opposition. The government's public posture was summed up by a letter written by Wu Zhaoshu, the chief of the Commerce Bureau, to the four merchants' associations regarding possible peaceful settlement of the case:

> In fact, the strike and breaking of economic relationship is a people's affair ... the people go to strike and the workers are angry as a result of the British government insulting Chinese characters in Shanghai, Guangzhou, Hankou and other places, and thus this kind of movement was as a result of the people's self aroused patriotism. The movement has nothing to do with the government. If Hong Kong government wants to settle the turmoil, it should not discuss with this government, it has to consult the striking workers; the government as a third party, should not engage in the negotiation at all.[24]

From the very beginning, there was a clear, albeit tacit, mutual understanding of divided roles and shared responsibilities between the KMT government and the Strike Committee. The government provided the strikers with moral, political, material, and legal support to facilitate the strike.[25] The Strike Committee provided the state with leadership, organization, and personnel to effectuate the strike. The clearest manifestation of this reciprocal relation was an appreciation note the Strike Committee sent to the KMT government on July 11, 1925, thanking the government for the use of free government telegram service for strike-related activities.

This short and simple thank-you note was very revealing of the motive of the Strike Committee and the nature of the working relationship between it and the National government. It clearly defined the role and mission of the striking workers. It affirmed that the workers had a political mission and public role to play: to remove the unequal treaties and to liberate the Chinese people. The Strike Committee, in announcing the government's support openly to its members and the public, gained a measure of legitimacy and credibility. The impact of the message was clear. The Strike Committee had been transformed into a social control agent of the state. The National government set the overall strike policy, the Strike Committee executed the strike.

The National government interjected itself sparingly and reluctantly throughout the strike—it was deferred to on matters dealing with the international community, and its sovereign authority was invoked as the final arbiter on national policy, law, and justice. Otherwise, because of political reality and expediency, the National government conceded near plenary powers to the Strike Community in conducting the strike. This aspect of the relationship is best illustrated by the decision of the National government to reopen Shamian to the public over the objections of the Strike Committee.

Overall, the Strike Committee could only make suggestions to the National government. More often than not, such suggestions were respected and followed but not in all cases. In the reopening of Shamian, the Strike Committee had to take remedial measures to make the best of a disagreeable situation. The National government unmistakably held the balance of power.

The relationship of the Strike Committee and the KMT government during the Canton-Hong Kong strike was a match made in heaven. The Strike Committee in effect became a de facto executive arm of the government and was allowed to function as a workers government within a national government. The concession of power, however substantial, was not total. It was always based on the unarticulated premise and mutual understanding that the Strike Committee willingly accepted the political legitimacy and military supremacy of the KMT government. In practice, this meant that the Strike Committee had to seek approval from the National government and was subjected to after-the-fact oversight on all matters implicating the state. It was clearly a senior-junior political relationship, with the National government holding the power to make the ultimate decision on any issue.

## Section 5—*Jiucha dui* as Governmental Social Control

> "The Strike Committee is the precursor of the future Chinese workers' government."
>
> *Sheng-Gang gongren dabagong ziliao* (1980)[26]

### Introduction

This section discusses the specific kinds of strike enforcement powers that were delegated to the Strike Committee in enforcing the Canton-Hong Kong strike. Specifically, it will look at how such powers were exercised as a way of understanding the Strike Committee's policing role, functions, and capacity during the Canton-Hong Kong strike. We will also be looking at how the KMT government assisted and supported the Strike Committee in enforcing the strike. Finally, we will apply the analytical frameworks developed earlier in Section 2 (Table 1) to assist in the assessment of the "governmental social control" capacity of the Strike Committee during the strike, and in so doing affirm the status and role of *jiucha dui* as a de facto policing agency.

### The delegation of specific strike powers

On July 8, 1925, the Guangzhou National Government endorsed the idea of an economic boycott directed against the British in Hong Kong. The National Government's standing committee issued the "Directive Authorizing the Guangdong Provincial Government to Carry Out Its Decision to Support the Guangdong-Hong Kong Strikers' Union

Headquarters" (hereinafter, "Directive") in support of the Sheng-Gang strike.[27] Item three of the Directive instructed the Guangdong provincial government to declare the following twenty-four ports and other coastal areas closed to the export of food:

Figure 1: Ports and areas subjected to boycott by the "Directive Authorizing the Guangdong Provincial Government to Carry Out Its Decision to Support the Guangdong-Hong Kong Strikers' Union Headquarters" of July 8, 1925

| | | | | |
|---|---|---|---|---|
| San Shui | He Kou | Jiu Jiang | Jiang Meng | Rong Qi |
| Xiang Shan | Shi Qi | Ao Men | Qian Shan | Wan Zi |
| Xia Peng Wei | Xia Xin Ning | Guang Hai | Chen Cun | Hu Men |
| Tai Ping | Bao An | Nan Tou | Zhen Chuan | Sha Tou Jiao |
| Sha Yu Pu | Ao Tou | Shan Wei | Ping Shan | Dan Shui |
| Da Peng | Hai Kou | Bei Hai | Guang Zhou-Wan | |

Source: Reconstructed from item (3) in "Guomin zhengfu guanyu weichi Shenggang bagong weiyuanhui ge jueyian xunlin" (July 8, 1925), "Zhonghua minguo guomin zhengfu xinling, di san hao" ("Guangzhou National Government's Directive Authorizing the Guangdong Provincial Government to Carry out Its Decision to Support the Guangdong-Hong Kong Strikers' Union Headquarters") ("Chinese National government instruction, no. 3") in *Wu-San-Shi yundong he Sheng-Gang bagong* (The May 30th movement and Canton-Hong Kong Strike) (Jiangsu guji chubanshe, 1985), 260–261.

The Directive is an important document for a number of reasons. It initiated the strike. It was skillfully written, however, in such a way as to absolve the National government of any responsibility for starting the strike. Also, the Directive clearly specified the role of the Strike Committee and the National government. It affirmed the National government's role in setting strategic policy while conceding to the Strike Committee the role of implementing the strike. It further vested the Strike Committee with legal authority, and political legitimacy, to act on behalf of the government in organizing the strike. The Directive also implicitly held the Strike Committee accountable for the successful prosecution of the strike, discipline of the strikers, and propriety of actions.

The Strike Committee accepted the KMT government's invitation and proceeded to fashion a strike plan. On July 9, 1925, one day after the Directive was issued, the Strike Committee settled on a strike date. The Strike Committee sent a "Circular telegram on implementing the blockade of Hong Kong," which declared that "From the tenth of this month, all boats and ferries will be forbidden to travel to Hong Kong and New Territories, so that it will die of starvation." It further asked the National government to instruct its army and police to assist in the blockade (hereinafter "Circular").

On July 13, 1925 the National government responded to the Strike Committee's call for military assistance. It directed the Guangdong provincial government to provide the Strike Committee with the necessary arm escort[28] (hereinafter, "Directive II").

The Guangdong provincial government acted promptly in response to the National government's Directive of July 23, 1925, and issued the following Prohibition (hereinafter "Prohibition"): "In regard to item three of the National government's instruction to protect the strikers, the provincial affairs meeting should wire and instruct all county heads, police bureau chiefs, merchants' association, and other groups, that whoever is found to have transported exported provision, is to be dealt with as high treason, and punished by death."

The Directive (July 8, 1925), Directive II (July 13, 1925), and the Prohibition (July 23, 1925) were the only government decrees making provisions for a blockade over food exports to Hong Kong. They can be properly viewed as enabling documents for the strike. What is noteworthy about these three enabling documents is that although they showed unmistakable support for the strikers, they lacked specificity on the goals and mission, role and functions, organization and process, powers and duties, supervision and accountability of the Strike Committee. Indeed there was no specific provision or explicit language appointing or authorizing the Strike Committee to take charge. In effect, the Strike Committee was given a blank check to organize itself to enforce the strike, with unspecified, albeit most encouraging, KMT government support. The Strike Committee eagerly took up the invitation and used its own initiative to implement the strike in the way it thought should be done. The KMT government rarely saw fit to intervene.

## The power to implement the strike

Taking hints from the KMT government, the Strike Committee took charge to orchestrate the strike. In the process the Strike Committee exercised a number of powers:

The Strike Committee exercised the power to declare a date certain to carry out the boycott. The Strike Committee further adopted a blockade plan without consulting the KMT government.

The Strike Committee exercised the power to change the scope of the boycott. On November 25, 1925, the Strike Committee decided to expand the scope of the boycott to other coastal ports.

The Strike Committee exercised the power to change the manner of enforcing the boycott. On March 15, 1926, the Strike Committee organized a naval patrol to provide for zone patrolling of the boycotted seaports.

The Strike Committee exercised the power to declare a date to terminate the boycott.

We can make a general observation on the nature of powers possessed by the Strike Committee from the manner they were exercised. Because the general police powers to implement the strike were self-endowed more so than explicitly delegated, the exercise of specific police powers was always subject to a potential veto by the KMT government. This made the KMT a knowing participant, albeit in a passive way, to the Strike Committee's exercise of state-policing powers.

### The power to finance the strike

The Strike Committee had the power to tax and spend to finance the strike.

On February 9, 1925, the Strike Committee promulgated the "Kaifang Sheng-O Hangxing tiaoli" ("Opening of Hong Kong-Macau Sailing Regulations"),[29] which permitted the resumption of the Canton-Macau steamline service in order to facilitate the return of strike workers from Hong Kong and Macau to Guangzhou. As a condition, the shipping company had to agree to free up space for Hong Kong and Macau strikers to go to Canton free of charge.

On September 21, 1925, the Strike Committee issued the "Sheng-Gang bagong weiyuanhui duiyu Ri, Mei, Fa deng guo lunchuan dianhu tiaoli" ("Regulations of the Strike Committee on Japanese, American and French's steamboats and shops"),[30] which permitted Japanese, American, and French boats to resume operation subject to certain conditions, one being that "One tenth of the worker's salary should be voluntary contributed to this Strike Committee, to obtain food provisions for all."

On March 22, 1926, the Strike Committee adopted the "Gang O chuanzhi huizheng fuye zi tiao li" ("Regulations on the return of Hong Kong Macau boat to resume service"),[31] which allowed non-British ships to resume regular service provided that the shipping companies agreed to pay a fee.

In order to end the strike, the livelihood of the unemployed striking workers had to be taken care of. The Strike Committee suggested a surcharge of a "erwu" (25 tax) on existing customs duties. Each strike worker was to be given 100 dollars from the levy. The KMT government was responsible for announcing and collecting the tax and gave the revenue to the Strike Committee for distribution.[32]

## The power to set strike law enforcement policy

The Strike Committee has the aythority and responsibility ro set and executive strike policy:

The Strike Committee had a key policy role to play in how to enforce the strike law.

The Strike Committee made clear from the start that they were boycotting for a public cause, not over private grievances. Thus on the issue of whether to continue to strike or not to strike, the Strike Committee declared that: "Because our strike concerns the whole issue of race and not our own personal problem, what to do next is a complex problem, and requires the help of overseas and local Chinese to resolve."[33] The Strike Committee expected and insisted upon maximum participation from the widest quarters.

The Strike Committee was most solicitous of the welfare of the public in determining how the strike should be conducted. Particularly, the Strike Committee was very much concerned with the adverse impact of the strike on the Guangzhou economy and the merchants' livelihood.

The Strike Committee did not hesitate to stop the boycott when it decided that it had outlived its utility.

## The power to make strike law

The Strike Committee was given great latitude and a free hand to promulgate organic laws for the establishment of strike agencies, administrative law for implementing the strike, and substantive and procedural criminal law for the punishment of offenders.

The Strike Committee promulgated various organic laws for the establishment, administration, and control of strike organs.

The Strike Committee also promulgated extensive and detailed administrative rules for the implementation of the strike:

On August 14, 1925, the Strike Committee set forth the standards and procedure for the issuance of the special permit with the "Sheng-Gang gongren weiyuanhui guanyu sheli texuzheng de tongzi" ("Notice of Sheng-Gang Strike Committee regarding special permit")[34] to facilitate and simplify the release of goods in storage and awaiting inspection and disposition.

In August 1925, the National government decided to reopen Shamian. The Strike Committee launched the most strenuous protest and suggested various measures to secure the Shamian opening from causing harm to the strike.

On February 9, 1925, the Strike Committee promulgated the "Kaifang Sheng-O Hangxing tiaoli" ("Canton-Hong Kong Sailing Regulations"),[35] which allowed the resumption of the Canton-Macau boat service in order to facilitate the return of strike workers from Hong Kong and Macau to Guangzhou.

### The power to interpret strike laws

The Sheng-Gang Strike Committee had great latitude in drafting administrative regulations and much discretion in allowing for departures from those regulations. The following are examples:

*Rules allowing for special dispensation to local residents:* The Strike Committee often made exceptions to the general boycott rules in order to alleviate the adverse impact of the boycott on local residents. For example, a total economic boycott would certainly have spelled disaster for the peasants in the Canton-Hong Kong border area, so the Strike Committee issued the "Sheng-Gang bagong weiyuanhui tezhun baoan nonghui nongmin jingguo yingjie tiaojian" ("The Sheng-Gang Committee: Conditions of special permission for Baoan peasants' association and peasants to pass through the British border") which allowed the border area peasants to obtain rice, fertilizers and salt across the Hong Kong border.

*Rules making special provisions for speedy inspection:* The Strike Committee adopted special rules to facilitate the speedy inspection of easily spoiled food, for example, salt fish. The long waiting period normally required for examination would create hardship for the coastal fishermen and merchants alike, causing spoilage of food or goods in the summer heat. Thus on April 17, 1926, the Strike Committee promulgated the "Sheng-Gang bagong weiyuanhui guanyu xianyu yunshu banfa xunling" ("Instruction of Sheng-Gang Strike Committee regarding the transportation of salt fish"), which allowed the free transport and sale of salt fish with nothing but a spot check.

*Rules granting individualized exceptions:* The Strike Committee often made individualized exceptions to alleviate any unintended impact or injustice occasioned by the draconian boycott rules For example, in the case of the Chen Jia Geng company, the *jiucha dui* seized illegally transported tires thought to have originated in Singapore. When certain mitigating information was brought to light about the tires and their owner, however, the Strike Committee proposed that the tires be exempted from confiscation and returned.

## The power to enforce strike laws

The "Jiucha dui zuzhi fa" ("The *jiucha dui* organic law")[36] specified the *jiucha dui*'s law enforcement duties as follows:

(a) To maintain order;
(b) To intercept provisions;
(c) To chase after running dogs;
(d) To arrest workers' enemies;
(e) To search and detain enemy goods;
(f) To blockade Hong Kong, Macao, and Shamian traffic.

From a reading of the original archives documents, however, the actual role, functions, and powers of the Canton-Hong Kong *jiucha dui* appear to be as follows:

The *jiucha dui* was involved in setting up blockades against the importation and exportation of prohibited goods.[37]

The *jiucha dui* was involved with inspection of incoming British and Japanese goods.

The *jiucha dui* was involved with interdicting and seizing smuggled provisions to the British colony, transportation of strike workers to and from Hong Kong, and the importation of enemy goods from Hong Kong.[38]

The *jiucha dui* was involved with investigating and reporting upon foreign spies and suspicious characters.[39]

The *jiucha dui* was involved with collecting intelligence on British arms transport.[40]

The *jiucha dui* was responsible for maintaining order and discipline within the strikers' ranks. It was particularly involved with the investigation and arrest of striker-impostors, troublemakers, and hooligans.

The *jiucha dui* was involved with preventing the local defense army and police from colluding with unscrupulous merchants in the transportation of food to Hong Kong and importation of enemy goods between Taipo (Hong Kong) and Sha Yu Yong, and between Huang Yu Yong, Ao Tou and Dan Shui.[41]

## The power to adjudicate and punish strike law violators

The Strike Committee had near plenary powers over the interpretation of strike law and the punishment of violators.

(1) The *jiucha dui's* law enforcement activities were subjected mainly to internal administrative review by a joint hearing office

(JHO) made up of five hearing officials (*cheng-shen yuan*) elected from strike workers from Canton (two members) and Hong Kong (three members), with occasional KMT government oversight.

The JHO, under the supervision and control of the Strike Committee, had a broad range of judicial powers to determine how strike laws should be interpreted. *First*, the JHO had exclusive jurisdiction over cases of strike law adopted by the Strike Committee, to the exclusion of the National government. *Second*, the JHO had broad jurisdiction over all cases arising from the strike. *Third*, the JHO conducted preliminary hearings in all cases and made referral to the special court in serious cases. *Fourth*, the JHO had original and final jurisdiction over all minor offenders (with punishment under ten days of confinement). *Fifth*, the JHO was not held accountable to the National government nor state law. The JHO was only held accountable internally and administratively to the Strike Committee.

(2) More significantly, there were no constitutional or institutional controls over the Strike Committee's exercise of strike powers. The constitutional documents of the time did not contemplate the existence of a private strike agency with plenary powers to effect a strike. As a result, it provided neither constitutional limitation of, nor structural check and balance to, the Strike Committee's assumption of governing police powers.

(3) In addition, there was no independent legal control of *jiucha dui* law enforcement activities. The *jiucha dui* was solely responsible for enforcing the strike laws and maintaining strike order. Also, there was no external administrative supervision over the discipline of *jiucha dui* misconduct. The *jiucha dui* committee, and the Strike Committee were only subjected to internal administrative review. The *jiucha dui* was discouraged from reporting to anyone outside the chain of command, including the KMT government.

(4) There was no legal review over *jiucha dui* administrative discipline. "The Jiucha dui jilu"[42] ("Jiucha dui disciplinary code") made the organization, direction, supervision, discipline, and punishment of the *jiucha dui* the sole responsibility of the *jiucha* committee, which was held accountable to the Strike Committee. The Strike Committee possessed broad and severe powers to discipline strike violators. The *jiucha dui* was subjected to severe punishment, including shooting, dismissal from office, imprisonment, and reprimand for any breach of discipline or violation of law. Also, the *Shui*

*Lu zhenchadui* (land-sea reconnaissance troop ) was subjected to "Shui lu zhen cha dui zanxing guize"[43] ("Provisional organic regulations of the land-sea reconnaissance troop"), which made the troop accountable to the *jiucha dui* committee. They were subject to the same discipline as the *jiucha dui*. The jiucha dui committee was in turn responsible to the striker representatives.

### The power to use coercive force

When the *jiucha dui* was first formed, it had 2,000 members. There were about 200 guns,[44] that is, one gun to ten *jiucha dui* members. They also had twelve armed patrol boats as a "navy." The *jiucha dui* was trained in military tactics and subjected to military discipline. The *jiucha dui* was not hesitant to use force to enforce the strike laws and suffered many casualties at the hands of local bandits, smugglers, shangtuan, and British soldiers.

### Lack of accountability

As might be expected, given the extensive delegation of police powers, the open charge to conduct the boycott, and a lack of structural oversight by the KMT government, there were many cases of *jiucha dui* abuse of power and citizens' complaints of the Strike Committee's misconduct.

The owners of private premises complained to the Guangzhou Public Security Office that the Strike Committee had been occupying private residences without payment.

There were constant reports of peasants' and workers' associations forcing others to participate in the shopkeepers' strike and interfering with the collection of taxes.

When private citizens were aggrieved with the *jiucha dui's* action, they had nowhere to complain but to the provincial affairs committee.

There were also many complaints over the *jiucha dui's* abuse of power from government officials.

The chief of public security, Wu Tiacheng, announced to the public that "The strikers were more violent than the soldiers of Liu and Yang."

On February 22, 1922, the Chinese custom and duties department at the Canton custom office announced that it would have to close the office because the Strike Committee had been encroaching on its legal mandate and authority.

More indicative of government officials' unease and frustration over the Strike Committee's blatant and consistent misconduct was the fact that the government's officials found it necessary to pursue self-help action, such as closing the Canton custom office or going directly to the public, for example, by complaints in the press.

### Strike Committee—*Jiucha Dui* as Governmental Social Control

The above detailed description of the Strike Committee's lawmaking and enforcement powers during the Canton-Hong Kong strike allows us to use the analytical framework developed in Section 2 to ascertain whether the Strike Committee was functioning in a "governmental social control" capacity (i.e., acting as a de facto state law enforcement agency).

Table 2: Strike Committee's governmental social control capacity (SC) in relationship to Canton-Hong Kong strike law enforcemen—an analytical framework

| | Responsibility | Power | Accountability |
|---|---|---|---|
| Defining norm | A (3) | B(3) | C(3) |
| Establishing norm | D(3) | E(3) | F(3) |
| Enforcing norm | G(3) | H(3) | I(3) |

SC3 = most governmental social control capacity
SC2 = some governmental social control capacity
SC1 = little governmental social control capacity
SC = government capacity
(Total possible SC) = SC 27 = most governmental capacity or approaching full governmental social control capacity, that is, sovereign state.

*Responsibility* is defined as the scope of state-controlled matters (over people, places, things, objects, matters) with which a party is charged. This is commonly associated with a state's political jurisdiction, manifested as constitutional limits and as translated into legal jurisdiction and administrative charge of all kinds, which is usually measured in terms of the scope (how many matters under control) and the nature (how important are things under control) of the party's jurisdiction.

*Power* is defined as the extent to which a party can effectively impose his will on others, which is usually defined along the dimension of legitimate force allowed to be used.

*Accountability* is defined as the extent to which a party is amenable to supervision by the state, which is usually measured by the degree of prior approval or subsequent review upon the party's action or decision.

*Defining norm* is defined as setting general social control expectations. The common indicators are adopting philosophy, setting policy, and deciding upon strategy.

*Establishing norm* is defined as setting specific social expectations. The common indictors are rule making and interpretation.

*Enforcing norm* is defined as seeking compliance with general or special social expectations. The most common indicators are policing, arrests, and punishment.

## A sample case analysis of more or less governmental capacity for the Strike Committee during the Canton-Hong Kong strike:

### Government delegation of police powers

1. The Strike Committee had the broadest responsibility in defining (A) strike control for union members, the public, and foreigners. This responsibility was manifested by the ability of the Strike Committee to advocate political-social philosophy, influence KMT national policy, and to set strike strategy on the full spectrum of strike issues. (A = SC3)
2. The Strike Committee had the broadest responsibility in establishing (D) strike control laws for union members, the public, and foreigners. This responsibility was manifested by the authority of the Strike Committee to promulgate strike laws and provided for exceptions to them on all matters affecting the successful prosecution of the strike. (D = SC3)
3. The Strike Committee had the broadest responsibility (G) in enforcing the strike laws for union members, the public, and foreigners. This responsibility was manifested by the unlimited authority of the *jiucha dui* to interdict any boats, inspect any goods, and seize any goods in all the designated boycott areas to effectuate the boycott. (G = SC3)
4. The Strike Committee possessed much power (B) in defining strike philosophy, policy, and strategy concerning the strike. This power was manifested by the Strike Committee's ability to face up to the KMT government in the Shamian incident. (B = SC3)
5. The Strike Committee had near total power (E) in promulgating strike laws. This power was manifested by lack of any prior consultation with the KMT government. (E = SC2)
6. The Strike Committee exercised total power (H) in enforcing the strike law. This power was manifested in the ability to use force (with

KMT assistance), imprisonment, and capital punishment to enforce the strike law. (H = SC3)

7. The Strike Committee showed very little accountability (C) in defining strike philosophy and policy. This accountability was manifested in the Strike Committee's ability to disagree with the KMT over issues of philosophy, policy, and strategy over the conduct of the strike. (C=SC3)
8. The Strike Committee showed very little accountability (C) in establishing the strike. This fact was manifested in the Strike Committee's public disagreement with the KMT over issues of philosophy, policy, and strategy over the conduct of the strike (F). (F = SC3)
9. The Strike Committee showed very little accountability (I) in the enforcement of strike law. (I = SC3)

From this sample case analysis it is possible to conclude that the Strike Committee enjoyed an SC score of 26/27, making it ipso facto a state agent with *full* state capacity. The conclusion drawn from this analysis only serves to confirm and reinforce what was publicly acknowledged during the time, that is, that the Strike Committee was functioning as a mini-strike government during the time.

## Government sponsorship of *jiucha* policing

From the very beginning the KMT was interested in doing what it could to assist the strikers and the Strike Committee. The National government provided in-kind service of all types for the strikers, for example, the dispensation of telegram fees[45] and the administration of strike funds. The National government led a concerted effort to harness funding from the private sector to provide financial support for the Strike Committee and displaced workers. It even started a public works project to support the unemployed strike workers. Varieties of support included a KMT investigation squarely laying the blame for the Shji massacre on the British in order to promote the cause of the strikers; financing of the Strike Committee's administrative costs and the strike's operational expenses; allowing the Canton-Hong Kong Strikers' Committee to use the Dong Yuan complex as a temporary office; sending fifteen graduating officers of the second graduating class at Whampao Military Academy to assist in the organization and training of *jiucha dui*;[46] collecting and distributing funds from KMT and Canton provincial government revenues and private sources on behalf of the strikers.

In June and July of 1926, the Canton government provided a total of 2.8 million yuan to the Strike Committee, or 58.6% of the 4.78 million yuan strike fund. It was also one of the most consistent sources of financial support for the Strike Committee. The government donated about 10,000 yuan each month to the strike fund. The July 1926 balance sheet of the Strike showed the following sources of contribution:

Table 3: Sources of strike fund collected by Strike Comittee, July 1926

| | |
|---|---|
| Collected in China | 250,000 yuan |
| Collected from overseas | 1.13 million yuan |
| Advanced by Canton government | 2.8 million yuan |
| Sale of seized merchandise | 400,000 yuan |
| Fines | 200,000 yuan |
| Total | 4.78 million yuan |

Source: Jean Chesneaux, in *The Chinese Labor Movement*, 293, 296.

Additional support efforts of the KMT and provincial government for the strikers included: the Canton government supporting a road-building project as work relief for the striking workers; military assistance from the KMT in the form of help to *jiucha dui* by government troops in local security efforts and even in clashes with the British on at least one occasion.[47]

The above detailing of KMT governmental political, moral, military, administrative, legal, and material support of the Strike Committee allows us to ascertain, with the analytical framework developed in Section 1, whether the Strike Committee received the endorsement of the KMT government in their strike law enforcement activities; thereby implicating the government in private law enforcement activities.

Table 4: KMT governmental sponsorship of Strike Committee strike enforcement—an analytical framework

| Theoretical concepts | Operational definitions | Example |
|---|---|---|
| Government endorsement (passive – sponsorship) | *Endorsement*—The extent to which the government accepts and approves of the existence of private social control. | *Public endorsement*—KMT government publicly supported the Strike Committee's strike enforcement role.[48] |

| | | |
|---|---|---|
| | *Countenance*—The extent to which the government tolerates the existence of private social control. | *Reluctant acceptance*—KMT knew of the existence of the Lin Heji case (capital sentence) but chose not to intervene while voicing strong objections through KMT Minister of Prosecution in the press.[49] |
| | *Approval*—The extent to which the government tacitly acknowledges the existence of private social control. | *Acquiesce to strike plan*—KMT did not object to strike date and plan announced by the Strike Committee. |
| | *Endorsement*—The extent to which the government affirmatively approves of the existence of private social control. | *Affirmative approval*—KMT made the Strike Committee the proper party to settle the strike. |
| Government involvement (active – sponsorship) | *Involvement*—The extent to which the government actively participates in bringing about the private social control scheme. | *KMT funding*—The KMT government provided funding for the Strike Committee. |
| | *Promotion*—The extent to which to which the government takes steps to establish, maintain, expand, or improve the private social control scheme. | *Dispute referral*—When private citizens were aggrieved with the *jiucha dui's* action, they were referred to mediation by the peasant-worker (nong-gong) and industrial (shiye) bureaus. |
| | *Sanction*—The degree to which the government made available legal sanctions and resources for private social control. | *Military backup*—The Strike Committee provided armed escort for the Strike Committee. |
| | *Enforcement*—The degree to which the government actively cooperates with a private social control agency in enforcing private social control regiment. | *Joint-operations*—The KMT police worked alongside the *jiucha dui* to enforce the Shamian opening. |

Table 4 clearly shows that the KMT provided extensive and consistent government assistance to the Strike Committee during the Canton-Hong Kong strike, sufficient to demonstrate a symbiotic relationship. In so doing, the KMT government gave the Strike Committee more than just material support; it gave the Strike Committee legitimacy and respect. In the process, it transformed what was essentially a self-help strike enforcement effort into a de facto quasi-governmental social control exercise.

## Conclusion

The above investigation into the Strike Committee's strike-enforcement role and functions during the Canton-Hong Hong strike shows that it was delegated substantial governmental authority and given unlimited governmental support to enforce the Canton-Hong Kong strike. The further analysis of the Strike Committee's law enforcement activities with "more or less governmental social control" analytical frameworks clearly demonstrates that the Strike Committee was engaging in governmental social control at the behest and with the support of the KMT government (i.e., as a state law enforcement agency).

Thus, it is accurate to assert that in 1925–1926, the Communists experimented with their first organized policing functions.

CHAPTER FOUR

# History of Communist Policing

## Introduction

The theory and practice of policing in any nation are shaped by historical events and driven by contemporary needs. Prior to October 1, 1949, the role and function, as well as the strategy and tactics, of public security, or police, in China were very much determined first by the war with the Japanese (1937–1945)[1] and later by the CCP-KMT (1946–1949)[2] civil war.[3]

Li Yiqing, the civil department head of the Jin/Ji/Lu border area government and chief of the public security general office from 1941 to 1945, observed that during the Japanese war the Party relied on the militia to eliminate traitors and spies.[4] During the civil war, the Party used public security, or police, to conduct land reform, exterminate bandits, and hunt down counterrevolutionaries. Still later, after 1947, public security was deployed to pacify cities and consolidate the power of the Party, on the way to forming a communist state in October 1949.

Throughout the whole period from 1937 to 1949, public security was preoccupied with defending the nation against Japan and protecting the Party from domestic (KMT, warlords') threats. Before 1946, public security was mainly concerned with external military challenges—elimination of pro-Japanese traitors and spies. After 1946, public security was chiefly occupied with internal political threats, primarily the elimination of KMT spies and counterrevolutionaries. Social security and public order problems were by comparison minor concerns.

For much of the time from 1939 to 1949, Communist public security was waging war on one kind of enemy or another. In terms of organization and method, there was no clear demarcation between civil policing and military security work. Public security activities were indistinguishable from military operations. There was a close and symbiotic relationship between the military and public security.

The lack of clear demarcation between military and civil capacity of public security has more ancient roots. Since antiquity, the Chinese people in general and the emperors in particular were much concerned with "disorder" (*luan*) of all kinds, from natural disaster to foreign intrusions to domestic uprising. *Luan* was dealt with by coercive force from military violence to criminal sanctions. Another reason that there was little distinction between military and civil security is that in imperial times the local magistrate was responsible for the well-being of the people. Every means, martial and civil, was at his disposal to quell any disorder.[5]

This chapter provides a brief history of Communist policing before 1949 and builds on Chapter 3's investigation of policing in 1925 and 1926. It focuses on public security development at the revolutionary bases in the border areas. Such a historical review aids our understanding of contemporary PRC police development. It helps us to answer such questions as why "strike hard" crime campaigns were conducted like military operations and why Falun gong members were treated as political subversives.

This historical review finds that PRC police have always served as an instrumentality of the state and in defense of the Party. Security, not crime and disorder, was the major concern of the CCP. In time of war and during the revolution, there were few attempts to separate the military from the police, in ideology, organization, function, or style. Ideologically, Communists, from Marx to Mao, have treated the army and the police as one and the same—a coercive tool of the state to suppress class enemies. In terms of organization and method, military and public security were fused into one.

Thus chapter is organized as follows: Sections 1 and 2 contextualize this study with a discussion of two defining characteristics of Communist policing during this era and beyond, the security-defense mindset and military-style operations. Section 3, "Policing in the Revolutionary Bases," explores the nature, role, and functions of police in the revolutionary bases in the border area, from wartime security to peacetime policing. Section 4, "First Organized Police," describes the first effort to organize policing in Yan'an. Section 5 is a discussion of lessons learned from this brief historical research.

## Section 1—Context One: The Security-Defense Mindset

### Introduction

The first defining characteristic of Chinese policing in this historical review is the security-defense mindset (*baowei*). How was the police–security organization under the CCP born? In December 1927, the CCP established its first *baowei zuzhi* ("security-defense organs"), the political special branch. In November 1931, the Chinese Soviet Republic provisional government formed the People's police administration department ("minjing guanli bu") and Political security department ("guojia zhengzhi baoweiju") in Jiangsi Ruijin, a revolutionary base; the former dealt with civil administration and the latter with security defense. The CCP set up the "sufan weiyuan hui" ("elimination of reactionaries committee") to purify the Party and eliminate counterrevolutionaries. The CCP's people's public security organs ("Renmin gongan jiguan") began to take shape and grow.

In February 1939, the CCP formed the *shehuibu* in charge of military intelligence against the Japanese and Party security. Later, during the civil war with the KMT, *shehuibu* spread all over the country.[6]

## The security-defense mindset

From the very beginning, the KMT was relentless in persecuting the Communists as subversives. Communists in China had to struggle for survival. The CCP was forced to operate underground and in secrecy. The CCP had to endure recurring political purges, legal prohibitions, police suppression,[7] and military campaigns.

In 1919, Chen Duxu and Li Dazhao published the "Declaration of the Beijing people" ("Beijing shimin xuanyan") in the aftermath of the May-Fourth movement. The declaration sought direct public participation to achieve basic political reform in China. The Declaration made five political demands: (1) securing Chinese sovereignty over Shandong from Japanese encroachment; (2) guaranteeing freedom of assembly and speech to the Chinese people; (3) allowing the people to organize their own *baoandui* in Beijing; (4) abolishing the infantry command and the garrison headquarter in Beijing; (5) relieving all the officials who were responsible for putting down the May-Fourth movement, including the undersecretary of the Army, Xu Shuzheng, the Beijing garrison commander, Duan Zhigui, and the infantry commander, Wang Haixing.

On June 11, 1919, the police arrested and imprisoned Chen Duxu, the pioneer of the Chinese Communist Party, for publishing his inflammatory Declaration. In February 1920, the police dispersed Beijing students for organizing a union for rickshaw drivers. In March 1920, the founders of the Chinese Communist Party met in secret to establish the Society for the Study of Marxist Theory at Beida. Still later, in July 1921, the French Concession police broke up a CCP meeting in Shanghai. The CCP had to conduct business on a boat on Niehu Lake.[8]

In every stage of its early political development as a revolutionary party, the CCP was subject to internal sabotage and external attack.

In August 1930, the KMT Central Government Council ("Guomin zhengfu huiyi") promulgated the "Emergency law for the Punishment of Crimes against the State," which targeted dissidents who disturbed law and order "with a view to subverting the Republic."[9]

On August 1, 1930, the Presidents of the Executive, Legislative, Judicial, Examination, and Censorial Yuan signed the "Secret Order from the Nationalist Government, Character MI, Number 11" decreeing that "Communists arrested ... should be immediately dealt with, according to military law."[10]

In October 1930, the "Shanghai municipality public security department, police officer and policemen service regulations"[11] forbade anyone to "publish, distribute, or paste any reactionary characters, to confuse and arouse the people."

In December 1938, the "Village and district anti-communist self-defense organization regulations"[12] established a local self-defense corps to assist the police and military in eradicating the Communists.

In April 1949, the "Shanghai municipality emergency order regulations"[13] provided capital punishment for "group riot," "strike," "inciting student movement," and "sabotage of social order."

All of the above national laws and local regulations were designed to eradicate the CCP, which was considered to be a subversive and destabilizing organization.[14]

In order to avoid detection and arrest, the CCP took on salient characteristics of a secret service organization: work units were highly compartmentalized, information was shared only on a need-to-know basis, and CCP leaders, such as Mao, worked and met at night.

## The lessons of history on Communist policing

The CCP's security mindset was also shaped by intimidation of workers in their early attempts to organize. On May 8, 1925, the Anyuan road miners' club was dismantled by government forces, three members were being killed and many more injured. Other workers were transported to Hunan. Zhu Shaolin, a labor representative at the Han Ya Ping strike, attributed the failure to the club's openness. Zhu's criticism was directed at Liu Shaoqi, who, as the foremost CCP labor leader of the Anyuan miners' club, insisted on selective openness in struggling against the KMT. The CCP learned that such openness was unsafe and changed their practices. Under the white terror regime (the KMT-controlled area during the Second Revolutionary Civil War, 1927–1937), the Party operated in secrecy to protect itself.

The CCP, nurtured by political adversity, naturally developed a paranoid character and siege mentality, as Li Lisan, a seasoned Communist organizer and labor activist, observed:

> The promotion of Communism should be an open and rightful affair. However, the CCP is still a secret organization. To join the CCP, one cannot tell

one's father and mother, and cannot talk even with a blade on the neck. If it is known, his head will be chopped off.[15]

In 1922 each new CCP member had to take a loyalty oath: "Seriously keep secret, obey discipline, sacrifice oneself, persevere in struggles, work hard for the revolution, never betray the party." The oath is indicative of the Communist mentality at the time. The oath had a profound impact on newly commissioned CCP members, no less than the oath of confidence administered by the Mafia or the blood ceremony of brotherhood taken by the Triads.

Then as now, the CCP sought physical security and political control at all costs. The CCP was and is obsessed with defensive measures. Secrecy was the rule of the day and deceit was standard. The establishment of a *baowei dui*, and its later militarization, is clear evidence of such a defensive mindset.

The CCP is a textbook case of political survival of the fittest. The CCP's success as a militant political organization was in no small part due to its tenacity and deviousness. In order to survive political persecution the CCP needed to establish a highly self-disciplined internal security and overlapping surveillance system.

The idea of *baowei* survived its early form as a defensive-protective mechanism and became in time an integral institutional feature of the PRC political and police system.

## The idea of *baowei*

There was *baowei* work ever since July 1, 1921, the day the CCP was born.[16]

In Chinese the character *bao* means to stand guard, and the character *wei* means to defend against or protect from. Together *baowei* means to stand guard over or protect from harm. Thus construed, *baowei* suggests a reactionary, self-defense force to protect one from external threats of all kinds.

## *Baowie zuzhi* and CCP policing

The CCP *baowei* organs differ from conventional police in material, significant, and discernible ways:

(1) The *baowei* organs were not a *sovereign* police force. Neither the CCP nor any of its affiliated labor organizations was a duly constituted sovereign entity. The *baowei* organs were security units performing police functions working within the CCP.

(2) The *baowei* organs were not an *institutionalized* police force. First, *baowei* organs were ad hoc, temporary, and voluntary organizations. Second, *baowei* organs had a close-ended mandate to protect the mother organization from internal strife and external threats. They were not meant to be a permanent police/security organization.
(3) The *baowei* organs had a *fluid* form, *open* structure, *flexible* process, and evolving mission, adjusting and adapting to political circumstances of the day. In order to survive the challenges, it learned to improvise, and not rule bounded.
(4) The *baowei* organs were not a *social* police force. The *baowei* organs were created to secure against political threats, not to enforce the law, maintain order, or serve the people.
(5) The *baowei* organs were not an *external* and *pro-active* police force. They were primarily concerned with internal security breaches generated by external militant political threats.

Table 1: Differences between CCP *baowei* organs and police

| Characteristics | Police | CCP *baowei* |
|---|---|---|
| **Political-legal status** | state entity | civil entity |
| **Organizational status** | institutionalized | noninstitutionalized |
| | (1) preplanned | (1) ad hoc |
| | (2) permanent | (2) temporary |
| | (3) structured | (4) unstructured |
| | (4) defined goals | (4) changing objectives |
| | (5) defined process | (5) undefined process |
| | (6) inflexible means | (6) flexible means |
| **Role & Functions** | social, political, and legal | political and militant |
| **Terms of reference** | externally directed | internally directed |

The fact that the *baowei zuzhi* were not institutionalized as a state organ serving legal or social functions, however, is not as important as the fact that *baowie* organs were functional, norm enforcing, and order-maintaining organs, from which the CCP borrowed heavily for ideas and experience in constructing its future formal public security organization.

Gradually, the *baowei* concept was embraced by the Communists as a necessary state function to secure Party secrets, to protect national security, and to guard against political subversion. This is the earliest known public security organization in Communist China.

From the beginning, political orientation, a security role, and the surveillance method have been the hallmarks of Communist *baowei zuzhi* and later policing work.[17]

Communist Chinese policing in general adopted much of the method of operation of the *baowei* organs of this era and this method later became the police system's defining characteristic. The *baowei* as a political security organ operated in a militant, covert, and, above all, politically paranoid manner.

Political security work operates entirely differently than social policing. Political security is concerned with Party survival. Social policing is concerned with social order. Political security is concerned with Party safety and revolutionary integrity. Social policing is concerned with social stability and personal safety. Political security is concerned with ideological dominance. Social policing is concerned with moral breach.

It is most unfortunate that Communist policing had to be associated with the CCP struggle for survival and power, first as a political organization and later as a revolutionary party. This early experience shaped the CCP leadership's idea of policing into a distorted pattern. In the end, Mao provided a theoretical model for the conduct of Communist policing. He observed that in dealing with the enemies of the state, the police should be dictatorial and oppressive, using all means at their disposal to defeat and eliminate the enemy.

Deng's economic reform has changed the political orientation of the police. In 1983, the PRC and Ministry of Public Security (MPS) called for the separation of MPS work and social/civil policing. On May 9, 1983, the Ministry of Public Security issued the directive: "Certain issues regarding the strengthening and reforming of public security work" ("Guanyu jiaqiang he gaige gongan gongzuo de rugan wenti"), which made clear that the strengthening and reforming of police work in the reform era required a proper understanding of the relationship between dictatorship and democracy.

The separation of political security from social policing was made possible with the establishment of the Ministry of State Security ("Guojia anquan bu"). On September 2, 1983, the NPC Standing Committee passed the "Decision regarding the State Security Organ to exercise investigation, detention, pre-trial, and arrest powers of the public security organ,"[18] which effectively transferred the political policing function from the Ministry of Public Security to the newly formed Ministry of State Security.

The State Security Organization was established by the Sixth NPC to be responsible for conducting investigations into espionage normally handled by public security.

On February 22, 1993, the "PRC State Security Law" ("Zhonghua renmin gongheguo guojia anquanfa") was passed. The law formally transferred political policing powers and responsibility from the Ministry of Security to the State Security Organization. State security work, as defined in the law, includes combating organizations and individuals engaged in activities deemed harmful to the PRC.

## Section 2—Context Two:

### Military-Style Operations—More Soldier than Police

Another characteristic revealed by this historical study is the fact that public security before 1949 was organized along military lines, managed with military discipline, and operated using military doctrines.

The Eighth Army helped organize and train the first public security organs in the defense against the Japanese base in Tai Xing qu.[19] Much of the organizational structure, operational practices, personnel staffing, and institutional nomenclature was borrowed from the military.

The public security organization chart resembled that of the PLA (People's Liberation Army). Public security operations were conducted with military planning, coordination, and execution. Military and public security forces were recruited using similar standards and processes. For example, the "The Chinese Communist Party, Shan-Gan-Ning border area committee, Shan-Gan-Ning border area government, People's liberation Army, the Eighth army, instruction for the mobilization of able-bodied men for behind the line security service"[20] called for the recruitment of 1,710 able-bodied men to fill the ranks of a military company and a security troop in order to strengthen the defense against the enemy and secure the border areas.

In the autumn of 1939, the Eighth Army organized the first *baowei ganbu xunlian ban* ("security workers' training course"). The trainees for the most part came from the military. Training involved reconnaissance and interrogation. Graduates were sent to public security organs to collect military intelligence and root out traitors and spies.

During this critical period of the fight for survival, there was but one overriding objective to public security/police/military operations and that was securing the base area from destruction from within and attacks from without.

This militaristic mentality of PRC public security—fixation on an enemy—became a defining characteristic of PRC policing and is evident even today, for example in the conduct of the "yanda" campaign of the 1980s and 1990s.

## Section 3—Policing in the Revolutionary Bases

The nature, characteristics, role, and functions of the public security forces during wartime was very well articulated in Party policies and administrative regulations promulgated in various revolutionary base areas, such as the Shan-Gan-Ning border area (Shanxi, Ganxu, Ningxia).

There was no separate public security contingent in the border areas in the 1930s, except in Yan'an. Public security work was performed by soldiers, militias, and the "mass" as general wartime security-defense measures (*baowei*). For example, on February 15, 1938, the Shan-Gan-Ning border area government promulgated the "Order of the Shan-Gan-Ning border area government—regarding border area administrative organization establishment,"[21] which did not provide for a separate police department or public security force.[22]

The Shan-Gan-Ning border area government's staff roster (February 1938) did provide for security guard details in the government administration (10 out of 66 positions) and a security guard section with the court office (21 out of 45 positions) for a total of 32 security guards out of 262 government staff positions, including other security details.

On May 10, 1941, the Shan-Gan-Ning border area Supreme Court ("Shan-Gan-Ning gaodeng fayuan") issued a "Directive on county level judicial work" ("Dui gexian sifa gongzuo de zhishi"), which provided for police power of arrest in the border government generally and was to be exercised by the armed force, defense-security details, and court officials.

Specific power of arrest was granted to court messengers (judicial police), people's associations, schools, organs (for internal affairs), and the army. The arrest of armed forces personnel was treated separately and subject to special actions, such as notification of local government and county defense security authority, and approval of the county chief.

Village heads and district chiefs could order the arrest of any offender but had to turn him over to the judiciary organ within twenty-four hours.

The county adjudicator and procurator could independently order the arrest of offenders to stand trial, but there was no specific provision for public security or police to make such arrests. This circumstance is another indication that public security and police as a separate and distinct institution as we know it did not exist then. With the Communists, public security during wartime was everyone's business.

Policing or, more appropriately, order maintenance was provided by social organizations and community members. The mass ideological teachings, isolated geographical landscape, and collective social structure of China made it unnecessary to establish a professional police force.

The idea of a bureaucratically organized and professionally trained police force was first proposed by Yan'an public security office chief Wang Zhuochao on February 25, 1941. The formal proposal made the following assertions and recommendations:

(1) The public security at that time was referred to as a *baowei gongzuo de jiguan* ("organ of defensive work").
(2) Public security was responsible for "securing the border area, strengthening anti-Japanese defense, safeguarding the Party, and protecting revolutionary leaders, organs, associations, and the people's interests."
(3) Police work should be specialized and professional.
(4) Police must be professionally trained by specialists, not by a general political cadre. Thus, political cadre schools for the training of administrative personnel and judicial officials did not meet police needs.
(5) Police training should be institutionalized. There was a need to set up a Yan'an police administration school.
(6) Police should be trained to handle diverse crime-related problems. Ffiteen of the sixty police administration class slots should be set aside for female officers who would handle sex and vice crime.
(7) Police must be trained over a six-month period before assignment to duty.

The Proposal was not well received. It was criticized for being too ambitious and unrealistic by the Shan-Gan-Ning government.[23] The border-area government was not ready for a professionally trained and independently organized police force. Wang's proposal to professionalize the police fell on deaf ears.

There was no separate police law at that time (before 1939), though criminal law existed for the punishment of robbers and thieves, which hinted at the existence of some type of policing. During this time, however, collective discipline, voluntary service, and self-help, rather than professional police, were the preferred recourse against criminals.[24] The lack of incentives and impetus to develop an independent professional police force had a lot to do with historical circumstances (resentment against the nationalist police), political ideology (police as instrument of oppression, self-help), social priority (war effort), and community resources (little burden on the people).

In 1937 the Shan-Gan-Ning border government existed and was functioning in a de facto mode. However, the formal structure of government was not officially established until 1939. Ad hoc policy directives and issues-oriented orders were used to provide for various vital government functions, services, and institutions. There were, for example, "Order of the Shan-Gan-Ning border area government" ("Shan-Gan-Ning bianqu zhengfu mingling") of September 12, 1937, on administrative zone division;[25] "General Order of the Shan-Gan-Ning of the border area government" ( "Shan-Gan-Ning bianqu zhengfu tongling") of September 20, 1937, on autumn harvest; and "Order of the Shan-Gan-Ning border area government and border area security command" ("Shan-Gan-Ning bianqu zhengfu, bianqu baoan siling bu mingling") and "Shan-Gan-Ning border area's organic regulations for defense force against the Japanese" ("Shan-Gan-Ning bianqu kanri ziweijun zuzhi tiaoli") of October 1, 1937, for coordination, command, and control of border defense forces.

A rudimentary structure of government during this time was first provided for by "Fundamental organic principle of the Shan-Gan-Ning border area senate and administration" of May 12, 1937 ("Shan-Gan-Ning bianqu yihui ji xingzheng ganyao").[26] No part of the law provided for the establishment of a police or public security force.

In 1939, the Communist Party formally established its first government structure in the Shan-Gan-Ning border area, with provisions for the first public security organization in Communist China. A "*Gongan ju*" ("public security office") was set up within the border-area government structure.[27] It is revealing to note that the "Shan, Gan, Ning bianqu zhengfu zhuji tiaoli" ("Shan, Gan, Ning border area government organization regulations"), promulgated on April 4, 1939,[28] provided for a defense-security command and defense-security department but not a police department.

Police administration was relegated to an incidental function performed by the "minzhengchu" (civil administration). The Security Command was responsible for coordinating border-area security, while the defense security department was responsible for investigation, uncovering, and arrest of traitors. Again, the role and function of police administration was nowhere to be found.

The functions and duties of the *baoanchu* were later more clearly specified in "Shan-Gan-Ning bianqu zhengfu zuzhi zanxing tiaoli" ("Shan-Gan-Ning border area government provisional organic regulations," 1941). A security defense office was to be set up in the border-area government. The county would establish security defense-security branch and the district security defense-security detail. The main duties of the security defense office were to: (1) eliminate traitors, (2) arrest bandits, (3) control check points, (4) stand sentry, and (5) maintain public order. Administrative and policy matters involving *zhian* (public security) were to be decided upon by the Shan-Jin-Ning border area administrative affairs meetings.

The Organic Regulations of 1941 as an enabling statute for *baoan* organs were supplemented by subsidiary legislation that give it force and effect. The complementary "Provisional organic regulations on Shan-Gan-Ning county government," passed at the same time, provided that the county should establish a defense security and a defense security company, coming under the direction of the county head.[29] The *baoan ke* (defense-security branch) was to be responsible for the policing duties specified in the preceding paragraph. The defense-security company (*baoan dadui*) was to be guided by the county head but commanded by the defense-security commander (*baoan siling*), who was responsible for area pacification, defense force, and the young pioneer troop.

The "Provisional organic regulations of the Shan-Gan-Ning border area county affairs committee" further provided that the county affairs committee should set up a special defense-security policy/administrative section (*baoangu*) responsible for the elimination of spies, provision of security, arrest of bandits, maintenance of check points, sentry duty, maintenance of public peace and order, and other police matters.

The turning point for public security work in the border area was 1946. The Japanese had been defeated and the border-area government could now turn its attention to civil war and domestic affairs.[30] The institutionalization of the police was part of a larger effort to reform and regularize the border government structure and process after the Japanese War. At the end of 1946, the Shan-Gan-Ning border government passed a number of laws, regulations, and orders to streamline the government process on education, taxation, land reform, and a number of other issues.

It was significant that the laws and regulations during this period were promulgated under the serial number of *sheng zi* (victory series), signifying a change in border area conditions and a corresponding change in government policy and administration.

The end of the war meant that the police had to pay more attention to civil matters and the social order. Two pieces of legislation during this time deserve mention: "The Shan-Gan-Ning border area violation of police regulations"[31] and "The Shan-Gan-Ning border area police work regulations" ("Police Regulations of 1946").[32] Together they carved out new roles and functions for the police.

Before these two police legislations there was no comprehensive police law providing for the role, functions, duties, and responsibilities of the police. Border areas public security activities were guided by ad hoc official policy pronouncements and issues-oriented orders.

In November 1946, the "Police Regulations of 1946" was passed. The law was designed as a set of general guidelines for police work. However, it turned out to be, in effect, a comprehensive police law.

"Police Regulations of 1946" has twelve articles and thirty-seven items. Together, they informed upon roles (Art. 1), discipline (Art. 2-4 items), work prescriptions (Art. 3-6 items), patrol duties (Art. 4-12 items), household registration duties (Art. 5-7 items), confiscation of weapons (Art. 6), responding to police alarms (Art. 7), police supervision (Art. 8), police use of arms (Art. 9), police reporting for duty (Art. 10), police rewards (Art. 11), and police punishment (Art. 12). The Regulations detailed what the police should or should not do in the course of duty. They give an illuminating picture of the roles, duties, and powers of police in China at the time.

On November 16, 1946, the Shan-Gan-Ning government committee issued the "Order of the Shan-Gan-Ning border area government" (Civil 74)[33] announcing the passage and promulgation of the "Shan-Gan-Ning border area violation of police regulations" (draft).[34]

On April 9, 1949, the "Provisional organic regulations for the Shan-Gan-Ning border government" was passed.[35] The Regulations provided that the Shan-Gan-Ning border government was responsible for promulgation and implementation of policies, including those involving public security. They provided for the establishment of a public security department (*gongan ting*) within the administrative structure of the border government to be responsible for the following duties, among others: arrest of spies, bandits, and other undesirables; maintaining the social order; immigration and border duty; and education of security personnel.

With the promulgation of "Police Regulations of 1946," "Shan-Gan-Ning border area violation of police regulations" (1946), and other related administrative orders, the Communist police system was increasingly taking shape, building a foundation for the PRC public security organs after 1949.

## Section 4—First Organized Police

The earliest known state-sponsored public security organization in Communist China was established in November 1931, by the Chinese Soviet Republic. This was the *Guojia zhengzhi baoweiju* ("State political security bureau"). Its main duties were to struggle against political adversaries (e.g., KMT spies, foreign enemies, and CCP traitors), and to secure the revolutionary base from sabotage and destructive activities.

In October 1937, the Communist Party Central issued "Shan-Gan-Ning border area government order—establishment of the Yan'an city government" (known as the Yan'an Order).[36] The Yan'an Order was drafted in response to the people's need for civil administration services—public security, air raid shelters, fire prevention, health services, and city construction. The Yan'an city government was supervised by the Shan-Gan-Ning border government.

The "Shan-Gan-Ning border area people's police" was established under the above Yan'an Order to maintain social order and provide for public welfare in the capital of Yan'an, including street safety, traffic order, household inspections, hotel control, and guard duties for Party organs and public meetings.[37] The first police chief was Liu Hupin.

The Yan'an Order was issued in October 1937. Chinese public security historical records, however, date the formation of the Yan'an police to May 1938. The two sources can be reconciled. The Yan'an Order provided for the formation of Yan'an government, including the police. The police history described the actual implementation of the Yan'an Order, including formation of the police.

The Yan'an police were commanded by the Yan'an public security bureau. The police were required to wear uniforms and were charged with maintaining peace and order. They worked alongside the mass-based "chujian weiyuanhui" ("eliminate traitor committee") to expose traitors, spies, and criminals.

On April 15, 1940, a police training school was proposed and approved by the Shan-Gan-Ning border government for the training of police cadres (*jingcha ganbu*) and officers (*jingguan*). This was the first attempt to professionalize the police and separate them from the other political offices, administrative organs, and military units, giving the police a new civic identity and many social functions.[38] It was also the first time the term *police* was employed to distinguish it from the *gongan* ("public security") or *baoan* ("defense security").

The nature and functions of revolutionary policing (*gemin jincha*) was first discussed in 1946.

## Section 5—Conclusion

This chapter investigates the development of Communist policing in China at the revolutionary bases in the border region before 1949. In the process, it looks into the nature, characteristics, role, and functions of the police from 1930 to 1949. During this time, the role and functions of the police in China were driven by wartime needs and shaped by the political agenda (CCP vs. KMT). Several examples illustrate this.

During the war with Japan, the 1941 "Jin, Ji, Lu, Yu border area government administration guiding principles" clearly stated that one of the most important tasks of the border government was "to defend the border area, persist in the northern China defensive war." These guiding principles were repeated in the "Guidelines of Shan-Gan-Ning administration policy"[39] of May 1, 1941. In the Shan-Gan-Ning border area, the number one guideline was to unite all classes, parties, and people to fight against the Japanese invaders and to utilize all human and material resources to defend the border area, the northwest region, and the whole of China, and to drive Japan imperialists from the country. It is important to note that none of the other twenty guidelines touched upon public security or social order issues and concerns.

Later, during the civil war, the 1945 CCP policy document "Important aspects of Jin-Cha-Ji border area executive committee administration" made clear that the primary tasks of the revolutionary government at Jin-Cha-Ji border area were to "liberate the cities" and "thoroughly destroy the enemy puppet organizations, establish a democratic political authority." The police tasks included the confiscation of enemy and puppet (KMT) organizations' property, discarding of monopolistic commercial practices, and doing away with exploitative measures.

In the fight against the KMT, the militant role and defensive posture of border-area administration was repeatedly confirmed in a series of government resolutions. In the 1946 "Resolution of the second meeting of the third Shan-Gan-Ning government committee,"[40] the committee resolved that the border-area government should improve military preparedness in the fight against the Nationalists, implement land reform, increase productivity to support the war effort, and work with the people and reduce the distance between them.

In 1949, Chairman Liu of the border committee reported to the Shan-Gan-Ning border government[41] that the first priority was to continue to mobilize all human and material resources to support the civil war effort and continue the revolutionary campaign. Among other tasks was the strengthening of defense-security work and the struggle against hidden counterrevolutionaries.

The most important observation here is that public security work in the border area had more to do with security-defense (*baoan* or *baowei*) than mainstream policing. This mentality afflicted the PRC police until well into the reform period in the 1980s.

A second and related observation is that when China's stated national priority shifted from fighting the Japanese to consolidating Communist power, so did the police role, mission, and function.

The lessons learned from this overview are that, first, the Communist police are an instrument of the Party; second, the role and functions of public security changed with wartime circumstances and necessity; third, in terms of goals or ends, the Communist police were more security conscious than crime oriented; and finally, in terms of means, the Communist police operated more like a military organization than a civil one.

CHAPTER FIVE

# Police Education

## Introduction

During the last thirty years of reform, China has undergone unprecedented changes that have affected every aspect of the society.[1] The process of reform, from liberalization of market to globalization of trade, from introduction of the rule of law to promotion of human rights, from derogation of Party authority to decentralization of government administration, poses tremendous challenges for policing and social control.[2]

The Chinese People's Republic of China police education system is particularly hard hit. It suffers from dated educational philosophy, obsolete instructional materials, ineffective teaching methods, and incompetent academic staff.[3] Overall, there is a gross mismatch between police education programs on the one hand and the nation's reform agenda and police operational needs on the other. PRC political leaders and police reformers are trying hard to catch up, but they are confronted with daunting challenges, from entrenched police culture to emerging economic interests.

A comprehensive review of literature shows that there is currently no Western academic study on PRC police education. More significantly, a review of selected comparative criminal justice textbooks shows that U.S. students are not being exposed to Chinese criminal justice and policing. The lack of literature on China obstructs comparative criminal justice research.

This chapter seeks to provide an overview of the PRC police education system. It is organized as follows. To anchor the study, Section 1 provides a brief review of literature on general theory and best practice of police education in the West. Section 2 traces the "History of Police Education in China" from the *Qing* dynasty to the PRC. Section 3 provides an overview of the "PRC Police Education System." Section 4, "PRC Police Educational Philosophy," discusses that philosophy, past as well as present. Section 5, "U.S. and Chinese Police Education Compared" compares and contrasts the police education in China and the United States. Section 6 reports on "Police Studies in China" as an emerging academic discipline. Section 7 reports the findings of a scientific survey conducted in China about police cadets' assessment of their educational experience. Section 8 discusses some of the "Police Education Problems and Issues" during the reform period. Finally, Section 9 presents some conclusions on the subject.

## Section 1—Literature Review on Police Education

Ever since August Vollmer introduced higher education to American policing in 1908,[4] debates over the necessity, content, impact, and effect have proceeded unabated.[5] Although Police Chief David Geary of Ventura, California, observed in 1966 that a four-year college degree could reduce personnel turnover and citizen complaint rates,[6] Professor Charles B. Saunders was quick to conclude in 1970 that "The reasons advanced for college education for police are essentially the same as those used to justify higher education as preparation for any other career. They rest more on faith than on fact."[7] The balance of judgment in 2008 is for well-educated police officers.

Over the years, policymakers, policing scholars, police executives, and street officers have given different reasons for police higher education, including the following:

(1) Higher education has been perceived as a "cure-all" for police ills of every kind and shape;[8] more education makes for better police officers.[9]

(2) Higher education contributes to upgrading of police services;[10] making them more efficient, effective,[11] and professional.[12] Kenneth Peak states,

> The administrators, however, found more overall advantages to having college-educated officers, including better communication with the public; better written report; more effective performance; more initiative; more professionalism; wiser use of discretion; increased likelihood of promotion; better decision making; more sensitive to minority and ethnic groups; and fewer disciplinary problems.[13]

(3) Higher education makes police work a more prestigious profession, thus more respectable to the public[14] and satisfying to officers.[15]

(4) Higher education helps police to understand their work better, making police work more meaningful to the officers.

(5) Higher education helps the police to broaden their mind and expand their vision, making them less dogmatic and authoritarian,[16] less prejudiced,[17] more flexible,[18] and less politically conservative and more socially sensitive.[19]

(6) Higher education helps police to be better thinkers and decision makers. It helps them to exercise their discretion more appropriately and use their power more properly.[20]

(7) Higher education helps police to build character and learn ethical conduct, making them more law abiding[21] and accountable,[22] and less susceptible to corruption of office and abuse of power.[23]

(8) Higher education inculcates democratic values in the police, making them less conservative and more progressive.[24]

In 1973, the debate was finally settled in the United States in favor of the educational reformers. The National Advisory Commission on Criminal Justice Standards and Goals recommended that "Every police agency should, not later than 1982, require as a condition of initial employment, the completion of at least 4 years of education (120 semester hours or a baccalaureate degree) at an accredited college or university."[25]

Once the decision is made to require higher education of the police, the issue is raised as to what kind of education best serves police needs.[26] As Charles Tenney observed, "There is agreement that education for law enforcement is an important feature of improving police performance and relations with and within the community. ... However, there is no real consensus on what "education" means for law enforcement. ..."[27]

The lack of consensus over police education—necessity, direction, content, and impact—results in part from a lack of shared understanding as to the role and functions of police. As Richard Myren, a noted police educator, once observed, "How can we say what education to do for policing until the public can agree on what it wants police to do for the community?"[28]

One of the major disagreements over police roles and functions is whether police should be professional law enforcement officers or the community's "philosopher, friend, and guide"?[29] As Michael Banton puts it,

> A division is becoming apparent between specialist departments within police forces (detectives, traffic officers, vice and fraud squads, etc.) and the ordinary patrolman. The former are "law officers" whose contacts with the public tend to be of a punitive or inquisitory character, whereas the patrolmen ... are principally "peace officers" operating within the moral consensus of the community.[30]

The other intractable issue is who is to decide upon police roles and functions in a community. In this regard, Professor James Q. Wilson observed that police perform multiple roles and operate with different styles in their community.[31] This leads to conflicting demands on the police and clashes of expectations between contending factions within the community.[32] As observed by the Kerner Report,

> The policeman in the ghetto is a symbol of increasingly bitter social debate over law enforcement. On one side, disturbed and perplexed by sharp rises in crime and urban violence, exerts extreme pressure on police for tougher law enforcement. Another group, inflamed against police as agents of repression, tends toward defiance of what it regards as order maintained at the expense of Justice.[33]

That observation suggests police role conflicts might be structural in nature and political in origin,[34] less amendable to positive articulation and definitive resolution.

Police role conflicts may have been self-induced: "It would appear that much of policing action is an attempt on the part of the police to dramatize certain of their actions and to conceal or make less than salient their other than frequent but less impressive activities."[35]

Finally, the ambivalence over proper police roles and functions has been increased in recent years by a shift in policing paradigm from traditional policing to community policing.[36] Police have reluctantly transformed their role from street crime fighter[37] to community problem solver.

Whatever the cause or reason, disagreements over police roles have a major impart on how police are organized, evaluated and trained. The question remains, what kinds of attitude, ability, and skills are required to be an effective officer? The lack of clearly defined police roles affects police educational goals and means. Effective education of police officers is difficult to achieve.

Currently, there are three answers to the question, what should police officers learn in college? (1) Police officers should be provided with a liberal arts education, making them model citizens, steeped in democratic values and reasoning; (2) police should be educated to the theory and practice of policing, making them competent professionals; and (3) police should be trained as police officers, making them consummate craftsmen.

## Section 2—History of Police Education in China

### Imperial China

The first interest in studying police as a professional field came during the police reform movement in the late *Qing* dynasty. With police modernization comes police professional education and academic study.

China's first Higher Police Academy (*Gaodeng xunjing xuetang*)[38] was established in the capital in April of 1906, and later one was set up in every province, providing recruit training to patrol officers or in-service training to police officials. The Higher Police Academy was a makeover of the Capital Police Academy, which experimented with the teaching of higher police subjects in 1903. With the establishment of the Higher Police Academy, the Capital Police Academy was closed down after it graduated a total of fifty-five higher diploma, or undergraduate, students. Students at the Higher Police Academy were appointed as a result of competitive examination, with only 240 candidates selected out of 6,000 applicants.

Police higher education degrees took three years to complete. The three-year curriculum included the following:

*Year 1:* Police studies, Great *Qing* Legal Code, police administrative law, military tactics, police judicial law, police fire prevention law, jurisprudence, public international law (peac), English or Japanese, and physical exercise.

*Year 2:* Police judicial law, civil procedure law, Great *Qing* Legal Code, public international law (war), civil law, commercial law, private international law, English or Japanese, and exercise.

*Year 3:* Criminal law, criminal procedure law, civil law, commercial law, prison law, general meaning of current Chinese legal system, administrative law, English or Japanese, physical exercise, and instructor command method.

The professionalization of the police through competitive entrance examinations and higher education demands spoke to the need for police academic research and scholarly publications; both were encouraged by the *Qing* police reformers. Thus in 1905, the Ministry of Police was established with a Police Studies Department, and the government Civil Affairs Department dedicated a special section to the translation of foreign police books. As a result of political leadership and administrative efforts, police studies as an academic subject started to grow.

The first published works in policing were translated books from foreign languages, for example, *Police Studies* (*Jingcha xue*) (1904) by Zuo Xin She. They were followed by professional police journals in every provincial police jurisdiction, for example, *Sichuan Police Work Official Journal* (*Sichuan jingwu guan bao*) and *Guangdong Police Work Official Journal* (*Guandong jingwu guan bao*) .

The objectives of the police journals were to: (1) promote police work; (2) spread police knowledge; and (3) develop police theories. For the first time in Chinese history, police work was made the subject matter of scholarly research, public debate, and mass circulation. As observed by a police author in the inaugural issue of *Sichuan Police Work Official Journal*, a public forum was needed to keep people informed about emerging social issues, to debate confusing government policies, to interpret unclear laws, and to analyze intricate police theories. The police could now work from a solid foundation of facts and theory, and people could build trust in the government and the police through scientific knowledge and academic debate.

This established a solid foundation for the development of a police academic discipline.[39]

## PRC

The development of PRC public security higher education and a police training system in China can be divided into five periods, each period shaped by prevailing political conditions and social needs at the time. The five periods are: (1) the initial building period (1930s to 1949); (2) the transformation period (1949 to late 1950s); (3) the adjustment period (early 1960s to before the Cultural Revolution); (4) the Cultural Revolution period (May 1966 to October 1976); and (5) the recovery and development period (October 1976 to present).

### (1) Initial stage period (1930s to 1949)

Public security education and police training first appeared in Communist China in the 1930s. The Soviet Chinese Communist border government organized two kinds of training courses for its political operatives: "security cadre training course" (*baowei gangbu xunlian ban*) and "public security cadre school" (*gongan gangbu xuexiao*) in the revolutionary base area. At this juncture, the newly established Communist government was very concerned about internal security and political survival in the face of KMT infiltration.

At the time, public security courses were aimed at promoting political commitment, particularly communist work style and party loyalty. Instruction on political theory and methods (dialectical analysis and historical materialism) was of the highest importance. Overall, party and public security cadres were taught how to be good communist members rather than effective police officers. They learned more about the direction, guidelines, and policies of public security work than any specific public security skills, laws, and regulations. During this time, Chairman Mao and other revolutionary leaders were personally involved in providing guidance for public security training.

(2) Transformation period (1949 to late 1950s)
The PRC government was formed in 1949. In the 1950s, the PRC engaged in nation building, purging the old and building the new. Public security, together with its education and training, was organized during this period. Most of the fundamental principles, methods, structures, and processes of PRC police education and training were established during this time. Public security education and training then focused more on imparting practical knowledge and applied skills than on theoretical knowledge. Though political and ideological training still figured prominently in the training process, public security skills became increasingly more relevant. The teachers were all experienced public security practitioners—experts, leaders, and front-line officers.

The first proposal to establish police schools came in the First National Public Security in October 10, 1949. The establishment of police training schools was then left in the hands of the respective major administrative regions. Later, in September 1953 and on occasion of the Second People's Public Security Work Conference, it was decided that the central government and large administrative regions would set up their schools. The provinces were not allowed to build police training schools.[40]

(3) Adjustment period (early 1960s to before the Cultural Revolution)
During the late 1950s and early 1960s, China suffered from economic crisis as a result of Mao's failed economic policy, the Great Leap Forward. The economic turmoil was exacerbated by bad harvests. Public security was in retrenchment. Police education was made the responsibility of Public Security Politic-Legal School (*Gongan Zhengfa Xuexiao*). Public security training responsibility was moved downward, that is, delegated to local public security, procuratorates, and legal cadres who organized "local security cadre training classes" or "central-local security cadre training courses" or "military security investigation skills classes." Police educators and students alike were asked to learn from practicing in the field.

(4) The Cultural Revolution period (May 1966 to October 1976)
During this period, Mao initiated the Cultural Revolution to reestablish his political control with the support of Lin Biao and Jiang Qing. The Red Guards, taking to heart Mao's instruction to "smash gongjianfa (police, procuracy, and courts)," destroyed the police along with the whole criminal justice system. The People's Liberation Army replaced the public security. Police education institutes were systematically de-

stroyed, though some police educators held fast to their convictions in fighting Lin and Jiang's gangs.

(5) The recovery and development period (October 1976 to present)
In October 1976, the "Gang of Four" was smashed. The country gradually returned to normal. Police education recovery started with the reopening of demolished politico-legal schools and the rehabilitation of humiliated public security education cadres. The resumption of politico-legal schools also marked the return of Party-directed police education, resulting in more emphasis on theory and less on practice.

Beginning with the 1980s, police education turned over a new leaf—its new mission was to prepare public security for the challenges of the twenty-first century, namely domestic market reform and global trade.

Police education reform in China dated from the First National Public Security Education Meeting in 1984. By 1997, there were four undergraduate police schools, thirteen higher public security professional training schools, seventy-six police training schools, and a number of public security cadre training centers.

By 1997, after ten years of public security education reform, public security education still suffered from the following problems, both old and new:

First, there was a lack of appreciation for high-quality police education. There was a tendency to keep schools running in a traditional way, with little change in methods or curriculum.

Second, except for the highly competitive and prestigious Ministry of Public Security (MPS) police schools, for example, the Chinese People's Public Security University (PSU), it was very hard to attract quality students.

Third, public security colleges and schools were funded by provinces and prefectures, making funds dependent on fluctuating regional economies.

Fourth, the public security schools were not able to attract quality teachers due to lack of resources and incentives.[41]

Some recommendations to rectify these problems were to appoint an important political leader to oversee the nation's public education affairs and place public education on the Party Central Committee's agenda so it would receive national attention; develop a clear set of public security educational objectives and make them a responsibility of public security political cadres; strengthen research and study in police education issues and problems; and produce a well-designed and -researched plan for the establishment of public security schools to meet market demand and social needs.

The "'95' gongan gongzuo gangyao" ("The '95' public security work agenda") clearly detailed the mission and vision of public security education reform and development. Particularly, the MPS was charged with the responsibility to develop a strategic plan for the establishment of public security schools and training nationwide. The direction was toward enhancing professional skills, e.g., modern management, and inculcating culture and values, e.g., rule of law. Since then, public security bureaus and offices all over the nation have placed increased attention on police education and training, including setting up special education work committees and distribution of additional earmarked funds. For example, Public Security Bureaus in Shanghai and Hunan have set up their own public security education committee, while Public Security Bureaus in Helungjian, Jiling, Liaonin, Shantung, Zhejiang, and Gangdong have increased their financial budget and staff establishment for public security schools and training sites.[42] Every effort was made to enhance the quality and competency of the teaching staff by sending teachers to graduate programs, teacher's training courses, and foreign exchange programs.

## Section 3—PRC Police Education System[43]

The PRC police education system provides three kinds of formal police schooling: police training schools provide basic training for new police recruits; post secondary colleges provide higher education for secondary school graduates; adult education courses provide higher education for civilians and in-service training for police personnel.

There are four levels to police training and education the secondary school technical education, post-secondary professional education, police undergraduate education, and police graduate education.

Table 1: Educational achievements of PRC public security 1983 vs. 1997

| Education level | 1983 | 1997 |
|---|---|---|
| *Da-zhuan* and above (universities and colleges) | 4.2% | 22.88% |
| *Zhong-zhuan* and *Gao-zhong* (technical secondary school and senior middle school) | 34.84% | 60.84% |
| *Chu-zhongand* below (junior middle school) | 60.84% | 17.84% |

**Source:** Li Wenneng, "Luli tigao jiaoyu zhiliang, shi gongan zui zhongyao di renwu" (Work hard to promote education quality, is the most important task facing public security education), *Gongan Jiaoyu* (Public Security Education) (Issues 42, 1997), 6.

By the end of 1996, the PRC boasted 300-plus public security schools of all kinds: 6 undergraduate institutions; 14 professional colleges; 75 police academies; 45 adult technical education centers; 39 armed police command schools; and 109 public security cadre training centers.[44] In a period of ten years (1986–1996), the PRC police education system graduated 7,000 undergraduates, 30,000 professional officers, and 150,000 technical students, and provided in-service vocational training for 600,000 police officers.

In the central government, the MPS is responsible for the planning and organization of police training and education nationwide. Currently, there are three police universities—Chinese People's Public Security University (*Zhongguo Renmin Gongan Daxue*), Chinese People's Police Officers University (*Zhongguo Renmin Jingguan Daxue*), and Police Criminal Police College (*Zhongguo Xingshi Jingcha Xueyuan*)—offering four years of police higher education.

These MPS-sponsored schools, similar to West Point and the United States Naval Academy, have two basic missions: (1) provide basic education for new officer candidates and transform them into officers with high morale, keen intellect, and a strong physique; (2) prepare officer candidates to assume future leadership positions within the MPS establishment.

Three kinds of people are eligible to apply to MPS schools: First, current high school graduates, unmarried and between the age of eighteen and twenty-two years old; second, serving officers (with two or more years of working experience) with a middle high education standard who are not older than twenty-eight years old; third, police officers who have served with distinction and have received achievement awards. They must have a high school certificate or equivalent standard.

The applicants must hold correct political views and possess good moral character. They must love the country and people, support the Party, uphold the constitution, and follow the rule of law. They must conduct themselves appropriately and be politically austere. Finally, they must possess strong organizational ability, self-discipline, and initiative.

PSU is run by the MPS. The predecessor of PSU was the Northern China Public Security Cadre School, (*Huabei Gongan Ganbu Xuexiao*) established in 1948. It had various names: Central Public Security Cadre School, Central People's Public Security School, and Central People's Cadre School.

In 1984, PSU was formally named. It has five departments: police management, public order, criminal investigation, police physical education, and law. It has research centers in police management, criminal investigations, safety and prevention, and population management. It publishes three academic journals: *Public Security University Journal* (*Gongan Daxue Xue Bao*), *Public Security Research* (*Gongan Yanjiue*), and *Police Digest* (*Jingcha Wenzhai*).

## Section 4—PRC Police Educational Philosophy

### Philosophy

PRC police educational philosophy is shaped by Chinese (Confucian) educational philosophy, and later Marxist political ideology. The purpose of education is to develop perfect—morally, spiritually, intellectually, culturally, and physically—police candidates. By definition, education is for the grooming of elites ("junzhi" or "gentlemen").

### Moral Education

To Confucius, the core of any education is to achieve perfection of self through self-cultivation. Under Communism and with the police, moral education is the development of a correct political viewpoint, superlative intellectual capacity, a wholesome moral compass, and a balanced psychological disposition.

Moral education is one of the most important aspects and unique characteristics of China's education policy and a foremost PRC police education goal. Theoretically, moral education is deemed essential for the development of a responsible socialist citizen and ethical police professional. Functionally, moral education is considered important to promote exemplary conduct, prevent abuse of power, and guard against corruption.

The vision of PRC police moral education follows the legacy of Confucianism. Moral education, since the days of Confucius, aims at building a well-rounded and virtuous person. It is designed to help people actualize their full potential through continuous self-reflection and the unrelenting search for improvement. Confucianism seeks to improve a person's character in its entirety—value system, thinking pattern, behavior, sense and sensibility.

### Socialist Education

The direction, content, and conduct of PRC police education are determined by educational policy set forth by the Communist Party, state, and local governments. The Communist Party approaches educational reform with a Marxist perspective. In 1957, Mao suggested, "Our education policy, should enable the educated to achieve moral education (*deyu*), intellectual education (*zhiyu*), and physical education (*tiyu*) development, becoming a laborer conscious of socialism and culture." In 1958 the Communist Party Central Committee and the State Council mandated that "the education policy of the Party is that education is to serve the proletarian class politics, integrating education with productive labor movement."[45] More recently, the "PRC Education Law" (effective September 1, 1995) provided that: "Education must be in the service of socialist modernization and construction, must be integrated with productive labor, in the development of comprehensive moral, intellectual and physical socialist enterprise builders and successors."

## Lei Feng Spirit and Policing

The ideal model for a consummate Communist police office is that of Lei Feng.[46] Lei Feng exemplified traditional Chinese virtues and contemporary Communist morality. Lei's Communist world view is best captured in his writing: "A man's usefulness to the revolutionary cause is like a screw in a machine. It is only by the many, many interconnected and fixed screws that the machine can move freely, increasing its enormous work power. Though a screw is small, its use is beyond estimation."[47]

In March 1963, Mao invited the nation to "Learn from Comrade Lei Feng" and emulate the "Lei Feng Spirit." Communist leaders honored Lei Feng as a folk hero for his relentless effort to uphold the Communist ideal of selfless devotion to duty and altruistic concern for the welfare of others.

Since 1963, successive Chinese leaders have used Lei Feng to remind the public of the need to return their ideological roots and draw upon the Communist ideal to meet reform challenges. Lei Feng resurfaced after the Tiananmen demonstration on June 4, 1989, and the Falun Gong sit-in on April 25, 1999.[48]

He is held up as an example for Chinese police officers as well as those in other careers. Other Communist heroes and even accomplishments are also used as role models for aspiring police officers, as the following table indicates.

Table 2: Exemplary attributes and qualities of selected Communist model heroes

| Model – Hero | Background | Attributes |
|---|---|---|
| **An Yemin (1938–1958)** | Served in the PLA Navy. Seriously injured in a battle with Taiwan but insisted on fighting to the last breath. He was made a PLA hero and a role model for all. | Heroism.<br><br>Self-sacrifice.<br><br>Dedication to duty. |
| **Daqing Oilfield, Heilongjiang Province** | Daqing was the first major oilfield opened up in China without foreign (USSR) assistance in 1963. | Self-reliance.<br><br>Hard work.<br><br>"In industry, learn from Daqing" (Mao, 1964). |
| **Wang Jinxi (1923–1970)** | "Iron Man" Wang and his famous No. 1205 Drilling Team worked subzero weather to produce oil for the motherland. | Perseverance in the face of challenge. |
| **Jiao Yulu (1922–1964)** | Jiao as Party secretary of Lankao County, Henan Province led the masses to combat natural calamities while battling cancer. | Indomitable spirit.<br><br>Tireless devotion to Communist cause.<br><br>A model Party cadre. |
| **Liu Yingjun (1945–1966)** | Liu was from a poor peasant background. He joined the PLA in 1962. On March 15, 1966, he sustained lethal injuries and died trying to save some children. | Sacrifice one's life for others.<br><br>A good student of Lei Feng. |
| **Wang Jie (1942–1965)** | Wang was a platoon leader of the 1st Company of the Engineering Battalion, PLA. While training militia a landmine exploded. Wang threw himself on the blast to save 12 lives. | "Fearing neither hardship nor death." |

## Section 5—United States and Chinese Police Education Compared

### Introduction

Confucius' approach to character building and moral development is not unlike those found in American higher education before 1900.[49] American universities then, just as PRC police schools now, instructed students on controversial moral principles and enduring character issues.[50] By the early 1900s, however, character considerations gave way to a focus on competency.[51] Still later (ca.1950), influential scholars in the United States wanted to be free from normative judgments when conducting scientific inquiry.[52] Since then, moral education has been taught almost solely in the form of informational courses and for moral clarification purposes.

In the 1970s, the Watergate scandal brought home the importance of ethics in personal choices and morality in public life. Professional bodies, public services, and private business started once again to demand professional ethics courses in universities. Overall, such initiatives seek to raise moral awareness, train students in moral reasoning, and promote moral decision making.

One of the major concerns is that moral education in universities might turn into value imposition, political indoctrination, and religious domination. Finally, people frequently take issue with the competency of moral instructors. It is in the above historical context that police ethical training evolved.

Moral education in criminal justice raises two questions: should ethics be part of the criminal justice curriculum, and how can ethics be effectively taught?[53] Jeffries Murphy argued for inclusion, observing that moral choices are indispensable in law, punishment, and justice, and that ultimately, political governance is about moral choices.[54] As to how morality should be taught, Professor Sherman suggested making students aware of varieties of moral issues, equipping them with skills to analyze a moral dilemma, instilling them with a moral obligation to do the right thing, and preparing them to tolerate moral ambiguity.[55]

According to H.R. Delaney, the study of moral and ethical issues in criminal justice is the study of "What is the nature of human actions and its relation to belief and knowledge?"[56] The questions to be asked include: What is a value choice? What constitutes fundamental human values? Are some values more important than others? How do we choose between competing moral choices or how do we resolve a moral dilemma?[57] Overall, the U.S. approach to moral education is to keep an open mind and to foster open dialogue.

In this regard, the Chinese follow a long tradition of seeking to attain a perfect moral order innate in the natural order of things (*tien ming*). An ethical people must be taught the moral rules and be encouraged to pursue them at all costs.

Table 3: Moral education and police: PRC vs. US

| | PRC | US |
|---|---|---|
| **Value postulate** | Social morality | Individual ethics |
| **Factual assumption** | Social nature of man—Collectivism and communitarianism<br>Effective personhood<br>Malleability of man and family socialization | Egoistical nature of man—hedonistic and utilitarian<br>Rational—calculating man<br>Self-determination and personal autonomy |
| **Role** | Dominant role | Secondary role |
| **Purpose** | Character building | Moral sensitivity training |
| **Scope** | All-encompassing | Issues oriented |
| **Means** | State indoctrination<br>Self-cultivation | State education<br>Personal reflection |

## Chinese vs. United States police education

There are substantial differences between the Chinese and the U.S. police education training systems. Specifically:

(1) *Educational philosophy.* Chinese educational philosophy is dictated by the Communist Party, expressed as ideology, and enshrined in the constitution. American police follow constitutional norms, the spirit of the law, and professional ethics. Beyond that, individual departments at every level of government are free to advance philosophical principles and defend value postulates.

(2) *Educational objectives.* The PRC police education objectives are more comprehensive and integrated. They are also clearly defined and narrowly construed. Police education is to prepare police officers to be politically committed, morally responsible, socially conscious, culturally rich, and professionally competent social change agents. There are few debates over vision and mission. Police education is subject to political control and responsiveness to people's needs. Police curriculum teaching must be grounded in theory and relevant to practice. In the end, the prime police educational objective is to give police educators, institutions, and students a sense of higher purpose and greater meaning to life as committed Communist agents.

The U.S. police education objectives are much more varied and subjective. There are as many articulations as there are varieties of theoretical perspectives and competing schools of thought. Educational objectives also change through time with evolving political philosophies, social values, and community interests. Given so many contingencies and uncertainties, police educational objectives inevitably invite contentious dispute and debate. Despite agreement on the necessity of police education, there are few agreements on police roles and functions and little consensus on what makes for good police officers. As a result, police educational objectives are difficult to define.

(3) *Organization.* Chinese police education is provided for by the MPS, and in the United States police studies are offered through state and private universities. In China there are three national police universities and many provincial colleges and local schools. In the United States there is no national police university (except for the FBI Academy) but many state and local police academies.

(4) *Instruction.* In China, all faculty members at national police universities and provincial police colleges are MPS officers and carry nominal rank. In the United States, except at service academies (e.g. FBI), where most instructors are law enforcement agents, faculty members at universities and colleges teaching police-related courses are all civilians, with a few adjuncts who are serving officers. They also must have proper academic preparation beyond a master's degree. Increasingly, there are many police officers who have earned higher academic credentials (J.D. or Ph.D.) and who teach after they retire from police work. Instructors and training officers at Peace Officer Standards and Training (POST) centers are a mixture of civilians and police.

The differences between the PRC and the United States in police education are revealing of other more fundamental differences between the two countries in national culture, political ideology, educational philosophy, and police roles and functions.[58]

Table 4: Comparison of Chinese and U.S. police education-training systems

| Comparative dimensions | U.S. | China |
|---|---|---|
| Philosophy/ policy | Follow constitutional norms.<br>Except for federal police agencies such as FBI, no national law enforcement policy.<br>State and local police follow respective state constitutions, local law, and police regulations. | Dictated by Communist ideology and Chinese philosophy.<br>Governed by MPS policy in professional areas, e.g., standards and style of work.<br>Governed by local policy in work-related issues, e.g., recruitment and traffic enforcement. |

| Comparative dimensions | U.S. | China |
|---|---|---|
| | **LEADERSHIP/SPONSORSHIP** | |
| **Education** | Certification by national or regional organization, e.g., the Middle States Commission on Higher Education is the unit of the Middle States Association of Colleges and Schools that accredits degree-granting colleges and universities in the Middle States region, which includes Delaware, the District of Columbia, Maryland, New Jersey, New York, Pennsylvania, Puerto Rico, the U.S. Virgin Islands, and several locations internationally.<br><br>Accreditation by professional organization, e.g., ACJS | Sponsored by MPS<br><br>Certified by the Ministry of Education |
| **Training** | Licensed by state Department of Education<br><br>Certified by respective police training board, e.g., Minnesota Peace Officer Standards and Training (P.O.S.T.) Board.<br><br>Approved by respective police agencies | Certified by the Ministry of Education |
| | **ORGANIZATION** | |
| **Education** | Independent, market driven | Dependent, state provided |
| **Training** | Decentralized, police department organized | Centralized—MPS at various levels of government |
| | **INSTRUCTION** | |
| **Education** | Provided by scholars with professional adjuncts, holders of Ph.D. or MA | Serving police officers with academic preparation. Ph.D. at the national level. MA at regional level. |
| **Training** | Police professionals with academic training with BA or MA | Servicing police officers with little academic training |
| | **CONTENT** | |
| **Education** | Non-specialized:<br>Liberal arts foundation, e.g., Police and Society<br><br>Professional preparation, e.g., Criminal Investigation | Specialized:<br>Professional, e.g., Criminal Law<br><br>Vocational, e.g., CSI |
| **Training** | Specialized:<br>Professional, e.g., Criminal Law<br>Vocational, e.g., Criminalistic<br>Technical, e.g., defensive driving | Specialized:<br>Vocational: criminal investigation<br>Technical, e.g., firearms use |

| Comparative dimensions | U.S. | China |
|---|---|---|
| **DEGREE CONFERRED** | | |
| **Education** | BA, MA, Ph.D. | BA, MA, Ph.D. |
| **Training** | Certification, e.g., Minnesota Peace Officer Standards and Training (POST) Board | Certification, e.g., Zhejiang Police College |
| **SITES** | | |
| **Education** | Civilian state universities | Three national police universities:<br>People's Public Security University<br>People's Armed Police College<br>People's Criminal Investigation University |
| **Training** | State licensed police training facilities | MPS sponsored colleges at provincial and municipality level |
| **Instructional Methods** | | |
| **Education** | Lectures<br>Case study<br>Independent study<br>Individual internship<br>Clinical study | Para-military discipline<br>Lectures<br>Structured internship<br>Field exercise |
| **Training** | Para-military discipline<br>Classroom instruction<br>Demonstration<br>Supervision skill exercise | Para-military discipline<br>Classroom instruction<br>Demonstration<br>Supervision skill exercise |

**Source:** Reconstructed from Lee Yingcai, "Comparative Chinese vs. United States police education and training system" ("Zhongme jingcha jiaoyu peixu bijiao"), *PSUJ*, 96:107—111 (2002).

## Section 6—Police Studies in China

### Introduction

Until recently, no police studies discipline existed inside China. First proposed in the late 1980s,[59] the study of policing is conducted under the rubric of the "public order studies" discipline (POS). POS is a subfield of study and research under the "public security (police)" academic discipline.[60] It was originally called "zhi-an guanli xue" ("public order management studies"). In 1998 it was changed to POS to reflect its broad coverage and multidisciplinary approach. POS is one of the two foundational subjects making up the "public security (police)" discipline, the other being criminal investigation.

Currently, the MPS is responsible for the development of POS, while the PSU is responsible for teaching and research. POS is not offered in other mainstream universities, such as Beijing University or the Chinese University of Political Science and Law.

As an emerging discipline, POS generated heated debate as to its nature, identity, purposes, boundary, and methods, paradigm and theory, and, ultimately, its contribution and utility as a scholarly enterprise. Currently, there is no systematic investigation into and scientific evaluation of *jingcha xue* as a scholarly enterprise, domestically or internationally.[61] For example, we do not even know how well developed police studies is as an academic field[62] and the extent of its contribution to police reform in theory or practice.

## Structure of POS as an academic discipline

The maturing of POS as an academic discipline and scholarly enterprise can be gauged in the following areas:

(1) POS has a well defined and confined subject matter of research and teaching:

POS has clear and distinctive research subject matter—phenomena of public order, causation, and response.

In terms of phenomena, POS studies the historical origin, social conditions, current patterns, and future trends of social order.

In terms of causation, POS investigates the functional relationship and statistical correlation between social conditions and public order. It also investigates the relationship between personal characteristics and social order problems, such as crime.

In terms of response, POS explores how varieties of state apparatus and a constellation of social forces can be brought to bear on social order problems and issues. In contemporary China it is the study of Comprehensive Social Control on crime and disorder.

In essence, POS is a unique subject of research and study in focus and scope that is not being adequately addressed by any one of the existing academic disciplines.

(2) POS is built upon a strong theoretical foundation with a distinctive conceptual framework.

In terms of theoretical foundation, POS is built upon a number of established scholarly traditions and emerging schools of thought. In early years, Mao resorted to Marxist theory of state and society to explain criminality. More recently, Western criminological and social order control theories have taken hold.

In terms of concept, terminology, and nomenclature, POS has adopted and embraced the following concepts and terms: public order administration, public order administration principles, public order administration subject, public order administration object, public order administration measures, public order eyes and ears, and a great number of others. These terminologies are an integral part of POS and cannot be found with other associated disciplines, such as public administration and law.

(3) POS uses a multitude of research methods from other disciplines.

POS research is conducted with the social survey method, content analysis, the historical method, the comparative method, the experimental method, and the systematic method.

(4) POS has its own academic literature.

After twenty years of development, POS boasts two authoritative journals: *Journal of Chinese People's Public University*, published by the PSU and *Policing Studies*, published by the Chinese Police Studies Association. Journal of Chinese People's Public University is one of the nineteen most authoritative legal-political publications and one of the one hundred most authoritative social science journals in China. The Chinese Police Studies Association is a first-class scholarly association. It is working hard to launch an associated second-class Public Order Association.

(5) POS is a comprehensive and integrated academic system.

POS is a relatively integrated study field with the following subject areas: (1) principles of POS; (2) history of POS; (3) public order legal studies; (4) public order management studies, which includes public order regulation and management, household management, road traffic management, fire prevention management; immigration control, and foreign resident management; and (5) comparative public order.

(6) POS works closely and collaboratively with other established disciplines.

POS works closely with and is complemented by other more traditional and well-established disciplines, such as public administration law, criminal law, political science, sociology, and management.

(7) POS has a well-defined research agenda and study focus:[63, 64] The subject matter of research and study defines and separates one discipline from another. What constitutes the subject matter of research of POS is a question still being debated. The following six schools of thought currently exist on the subject: Management school; Public order school; Public order regularity school; Contradiction school; Social order prevention school; and Social order phenomenon, causation, and response school.

## Debates, problems, and issues

In order to promote the building and strengthening of POS as an academic discipline, the Chinese Public Security University organized a "National conference on new century public security studies academic discipline building" at PSU in 2007. The conference was well attended by leaders, staff, and faculty of PSU, as well as many regional police colleges, including Beijing Police College and other provincial police colleges from Shanghai, Tienjin, Zhongxing, and other provinces. Additional representatives attended from Beijing University, Wuhang University, Suzhou University. Yanzhou University, Zhongnan Commercial, Politics and Law University, and Xibei University.[65]

The conference participants exchanged views on a number of issues and problems related to building POS as an academic discipline, including study subjects, boundary, focus, methods, organization, and connections with other related and associated disciplines. Various discussions were held on POS's vision and mission, staff recruitment and training, and curriculum design and teaching methods.

One of the major debate issues was on the subject matter of study and research. POS has a well-defined and special subject of study, but there is yet no uniform agreement on the focus and scope of POS in China. Again, there are a number of schools of thought:

- POS studies phenomena, causation, and response.
- POS is the study of phenomenon, patterning,[66] and response of public order.
- POS theory should be built around public order, public order management, and public order issues.[67]
- POS seeks to ascertain and realize public order strategy in the new century and to develop and train public order human resources.
- The concept of public order prevention studies is the study of disruption of public order and harm, and related principles and practices of preventive measures.
- POS has three sets of different research focuses: (a) public order practice theory; (b) interaction between public order subject and object known as contradiction theory; and (c) public order maintenance and management theory.

In summary, POS should be concerned with "comprehensive control" of crime and disorder in six respects: strike, prevent, manage, educate, reform and build, with prevention and management being the major focus.

## Section 7—Evaluation of PRC Police Education: A Case Study

### Introduction

To date, there is no published account of assessment of PRC police education system and process. In 2003 *Public Security Education* published a scientific survey of police students from Chinese Criminal Investigation Police College, Jiansu Police Officer College, and Shandong Public Security Professional College with a "Questionnaire on the current status and analysis of criminal investigation technical education at public education higher education institutes" that asked the respondents their opinions on overall satisfaction with their police education in terms of relevancy and utility, curriculum design, course content, teaching methods, school facilities, faculty capacity, and teaching evaluation.[68]

The survey found that, while a majority of students were satisfied with the education received, many of them were not happy with what and how criminal investigation education was taught.[69]

### Findings

Table 5.1: Students' self-assessment of overall education quality

| **Capable of working at public security agencies — criminal investigation work** | Able ("neng") | Basically able ("jiben neng") | Not quite able ("bu tai neng") | Not able ("bu neng") |
|---|---|---|---|---|
| Responses | 104 | 72 | 59 | 25 |
| Percentage | 40 | 27.7 | 22.7 | 9.6 |

**Source:** Zhao Xiuping 40R

Table 5.2: Students' understanding of educational objectives

| **Are the professional educational objectives clear?** | Yes ("shi") | Basically so ("jiben shi") | Not very much ("bu taishi") | No ("bushi") |
|---|---|---|---|---|
| Responses | 107 | 102 | 45 | 6 |
| Percentage | 41.2 | 39.2 | 17.2 | 2.3 |

**Source:** Zhao Xiuping 41L

Table 5.3: Degree of student identification with professional education

| **If you had to do it again, would you pick the same professional subject?** | Would ("hui") | Basically would ("jiben hui") | Not very likely ("bu tai hui") | Would not ("bushui") |
|---|---|---|---|---|
| Responses | 156 | 51 | 42 | 11 |
| Percentage | 60 | 19.6 | 16.2 | 4.2 |

**Source:** Zhao Xiuping 41L

Table 5.4: Students' evaluations of basic curriculum design

| **Does the basic curriculum meet needs?** | Able to ("neng") | Basically able ("jiben neng") | Not quite able to ("bu tai neng") | Not able ("bu neng") |
|---|---|---|---|---|
| Responses | 11 | 126 | 109 | 14 |
| Percentage | 4.2 | 48.5 | 41.9 | 5.4 |

**Source:** Zhao Xiuping 41R

Table 5.5: Students' attitudes toward the status of electives

| **Are electives meeting needs?** | Able ("neng") | Basically able ("jiben neng") | Not quite able to ("bu tai neng") | Not able ("bu neng") |
|---|---|---|---|---|
| Responses | 39 | 78 | 65 | 80 |
| Percentage | 15 | 29.2 | 25 | 30.8 |

**Source:** Zhao Xiuping 41R

Table 5.6: Students' attitudes toward demand of practical education

| **Should practical education be strengthened?** | Necessary ("xu yao") | Basically necessary ("jiben xuyao") | Not quite necessary ("bu tai xuyao") | Not necessary ("bu xuyao") |
|---|---|---|---|---|
| Responses | 234 | 26 | 0 | 0 |
| Percentage | 90 | 10 | 0 | 0 |

**Source:** Zhao Xiuping 42L

Table 5.7: Students' attitude toward professional subjects teaching methods

| **Are you satisfied with how professional studies are being taught?** | Yes ("shi") | Basically so ("jiben shi") | Not very much ("bu taishi") | No ("bushi") |
|---|---|---|---|---|
| Responses | 39 | 114 | 86 | 21 |
| Percentage | 15 | 43.8 | 33.1 | 8.1 |

**Source:** Zhao Xiuping 42L

Table 5.8: Students' attitudes toward faculty teaching performance of professional subject matter

| **Is faculty teaching performance of professional subject matter high?** | Yes ("shi") | Basically so ("jiben shi") | Not very much ("bu taishi") | No ("bushi") |
|---|---|---|---|---|
| Responses | 105 | 117 | 38 | 0 |
| Percentage | 40.4 | 45 | 14.6 | 8.1 |

**Source:** Zhao Xiuping 43L

Table 5.9: Students' assessment of practical experience of faculty professional subject matter

| **Should practical experience of faculty with professional subject matter be strengthened?** | Yes ("shi") | Basically so ("jiben shi") | Not very much ("bu taishi") | No ("bushi") |
|---|---|---|---|---|
| Responses | 172 | 55 | 29 | 4 |
| Percentage | 66.2 | 21.2 | 11.1 | 1.5 |

**Source:** Zhao Xiuping 43L

Table 5.10: Students' assessment of experimental education conditions )

| **Are the facilities and equipment for experiment of this professional study sufficient in meeting teaching needs?** | Able ("neng") | Basically able ("jiben neng") | Not quite able ("bu tai neng") | Not able ("bu neng") |
|---|---|---|---|---|
| Responses | 33 | 56 | 91 | 80 |
| Percentage | 12.7 | 21.5 | 35 | 30.8 |

**Source:** Zhao Xiuping 43R

Table 5.11: Students' assessment of examination

| **Are the facilities and equipment for experiment of this professional study sufficient in meeting teaching needs?** | Reasonable ("heli") | Basically reasonable ("jiben heli") | Not very reasonable ("bu tai heli") | Not reasonable ("bu heli") |
|---|---|---|---|---|
| Responses | 15 | 56 | 109 | 57 |
| Percentage | 5.8 | 30.4 | 41.9 | 21.9 |

Source: Zhao Xiuping 43R[70]

## Discussion

Overall, a majority of the student respondents felt that the education they received adequately prepared them for criminal investigative work ("able" 40%, "basically able" 27.7%). A sizable minority (32.3%), however, disagreed (Table 5.1). The satisfaction with their criminal investigation education is still higher. Of the student responses, 79.6% said they "would ... pick the same professional subject" (Table 5.3). However, when further examined, the students had mixed feelings about the curriculum design. However, only 52.7% thought that the basic curriculum was meeting the needs (Table 5.4). In fact, most felt that that the electives were not meeting their needs (Table 5.5: 55.8%).

The students reserved their harshest criticism for the relevancy and usefulness of their education. Without exception, the students were of the opinion that practical criminal justice education should be strengthened (Table 5.6: 100%), starting with strengthening the connection between school and frontline public security agencies.

Finally, while the students were basically happy with the competence (Table 5.9: 87.4%) and performance (Table 5.8: 85.4%) of the faculty, they were less satisfied with the teaching methods (Table 5.7: 41.2% dissatisfied) and campus facilities (Table 5.11: 63.5% dissatisfied).

## Section 8—Police Education Problems and Issues

*Crisis of identity*. Police education in China, especially at the local levels (provincial and municipal), suffers from an identity crisis. With lack of guaranteed job placement, police colleges are forced to lower their admission standards to attract qualified candidates. With pressure to make police education more relevant to the reform, police colleges are returning to more basic vocational education. Both of these strategies to stay affordable serve to reduce public security colleges' distinctiveness as places of higher education.

*Lack of placement.* Police education in China prepares students for police work. For example, if students graduated from People's Public Security University, they are guaranteed a job as a police officer. This is not the case with local (provincial and municipal) police colleges. For example, in certain provinces there were thirty-seven police colleges but only thirty-one police vacancies. Those who failed to find placement would be unemployed.[71] The placement situation is exacerbated by the fact that the police profession is being opened to people from all walks of life, consistent with market principles to attract the best and most suitable staff. Repeatedly, students from other universities have been hired as police officers. There is currently no official policy to hire police college graduates over those from non-police colleges. The lowering of admission standards further makes the police college graduates less competitive.

There are currently two strategies to deal with recruitment issues. Under the theory of education industrialization, the state has to increase in educational capacity of the nation through increased investment. The increase in police education investment in building larger schools and faculties will serve to attract more enrollments. The other strategy is to expand recruitment to attract non-police bound students, or said another way, "recruiting students is not the same as recruiting police."

Both strategies have fundamental flaws. The first is a waste of resources. Blind investment in police education does not solve the fundamental issue of how to create sufficient police employment for the ever-expanding number of police college graduates in the long term. In the short term, there might not be enough qualified staff to educate the new glut of police students. More graduates with lesser quality spell trouble for police education.

The second strategy raises fundamental issues of what police college and education are all about. If police education is not only for police-bound students, there is a real question as to why paramilitary discipline and police curriculum are necessary. More practically, why teach police tactical skills—marital arts, shooting, driving—when students do not intend to become police? In the end, there is a real question as to whether police colleges should change their major focus to non-police teaching to accommodate an increase in enrollment of non-policing students.

*Liberalization of police curriculum.* There is also a vibrant debate on the role and function of police colleges. Is it only to prepare students to be police officers? Or is it preparing the students for life. The tendency is to reduce specialization and make the curriculum more fundamental.

## Section 9—Conclusion

As indicated, there are very few studies of any kind in Western literature on PRC police education and scholarship. This study investigates the PRC police education system, particularly its educational philosophy and practice, scholarship nature, and methods as a means to understand how PRC police educators hope to meet the challenges posed by the fast-transforming Chinese economic, political, and social order. With respect to PRC police education, making the old to fit the new is the foremost challenge.[72]

(1) Traditionally, police higher education catered to young and uninitiated students, not mature and professional ones. The current educational system fails to meet the needs of field officers who are more interested in acquiring operational skills than engaging in theoretical debates.

(2) Traditionally, police education has been instructor-centered and not student-oriented. This emphasis is not adequate in meeting the needs of students with diverse backgrounds, different interests, and individual needs.

(3) Traditionally, police education has been conducted in fixed locations with standardized course materials and structured program delivery. This formula does not address the individual education needs of many adult students who seek non-traditional, off-campus, and special education options.

(4) Traditionally, police school teaching style has been characterized by "preaching, imparting, and analyzing" activities. This style of instruction presupposes a finite set of knowledge, one way of learning, and one best way to solve problems. It does not fit well with information explosion, global communication, and interpenetration of knowledge dominants.

(5) Traditional police education is hampered by a set of uniform academic yardsticks. It fails to take into account individual intellectual capacity and personal developmental needs.

(6) Traditionally, police education goal, organization, content, and method are considered uniform in nature, which is inadequate in addressing changing economic and social conditions of the society.

(7) Traditionally, the police education system has been a closed system. A closed system is ill-equipped to deal with open-market conditions and changing social context.

(8) Traditionally, the police education system is driven by centralized policies, top-down guidelines, and absolute commands. It does not reflect local conditions and special concerns. It is not suited to mutual communication and joint problem solving.

The study makes clear that education and scholarship development in China lag far behind the pace of reform. Reformers are struggling to keep up. There are many thorny challenges but few effective solutions. Appeals to political ideology have lost much of their luster in the market economy and a materialistic world.[73] Communist political ideology and ways of doing things (e.g., Lei Feng spirit and self-sacrifice) have little relevancy and still less resonance with a learning community, most of whom were born after Mao and brought up during Deng's reform period. The mantra of communism, much like the recitation of Confucianism, is poisonous to a critical mind and suffocating to creative spirits. Campaign-style mobilization does little good in changing people's conduct and making inroads in institutional behavior, still less in making a difference to organizational culture and individual attitudes in universities. Reform by slogan is destined to fail; it focuses too much on form over substance, preferring symbolism to realism, and propaganda over discourse. Ultimately, police education reform efforts are severely limited and compromised by what is going on in the society.[74]

The way forward is to take Mao and Deng at their word. Mao preached about the need to make knowledge "scientific" and "relevant," that is, grounded in reality and tested in practice. Deng called for discarding the old to make room for the new—having an open mind. Both approved of action-oriented research, a learning-as-one-goes strategy, or "crossing the river by felling the stone," one stone at a time.

# CHAPTER SIX

# Police Culture

## Section 1—Introduction

There are repeated claims that the police (*gongan*) in the People's Republic of China (PRC) abuse their legal powers.[1] At the "First National Procuracy meeting on rights violation and dereliction of duty" (1990),[2] it was reported that from 1979 to 1989 there were 75,117 cases of "rights violation" and "dereliction of duty" involving the police. In the "Second National procuracy meeting on rights violation and dereliction of duty"[3] (1991), it was reported that only 16,044 of the 45,033 official abuse cases for the year were being investigated. The meeting called attention to the adverse effects of police abuse of power on social stability and economic development. Government leaders at all levels were instructed to strengthen supervision in five kinds of cases: inquisition by torture; illegal imprisonment; fraudulent activities for personal gain; abusive use of official power; and important cases involving significant liability.

This concern has prompted the Guangdong province public security department, and other government bodies, to issue remedial regulations, with such descriptive titles as "Guanyu yanjin dama qunzhong, xingxun bigong de guidingg" ("Regulations on strictly forbidding the police from beating and yelling at the people, and conducting coerced confession"). Generally, these regulations prohibit the police from violating people's rights in performing their duty, especially in obtaining coerced confessions.

In China, police abuses have been attributed to a lack of institutional supervision and a failure of legal control. Many PRC police officers consider legal procedures a waste of time and an obstacle standing in the way of justice. In most cases, the police seek substantive justice over procedural justice.

Since the 1980s, there have been repeated calls for better supervision and more effective control of police powers.[4] Yang Yichen, Chief Procuratorate, observed,

> In the last five years [1979–1988], we have spent relatively more time and effort in fighting crimes ... but legal supervision is not sufficient. The main reasons are: (1) There is no sufficient appreciation about the importance and meaning of legal supervision. (2) Our leaders cannot keep pace with the development of the time. They are not able to respond to new situations and provide for appropriate solutions to problems. (3) Legal procedures and methods are

> not adequate. The effect of legal supervision is not strong. (4) There are not enough party cadres. Their quality is not high. (5) There is a lack of equipment and resources.

Three decades later (2005), police abuse of power is still rampant, requiring more vigilant supervision of the People's Procuracy. In 2004, Supreme People's Procurator Jia Chunwang reported in "Supreme People's Procuracy Work Report" (March 10, 2004)[5] that the nation's procurators have investigated 39,562 cases (involving 43,490 persons) of official occupational crime, from corruption (18,513), to dereliction of duty (7,120), to coerced confession (1,408). They also have rejected police case initiation in 2,552 cases and initiated 22,575 cases declined by the police. They have refused arrest applications in 58,872 cases and declined prosecution in 27,957 cases. They have issued 7,055 formal notices of criminal investigation and prosecution irregularities. Finally, the Supreme People's Procurator has established a zero tolerance policy in illegally prolonged detention cases and has sent notice of ratification on 25,181 such cases.

Police abuse of power is also a chronic problem in the West. The *Report on Lawlessness in Law Enforcement* (Wickersham Report [1931]), found the police frequently to be in "flagrant violation of the law."[6] In the United States, many national commissions and still more police studies[7] suggest that police abuses escape effective administrative or legal control for a variety of reasons. The President's Commission on Law Enforcement and Administration of Justice[8] observed that police violence and abuse of rights were institutionalized and attributable to larger historical, social, and cultural forces, such as economic disparity, racial discrimination, and a culture of violence both within police organizations and in society in general.

In the 1970s, the New York City Knapp Commission (1969–1972)[9] uncovered widespread, open, and systematic corruption as a way of life inside the New York Police Department (NYPD). In spite of repeated and emphatic promises to reform, however, police corruption remains, due to a culture of corruption and the "blue code of silence." Robert J. McCormack noted that high profile police brutality cases, like the Rodney King case, further show that police abuse of power cannot be effectively addressed without changing organizational culture and police attitudes.[10]

In the 1960s the Supreme Court invoked the Constitution (e.g., *Miranda* v. *Arizona*, 384 U.S. 436, 1966, *Mapp* v. *Ohio*, 367 U.S. 643, 1961) to "police the police." This effort has had limited success.[11] Constitutionalization of police procedure has met with stiff resistance and crafty avoidance from the police[12] (e.g., the exclusionary rule did not stop the police from obeying the constitutional rules in the breach).[13]

Studies have since found that personality, the police subculture, and organizational structure have more to do with police misconduct than do formal rules and regulations. For example, while William A. Westley observed that stressful working conditions and hostile public relations combine to produce violent police disposition and behavior,[14] Jerome H. Skolnick found that elements of the working environment of police officers—danger, authority, and efficiency—combine to generate distinctive cognitive and behavioral responses in police, leading to a "working personality" that often includes authoritarianism, suspicion, hostility, insecurity, conservatism, and cynicism.[15] Rookies are quickly socialized into the police culture while on the job, effectively replacing official rules with informal customs.[16]

This chapter identifies two cultural reasons—the lack of an entrenched legal culture in the rule of law and the absence of an engrained constitutional spirit in limited government—to explain PRC police abuse of power.

The chapter is organized into five sections. After the introduction (Section 1), Section 2 identifies the problem under discussion–the seriousness and prevalence of abuse of power by PRC police—by offering a case study of a Hong Kong merchant illegally detained in the PRC in 1999. Sections 3 and 4 discuss two distinctive cultural-jurisprudential reasons, "Lack of the Rule of Law" and "Lack of Constitutionalism," to account for the observed abuse of power by police in China. Section 5 concludes by addressing the need for a change in police culture through education, supervision, and discipline, and not only through legal punishment or constitutional checks and balances as suggested by some Western scholars.

## Section 2—Police Abuse of Power in China: A Case Study

On Sunday, October 24, 1999, Lok Yuk-Sing, 63, returned home to Hong Kong after 16 months (487 days) of detention by PRC police, without trial, in Inner Mongolia, China. Allegedly, Lok was detained over the Lai Sun Group's (Lok's ex-employer) $4 million commercial debt dispute with China. Lok was released after his family paid a $50,000 "bail" to local public security officials. Both the PRC and Hong Kong governments insisted that the mainland authority acted in accordance with PRC law, to which Lok's family has taken exception.

Was Lok arrested and detained legally in China? If not, how prevalent is the problem of illegal arrest and detention in China? What are the causes of such police abuse of power? What steps have been and could be taken to control this and other police abuses? This section will investigate these questions in turn.

The question of whether Lok was arrested and detained legally needs to be analyzed in two ways, substantively and procedurally.

Substantively, it is not altogether clear whether the Inner Mongolia police had the legal right to charge the Lai Sun Group, and by extension its responsible agent in China, with a criminal offense for an alleged commercial fraud. More pointedly, there is no evidence of Lok's personal involvement, personally or as an agent, directly or indirectly, in the alleged fraud. In this regard, Chinese political and police leaders have long frowned upon invoking the criminal process and using local police to secure the return of commercial loans.

Procedurally, it is apparent that the PRC Inner Mongolia police acted beyond the PRC Criminal Procedure Law (1996) (CPL) in subjecting Lok to lengthy investigative detention without prior approval or subsequent charge or trial. According to Lok (who who provided information to this author), he was not tried and the People's Procuratorate refused to approve of Lok's arrest three times. Thus, Lok was not properly detained, arrested, or otherwise subjected to "compulsory measures."

Under the CPL Chapter VI and People's Police Act (1995) (Article 12), the PRC police have the legal authority to employ appropriate compulsory measures—summoning for investigation, detention, arrest, guarantor pending trial, or residential surveillance—against a criminal suspect for investigation purposes. Strict legal procedures, however, must be followed, and in this case it appears they were not.

First, the Inner Mongolia police arrested Lok in Dongguan without a warrant; at least there was not one to Lok's knowledge. This action is a blatant violation of CPL Articles 64 and 66, which require police to gain permission and to obtain a warrant before an arrest. Cross-province arrest further requires the affirmative approval of senior level police administrators of both provinces. There was no record of such approvals being sought and granted.

Second, CPL Articles 64 and 71 require the Inner Mongolia public security to inform a suspect's family of the reason and place of detention within twenty-four hours of arrest. This was not done.

Third, CPL Article 2 states that "the aim of the Criminal Procedure Law ... is: to ensure accurate and timely ascertainment of facts about crime ... protection of innocent against being investigated for criminal responsibility. ..." Thus, CPL requires the Inner Mongolia public security to interrogate Lok within twenty-four hours after his detention (Article 64) or arrest (Article 72), and to release him if no incriminating evidence is found or criminal charge is forthcoming. If there is a further need for investigation, other less imposing and restrictive compulsory measures are to be used, such as enlisting a guarantor pending trial or imposing residential surveillance. Lok was finally placed under residential surveillance, albeit at a much later date and long beyond the time limit provided for by law.

Fourth, CPL Article 124 provides that holding a criminal suspect in custody during investigation after an arrest should not in any event exceed two months. The People's Procuratorate at the next higher level can grant another month of extension to facilitate difficult and complex investigation. In this case, Lok was detained for a total of sixteen months. This far exceeded the maximum time limit for investigative detention allowed by law.

Finally, CPL Article 75 provides that "if the compulsory measures adopted by ... a public security organ exceed the time limited prescribed by the law, the suspect. ... shall have the right to demand cancellation of the compulsory measures ..." Lok had every right to challenge the legality of his release granted under guarantor (CPL Article 56) pending trial. He did but to no avail.

Lok's case is not an isolated incident. He is not the first Hong Kong businessperson to be detained in China without trial for a long duration of time over contractual disputes and commercial debts. According to the HKSAR, the government was aware of fifty-one such cases of illegal detention in 1999. According to the Hong Kong Human Rights Watch, over eighty cases were reported.[17]

More generally, illegal detention including overextended detention is not new, nor is it a small problem in China. For example, in 1986 the Chinese government acknowledged that of the thousands of "detention for investigation" cases nationwide, only 36.3% met all legal requirements, with some provinces falling below 10%. The illegal detention problem was more prominent in the southern part of China than in the north; for example, official self-reported data showed that in 1990, 5.7% of all arrests in Beijing were illegal/overextended detention, while 23.8% of arrests in Guangdong were illegal. Illegal arrest and detention have variously been used as retribution, as summary punishment, in aid of investigation, and as settlement of commercial disputes.[18]

Cases studied show that illegally detained persons were often forced to share rooms with, and were subjected to abuses of, dangerous criminals, and that the former were left with little food to eat and unsanitary living conditions.[19]

The problem of using police powers in China to settle contractual disputes stemmed in part from the following reasons:

First, from the perspective of the Chinese contracting party, some of the commercial contracts were tainted. They were secured by corruption or based on grossly unfair bargains. This circumstance provided the Chinese party a righteous reason to invoke aid from the police.[20]

Second, the PRC commercial dispute resolution system, from arbitration to litigation, is not adequate to satisfy the needs and expectations of the people. It is commonly viewed as insufficient to protect the legitimate interests and rights of the litigants[21] because of its expense, inefficiency, or unfairness.[22]

Third, the inadequacy of the legal system is aggravated when it comes to cross province/region commercial disputes. The legal obstacles caused by having to operate across provincial boundaries have led to concerns that out-of-state party litigants might be able to avoid liabilities by skipping town. As a prudent measure, the police are often called upon to detain the out-of-state party until the commercial dispute is resolved. Because such detention is frequently illegal, the police subvert the criminal law process in aid of the civil court proceeding.[23]

Fourth, the PRC police are subject to the dual control MPS (professionally) and the local Party and government (politically).[24] In terms of professional development and strategic direction, the central command and control system takes hold. On operational issues, however, the local political and government authorities have the dominant influence. When well-connected local businesspeople or state enterprises get into trouble, they will turn to the police for help.

The PRC political leadership, legal authority, and police administrators are not unaware of the problem. For example, the PRC People's Procuratorate has been diligent in using its correction or legal violations powers to correct some of the more blatant and persistent illegal arrests/overextended detention cases. In 1990 of all the "correction for legal violation" actions taken against the police for abuse of power, 89% were for illegal arrest and detention, and in 1991 it was 85.6%. Prosecution of illegal arrest, detention, and search cases increased from 21.2% of all democratic rights violation cases in 1979 to 67.9% in 1985.

The MPS People's Procuratorate and People's Court have issued repeated notices and stern warnings against the misuse of police powers, especially for the settlement of commercial disputes. In 1996, the PRC Criminal Procedure Law was revised to abolish the "sheltering for examination" powers. In spite of these efforts, however, police abuse of powers has not been abated to the extent that China-bound traders and businesspeople can feel secure.[25]

Finally, as reported by Xinhua in "Illegal detention cases cleared from China's judicial system" (January 5, 2004): "In 2003, the Supreme People's Court, the Ministry of Public Security and the Supreme People's Procuratorate, jointly issued a notice to subordinate bodies for the review, resolution and prevention of illegally prolonged custody cases in every investigation and trial. By the end of last year, China's courts had reviewed and solved 4,100 unlawfully prolonged detention cases, releasing 7,658 detainees."

## Section 3—Lack of the Rule of Law

### Legal Culture Defined

Legal culture has been defined by Lawrence Friedman as "those parts of the general culture—customs, opinions, ways of doing and thinking—that bend social forces toward or away from the law and in particular ways."[26] The rule of law, as a unique kind of legal culture, is mainly a Western concept and practice.[27] The concept has come to stand for responsible and accountable governance. It incorporates and encompasses a number of fundamental principles: (1) No one is above and beyond the law.[28] (2) It is a government of law, not man.[29] (3) It is an ethical principle standing for liberty, fairness, and equality.[30] In its essence, the rule of law is not just a jurisprudential, political, or ethical *principle*. It is all these and more. It is the *spirit* of a people and the *way of life* of the community.

### Some empirical evidence of the lack of the rule of law

There is no readily available index of the rule-of-law culture in China. However, we can look at four sets of PRC official data to inform ourselves of people's general attitudes toward law.

First, we can look at how party cadres were treated when they offended the state law or violated Party discipline. The rule of law requires that *all* party cadres are to be treated equally before the law.

Second, we can look at how much confidence the general public has in the legal system. A sound legal system should inspire confidence and promote reliance. People should feel comfortable in airing their complaints about the legal system.

Third, we can look at how responsive the legal system is in redressing people's complaints. An accountable legal system should provide a meaningful way for the public to correct administrative decisions and legal errors.

Fourth, we can look at how citizen complainants fare with Administrative Litigation Law in courts. An effective legal system should protect the rights of the people.

**How cadres are being disciplined**

In the PRC one way to hold government officials accountable is by filing a complaint with the Party's supervisory organs. The *Law Year Book of China* reports on citizens' complaint statistics. The starting hypothesis is that if the rule-of-law culture prevails, supervisory activities and disciplinary actions over official misconduct will be based on merits and not on the relative status of the officials involved.

The statistics show a different picture. Higher officials have been treated much more leniently than lower officials. In 1990, about one in every two (47.6%) complaints by citizens on police misconduct was actually processed. Of those, about a quarter (23.1%) of the cases made it to the *lian* stage (initiating an investigative file). Of significance is the fact that punishment was recommended in over 91% of the *lian* cases. Thus, for all intents and purposes, *lian* means that a case is very well substantiated.

The 1990 statistics on complaint processing (Table 1) show that the *lian* rate deteriorates as the cadre status escalates. Thus, while in general an average of 23.1% of the processed complaints ended up with *lian*, only one in twenty (5%) complaints processed at the *Ting/Ju* (Bureau) level did; in fact, the *lian* rate deteriorates at each step up the cadre status levels. The punishment rate for convicted officials also shows a similar pattern. Thus, whereas over 91% of *lian* cases overall received some form of recommended punishment, in cases involving the *Ju* (bureau), *Chu* (office), or *Ke* (branch) officials, punishments were recommended in 74.4%, 64%, and 76% of the *lian* cases, respectively. More significantly, whereas overall about 15% of officials were recommended for punishment below the *Ke* level, with the *Ju* level it was only 1.7%.

The disparate treatment of complaints against officials is a good indication of unequal treatment of the law.

Table 1: 1990 Complaint cases handled by supervision organs nationwide

| Cadre Status (*Ganbu Ji*) | Total Complaints | Complaints Processed | Complaints Recorded (*lian*) | Punishment* |
|---|---|---|---|---|
| *Ting/Ju* | 7,529 | 3,115 (41.4%)** | 176 (5.6%) | 131 (74.4%) (1.7%)*** |
| *Xian/Chu* | 56,909 | 22,054 (38.7%) | 2,784 (10.4%) | 1,781 (64%) (3.1%) |
| *Xiang/Ke* | 176,696 | 72,845 (41.2%) | 13,947 (19.1%) | 10,588 (76%) (6%) |
| *Others* | 226,575 | 124,569 (55%) | 34,518 (27.7%) | 34,485 (99.9%) (15.2%) |
| *Total* | 467,709 | 222,583 (47.6%) | 51,425 (23.1%) | 46,985 (91.4%) (10%) |

**Source:** abstracted from *Law Year Book of China 1991* (Beijing: Law Year Book of China Publication), 957.

**Note:** * Punishment includes recommendation for disciplinary actions.
** Stage wise attrition rate = present stage over last stage.
*** Cumulative punishment rate = punishment over total complaints

## How much confidence the public has in the law

The people in China have little confidence in the rule of law.[31] This is evidenced by their reluctance to approach judicial agencies—procuratorate and court—to redress their grievances against officials. As one person complained in a *Times* China blog:

> There are a few people winning justice through petitioning in China. It is those who work with right government officials in a right place at a right time. Ironically, some of them still need to give of their briberies to get the attention of the government officials and have wrongdoing punished. The government may try to expose a couple of corrupt officials and invest jobs of wrongdoing, but there are thousands of them and jobs of wrongdoing carrying on under their eyes, and they choose to keep quiet with their eyes closed. Don't even think about do the right things and right things will happen in China in most time. It has already been left for movie directors to entertain their audience.[32]

The data from the Supreme People's Procuracy showed that between 1986 and 1991, people's visits (*xinfang* or letter visit, *shangfang* or personal visit) with the nation's procuratorate organs and courts dropped sharply (Table 2), from 1,008,483 in 1986 to 763,365 in 1991, a drop of 24.3%. In the case of the courts, the decrease was still more pronounced, dropping from 9,071,038 in 1986 to 4,321,957 in 1991, a decline of 52.3% (Table 3).

In 2005, Xiao Yang observed in the Report of the People's Supreme Court to the Tenth National People's Congress, "Local courts across the country received 3,995,244 letters, visits and calls of complaints in 2005, down 5.33 percent year-on-year."[33]

Table 2: 1986–1991 Letters or personal visits with people's procuratorial organs nationwide

| Visits | 1986 | 1987 | 1988 | 1989 | 1990 | 1991 | 1986 - 1991 |
|---|---|---|---|---|---|---|---|
| Letter | 773,336 | 725,044 (- 6.2%) | 701,728 (- 3.2%) | 1,041,126 (48.4%) | 738,436 (-29%) | 596,108 (- 19.3%) | -177,228 (-22.9%) |
| Person | 235,147 | 224,430 (- 4.6%) | 232,297 (3.5%) | 220,716 (- 5%) | 171,984 ( -22.1%) | 167,257 (- 2.7%) | -67,890 (-28.9%) |
| Total | 1,008,483 | 949,474 | 934,025 | 1,261,842 | 910,420 | 763,365 | 245,118 |

Table 3: 1986–1991 Letters or personal visits with people's courts nationwide

| Visits | 1986 | 1987 | 1988 | 1989 | 1990 | 1991 |
|---|---|---|---|---|---|---|
| Letter | 4,734,847 | 4,520,822 | 3,570,685 | 2,287,737 | 2,230,383 | 2,005,340 |
| Person | 4,336,191 | 4,546,280 | 4,175,204 | 2,681,484 | 3,046,858 | 3,115,277 |
| Total | 9,071,038 | 9,067,102 | 7,745,889 | 4,969,221 * | 5,277,241 | 4,321,957 |

**Source:** Abstracted from *Law Year Book of China (1987 to 1992)* (Beijing: Law Year Book of China Publication), (1987:884); (1988:817); (1989:1083); (1990:995); (1991:937); (1992:861).
**Note:** * This does not include non-complaint (*feisu*) visits, a new distinction drawn in reporting.

From the visitation data, it appears that increasingly the people are disillusioned about their legal institutions. They have little confidence in the legal system to solve their problems and address their concerns, especially against government abuses. In brief, the public has very little faith in the rule of law and associated legal processes.

In 2005, the right of the people to petition the government was further curtailed by the government's systematic effort to restrict resolution of petitions at the local levels with the promulgation of revised "Regulations of Petitions" which makes local officials responsible for dealing with people's grievances.

"For example, the xinfang responsibility system adopted in February 2006 by the Ningnan county government in Sichuan province provides that local authorities receive a warning if 10 or more petitioners from their jurisdiction collectively petition provincial or higher authorities, if 20 or more petitioners collectively petition prefectural authorities, or if 30 or more petitioners do so at the county level. If petitioners present three or more collective petitions within a year to provincial or national officials, local officials lose eligibility for promotion or other awards."[34]

The new "Regulations of Petitions"(*Xinfang taoli*) (2005) have the unintended effect of denying access to petitioners altogether. In frustration the people turn to mass actions and violent confrontations. For example, in the "Weng'an" Incident of June 28, 2008, the local populace attacked and burned down a police station and a county government office building in Guizhou as a result of dissatisfaction with police investigation into the death of a local student. In the "Fugu Incident" of July 3, 2008, police and villagers clashed over the failure of the police to inform the next of kin of the deceased upon the discovery of the dead body. Finally, in the "Huizhou Incident of July 16, 2008, 100 people attacked police officers, overturned a police wagon and raided a police station over the controversial death of a motorcycle driver in Huzhou, Guangdong.

## How the procuratorates react to citizens' requests for legal review

The people's disillusionment with the legal system is not groundless. Citizens' complaint processing rates and case attrition statistics published by the *Zhongguo Jiancha Nianjian* for 1990 to 1991 show that the chances of having a prior police action reversed were very slim. The overall success rate for having an original adverse police/procuratorate decision amended in 1990 and 1991 was less than 1% (Table 4). In challenges to detention and arrest decisions, the percentage drops still lower. In 1990, 3 out of 3,950 detention decisions were amended, which is a 0.07% rate. In 1991, the amendment rate, though better, was not encouraging: 9 out of 2,660 cases were amended, for a 0.34% rate. The refusal to accept arrest decisions follows the same pattern. In 1990, only 3 out of 9,932 complaints were amended. In 1991 it was 24 out of 8,211 cases.

Table 4: 1990--1991: Complaints handled by the people's procuratorial organs nationwide: Stage-wise attrition rate and cumulative success rate

| Nature of cases | Year | Cases accepted | Cases filed | Cases disposed | Decisions amended | Success rate |
|---|---|---|---|---|---|---|
| Total | 1990 | 73,355 | 9,246 (13%) | 4,144 (45%) | 809 (20%) | 1% |
| | 1991 | 130,827 | 12,307 (9%) | 4,593 (37%) | 1,124 (24%) | .86% |
| Refuse to accept detention (*juliu*) | 1990 | 3,950 | 168 (4%) | 31 (18%) | 3 (10%) | .07% |
| | 1991 | 2,660 | 127 (.5%) | 33 (26%) | 9 (27%) | .34% |
| Refuse to accept arrest (*dibu*)* | 1990 | 9,932 | 168 (2%) | 31 (18%) | 3 (10%) | .03% |
| | 1991 | 8,211 | 1,046 (13%) | 157 (15%) | 24 (15%) | .29% |

***Source***: Extracted from *Zhongguo Jiancha Nianjian (1991) (1992)* (Procuratorial Yearbook of China 1992, 1993) (Zhonggou Jiancha Chubenshe, 1993, 1994), 347 (191), 367 (1992).

## How citizens fare with administrative litigation[35]

The ultimate test for a rule-of-law regime is how legal actions against the government are tested in court. In April 1989, the NPC promulgated the Administrative Litigation Law (ALL) or Administrative Procedure Law of the PRC.[36] According to Article 1, the purposes of the ALL were "safeguarding correct and timely trial of administrative cases, protecting the lawful rights and interests of citizens, legal persons and other organizations, and ensuring and supervising the exercise of administrative power by administrative organs according to law." Article 11 of the ALL allowed citizens aggrieved by the government to file a number of kinds of administrative claims, such as refusing to accept certain administrative penalties, refusing to accept compulsory administrative measures affecting personal freedom or property rights, and deeming that an administrative organ has demanded the performance of duties in violation of law, among several others.

Minxin Pei investigated the implementation of the ALL and found that while the ALL has been well received by aggrieved citizens (administrative cases accepted for litigation in the courts jumped from 632 in 1986 to 5,240 in 1987; to 35,083 in 1994; and to 52,596 in 1995),[37] the disposition of the complaints by the courts raises substantial questions about the efficacy of the courts in adequately addressing complainants' grievances.

According to Table 5, below, the chances of winning RAA cases by citizens remained low, averaging 17% during the period 1988–1995. UAA rates did show declining support of administrative agencies. Government won 49% in 1988, but only 17% in 1995, or from a 5 to 1 winning ratio against citizens in 1988 to nearly a 1 to 1 ratio in 1995. However, the winning ratio by citizens is a pyrrhic victory, because most of the government "losses" resulted from SWP or "suits withdrawn by plaintiffs," or as some might suspect, informal negotiated settlement. Table 5 shows that in 1988 there was a 27% SWP rate; by 1995, it rose to 51%.

Regarding the police, citizens' administrative complaints against them were losing ground, more so than any other kinds of administrative claims (Table 6). Thus, the courts were more inclined to rule against citizens (UAA) and in support of the police (1992—31% vs. 1995—20%), while their actions against the police in favor of the citizens remained relatively unchanged through the years (RAA) (1992—19% vs. 1995—16%). Most tellingly the inclination of the citizens to SWP was high and getting higher each year (1992—39% vs. 1995—50%), demonstrating clearly that citizens placed little faith in the court system to validate their complaints.

Table 5: Disposition of tried cases (%)

| Year | RAA | UAA | SWP | CAA | Others |
|---|---|---|---|---|---|
| **1988** | 11 | 49 | 27 | 5 | 8 |
| **1989** | 14 | 42 | 31 | 6 | 7 |
| **1990** | 17 | 36 | 36 | 3 | 8 |
| **1991** | 19 | 32 | 37 | 2 | 10 |
| **1992** | 21 | 28 | 38 | 2 | 11 |
| **1993** | 19 | 23 | 41 | 2 | 15 |
| **1994** | 19 | 21 | 44 | 1 | 15 |
| **1995** | 15 | 17 | 51 | 1 | 16 |

**Source:** Extracted from Table 4: "Disposition of Tried Cases," (%) in Minxin Pei, "Citizens v. Mandarins: Administrative Litigation in China," *The China Quarterly*, No. 152: 832–862 (1997), 842.

**Notes:** RAA: Revoking administrative actions (in China); UAA: Upholding administrative actions; SWP: Suits withdrawn by plaintiffs; CAA: Administrative actions revised by the court.

Table 6: Dispositions of major categories of ALCs (%)

| Year | UAA | RAA | SWP | CAA | Others |
|---|---|---|---|---|---|
| | | 1992 | | | |
| Law enforcement | 31 | 19 | 37 | 3 | 10 |
| ALL* | 28 | 21 | 38 | 2 | 11 |
| | | 1993 | | | |
| Law enforcement | 26 | 17 | 43 | 2 | 12 |
| ALL | 23 | 19 | 41 | 2 | 15 |
| | | 1994 | | | |
| Law enforcement | 20 | 16 | 47 | 2 | 15 |
| ALL | 21 | 19 | 44 | 1 | 15 |
| | | 1995 | | | |
| Law enforcement | 17 | 16 | 50 | 2 | 15 |
| ALL | 17 | 15 | 51 | 1 | 16 |

**Source:** Extracted from Table 4: "Dispositions of Major Categories of ALCs (%)" in Minxin Pei, "Citizens v. Mandarins: Administrative Litigation in China," *The China Quarterly*, No. 152: 832–862 (1997), 846

**Note:** * Includes law enforcement, land use, industrial, and commercial.

Some reasons for the lack of an entrenched legal culture in the rule of law:

China does not have an entrenched legal culture in the rule of law.[38] There is no well-developed intellectual history or firmly entrenched cultural heritage favoring the use of law to govern the state, rule the people, solve problems, or resolve disputes in China. Instead, good conduct and morals, obedience, and a strict social hierarchy formed the bedrock of Chinese tradition and society.

More pertinently, the spirit of the rule of law, as discussed above, never gained a strong foothold in China.[39] There are many reasons for such a conspicuous absence:

(1) *The Chinese society has few needs for law to maintain social order.* Societies exhibit different propensities for conflict, deviance, and disorder. Historically, China has been highly structured, tightly integrated, well settled, and very stable.[40] In sum, it is a very well-ordered society, needing few laws to maintain that order.

(2) *The Chinese people do not think legally.* Thinking legally is an endowed capacity, an acquired skill, and a developed habit. Thinking legally requires an ability to think conceptually, abstractly, universally, and theoretically. The Chinese think in more concrete, particularistic, holistic, and practical ways. Their thinking process is characterized by the acceptance of actuality rather than a striving for abstractions associated with the law.

More importantly, the Chinese are not emotionally drawn to solving problems rationally and systematically. Western thinkers seek a structured legal order imposed from without while the Chinese accept natural ordering emulating from within.[41] The Chinese socialization process effectively inculcates in them psychological characteristics to function in a society circumscribed by internalized moral norms of correct conduct as structured by proper relationships.[42]

(3) *The Chinese have no personal identification with the law.* There is no personal resonance—cognitive understanding, emotive appreciation, or moral identification—with the rule of law at the grassroots level. Philosophically, law and litigation are to be avoided at all costs. Conceptually, law means punishment.[43] Emotionally, law is associated with shame. Morally, law is equated with evil.[44] Consequently, the Chinese people do not rely upon the law as an effective means of social control or a preferred way to resolve disputes.[45]

(4) *The Chinese have had bad experience with the law.* China's first experience with law under the *Qin* dynasty (221 B.C.—206 B.C.) was a disastrous one. The First Emperor (*Shihuandi*) of China ruled the country ruthlessly with an iron fist by means of harsh and uncompromising legal rules. Since then, successive generations of Chinese people have experienced law as imposed from above and beyond their reach.[46]

In Imperial China, the law, in the form of the emperor's decrees, was never meant to be, and did not function as, a replacement for the universal moral code and entrenched tradition in policing the people, ordering society, and resolving disputes.[47]

In modern China, law under Communist rule is unreliable much of the time, inconsequential for most people, and inadequate to address many of the people's problems. In the early days of the PRC, Mao effectively used individual voluntarism and mass mobilization to move the country ahead. More pertinently, mass struggle and self-criticism, not legal norms and judicial processes, were used in ordering society.[48] Contradictions with the enemy were resolved by force. Contradictions within the people were settled through education, persuasion, and mediation.[49] The nation's legal institution was completely destroyed during the Cultural Revolution (1966-1976) and the Gang of Four era. Politics was in control and revolutionary fervor prevailed. In all, during Mao's reign (1949–1976), the people were expected to follow Party policy,[50] conform to collective will, and abide by individual discipline[51] in constructing a new socialist state.[52]

More recently, Deng's effort to promote the rule of law was repeatedly tested and found wanting. From 1984 to 1987, the Party and state sponsored a series of anti-crime campaigns at the behest of Deng. There was very little concern with legality in the zealous pursuit of social order.[53] In 1989 the Party put down the June 4 student uprising with military force. Political dissidents and counterrevolutionaries were routinely detained, arrested, and tried without due process of law. Minimal attention was paid to constitutional rights in seeking political stability. In the 1990s, police powers and law were exploited to serve individual, organizational, and local economic interests.

The Chinese, then and now, have experienced and understood law as a means of coercion in the hand of the governing authority. Law is to be avoided, not embraced.

(5) *China has no national ethos or political ideology upholding the rule of law*. Traditionally, Confucian teachings slighted the role of state and law and opted instead for the family and *li* as the final arbiters of individual behavior and social control.[54] More recently, Marxist ideology predicted the withering away of the state and the disappearance of law in the utopian communist state.[55] Mao endorsed a limited and much circumscribed role for the state. However, he was quick to reject the legal system as dysfunctional and the criminal justice process as bureaucratic.

Deng never questions the role of the state and the utilities of law. He wants above all else to make certain that laws exist, that they are followed, and that those who violate them are punished. However, under his stewardship, law was to be used as an instrumentality of the state to serve the country's political, social, and economic needs, that is, "rule by law" and not "rule of law."

(6) *China has no individual or fundamental human rights tradition*. Traditional Chinese feudal society was characterized by a natural economy, a patriarchal system, and an autocratic rule. The ideas of individual dignity, freedom, and rights did not exist. According to "*weihu quanti quanli de fazhi lilun*" (legal theory of maintaining group rights), China labored under different social history, economic conditions, and political traditions and as a result her conception of human rights is necessarily different from that of the West.

Western capitalist societies experienced rapid industrialization and commercialization in the eighteenth century. The change in the economic system resulted in a change in the political structure, requiring the breaking down of traditional authorities. The ideas of human dignity, individual rights, the social contract, and a republican form of government came into prominence.

China faced a more complex historical, social, and political reality. There was no rapid industrialization and commercialization that provided the impetus for human rights development. Rather, there was a long-enduring concern for maintaining the imperial order and feudal tradition, while the nation struggled for survival against internal dissension, external threats, and natural disasters. The historical legacy of imperialism and feudalism stifled human rights development. The ongoing concern for national survival led to the promotion of collective and group welfare over individual rights. Thus, traditional Chinese philosophy emphasizes loyalty to the emperor, respect for the family elders, and *datung* or sacrificing the individual for the group.

In the PRC the concepts of rights and duty are reciprocal, not independent. They are contingent and not absolute. Article 33 (3) of the PRC Constitution provides, "All citizens are entitled to the rights and at the same time must perform the duties prescribed by the Constitution and the law." In practice this means that when the citizen exercises his rights, he may not "infringe upon the interests of the state, of society or the collective, or upon the lawful freedoms and rights of other citizens" (Article 51, PRC Constitution, 1982).

When such a constitutional principle is applied in the daily course of criminal justice work in China, it takes on a pragmatic appeal and intuitive logic. Theoretically, why should the law protect the rights of a defendant at the expense of society's interests? Practically, why should procedure rights stand in the way of investigation, arrest, and prosecution of criminals? Such a "reciprocal right" principle also reflects the Chinese cultural tradition and converges with public sentiments that justice requires that criminals be treated differently from "good people."

In summary, China does not have a "fundamental rights" concept, akin to that of the West.[56] Individuals do not enjoy rights separate and distinct from the group. There is no concept of natural, inalienable, or absolute rights. An individual is not allowed to stand in the way of society's interests and collective welfare. In traditional Chinese society, as with the contemporary socialist state, the individual labors for the welfare of others (family, relative, friends, country) and suffers under the interests of the collective whole.[57]

## Section 4—Lack of Constitutionalism

Constitutionalism is new to China. Until very recently, the idea of the constitution as a limit to state powers was unheard of in China.[58] The nature and functions of a socialist constitution is a much debated subject. Jerome Alan Cohen, a prominent Chinese legal scholar, has asked openly, "What functions does a constitution serve in the Chinese political-legal system? Is it a sham not worth the paper on which it is printed? Is it an artifice of propaganda designed to impress and mislead foreigners?"

Another more skeptical Western scholar even dismissed the communist constitution as totally useless in protecting citizens' rights and checking government abuses:

> What could be the function of a constitution in a communist state? It cannot restrict the actions of the dictatorship. Nor can it impose goals upon the party. It can set up the major institutions, but the dictators are free to change function as they see fit, and to make these institutions function in any way they desire. The *uselessness* of existent communist constitutions is most glaringly revealed in the norms they proposed on the fundamental rights of citizens, many of which are dutifully though ambiguously recited, but all of which are systematically disregarded in the day-to-day actions of the party, the state, the judiciary, and the police, not just during periods of emergency but permanently.[59] (Emphasis mine)

There are other more thoughtful evaluations of the functions of a socialist constitution. For example, one Chinese political science scholar observed that it is inappropriate to judge socialist constitutions by Western standards. Thus, it is biased to view and judge the socialist constitution as a mirror image of those of the West, as an enduring document of state powers and limitations. A socialist constitution should be viewed historically and evolutionary.

In its early stage the constitution is concerned less with restricting state powers than with liberating the human spirit. Next the constitution reports upon the achievements of past progress of revolution and further spells out a program for future development. Eventually, the constitution serves as a framework for state building. Significantly, none of the socialist constitution stages here mentioned functions as a *limitation* to state powers.[60]

Table 7: Comparative study of role and functions of PRC constitutions

| | 1949 | 1954 | 1975 | 1982 |
|---|---|---|---|---|
| **Historical context** | China liberated | Revolution secured | Cultural revolution in progress | China modernization reform beginning |
| **National needs** | Political consolidation<br><br>Social purification | Socialist state construction: Institutional building; Economic planning | Ideological struggle | Political order<br><br>Social stability<br><br>Economic development |
| **Nature of constitution** | Affirming revolutionary achievements<br><br>Liberating people's spirit<br><br>Defining a vision of the future | Providing a blueprint for state construction | Political manifesto:<br><br>Declaring political identity<br><br>Instilling political order<br><br>Affirming political ideology | Constitutional framework of government |
| **Limitations to power** | Ideological Control and political supervision | Party discipline and administrative supervision | Mass struggle | Constitutional supervision and rule by law |

As indicated in Table 7, taking law as reflective of changes of material conditions and the production relationship in society through time (i.e., historical materialism), the PRC Constitution performed different roles at different times in PRC history. In 1949 China was liberated from the KMT. The CCP was busy with consolidation of power and purging of counterrevolutionaries. Thus the Common Program (1949) as a constitutional document was less interested in protecting rights and still less in limiting government, and more in empowering the people to build a utopian society by purging the old feudal system and building the new China. During the reform period, the 1982 Constitution had a fundamentally different task—laying the necessary foundation for Deng's reform. As such, political order and social stability, the pre-conditions for sustained economic development, had to be protected by law.

Western jurists have come to associate a constitution with a limited government by law. The constitution is a social contract adopted by the people to limit the powers of government and protect the rights of the people. Before 1982, the PRC leadership shared no such understanding, nor did the people harbor such expectations. The same mentality and attitude remained after 1982. The PRC Constitution since 1982, being 1988, 1993, 1999 and 2004.

First, communist ideology considers the evils of government to be structural in nature and material in origin. Constitutional government is a historical-material product and a capitalist invention. With the capitulation of the capitalist state and the arrival of a communist utopia, the state with all its attending evils will fade away. There will be no need for coercive laws, much less a restrictive constitution.

Second, with the advent of the socialist state on the way to a communist regime, there is no distinction between the governor and the governed. They are all part of the proletarian, or the people. Party cadres and state officials administer the country on behalf of and for the interest of the people. There is no adversarial relationship, only a common bond.

Third, Mao would find it odd to talk about restraining the powers of government, especially in criminal justice matters, when the people are the master of their own affairs.[61] In theory, people's justice means simply that the people can do no wrong; the act and judgment of the people are, ipso facto, just and proper. Mao's classic statement in his "Report on an Investigation of the Peasant Movement in Hunan" bears repeating: "The peasants are clear sighted. Who is bad and who is not quite vicious, who deserves severe punishment and who deserves to be let off lightly—the peasants keep clear accounts and very seldom has the punishment exceeded the crime.[62] Mao did suggest that some form of "check and balance" was necessary to forestall people making hasty and wrong decisions in the heat of passion, but he was less concerned with institutionalized official abuses.

Fourth, Communist doctrine advocates democratic centralism as the fundamental rule in organizing government. It rejects categorically the concept of separation of powers as a way to counterbalance the concentration of powers in the state authority. It considers such an arrangement counterproductive and a plot of the capitalists to gain control over the people.

Fifth, Mao would readily concede that there are many instances when party cadres, state agents, and government officials might make mistakes. These mistakes are of an accidental nature and incidental kind, not systematic and structural in origin.

Sixth, Marx observed that human nature and consciousness change with the material conditions and social relationship of a society.[63] Mao believed that individual personality is shaped and conditioned by one's class status.[64] Both subscribed to the idea that the "central function of government will be treated as the transformation of the social natures of the citizen." This entailed destroying capitalistic institutions on the way to fostering socialist morality.[65] This understanding of the role and functions of government precludes the Communist leaders from looking toward the constitution as a means to address government abuse. Coercive laws do not change human nature; education does.[66]

The disappearance of an exploitative class of enemy, the mutuality of interests between the governed and the governors, the integration of the people with the officials, the commitment to democratic centralism as a political doctrine, the nonantagonistic nature of official misconduct, and the belief in the malleability of human nature all argue against the adoption of a limiting constitution on state powers.

## Section 5—Conclusion

This chapter, in reflecting upon the reasons for the lack of control of police powers in the PRC, starts with the premise that the law is quintessentially a cultural product. As such, the operation of the law is informed by past history and driven by prevailing ideology. The lack of a legal culture and a constitutional spirit materially affects the control of police in China. For example, the lack of a constitutional spirit of limited government affects how police misconduct is perceived and controlled. Police misconduct is viewed as personal wrongdoing, not as structural or organizational malfunctioning. The solution to police abuses of power is more education, supervision, and discipline, not legal punishment or constitutional checks and balances.

China has a long history of rule by man and institutionalized despotism. More recently, it has practiced legal nihilism and jurisprudential pragmatism. The lack of a historical national ethos in the rule of law and constitutional government, as reinforced by a contemporary political ideology calling for legal nihilism, provides little constraint on police powers. The emergence of political pragmatism further offers the police a politically correct justification to depart from doing what is right by the law to pursue what is effective and expedient in each situation.

The solution to the PRC's police lawlessness problem is thus not only to have more laws on the books or to assure more stringent law enforcement by officials, but to develop a more rooted legal culture, starting with a supportive political ideology that makes fidelity to law a categorical imperative and transcendental value more than merely a convenient instrument and expedient measure.

**Postscript**

On February 28, 2008, the State Council released China's most comprehensive assessment of the development of rule of law in China. The "White Paper: China's Efforts and Achievements in Promoting the Rule of Law" has this to say about China's intention and achievements in pursing a rule of law regime: (1) Rule of law has been firmly established as a fundamental principle of governance. (2) The CCP pledged to lead the nation with law and operate within the PRC Constitution. (3) Under the PRC Constitution, human rights are protected by law (Article 33: "[T]he state respects and protects human rights") and in conformity with United Nation conventions and protocols, including International Covenant on Political and Civil Rights (signed October 5th 1998), and the International Covenant on Economic, Social and Cultural Rights (signed October 27th 1997). (4) The environment of rule of law is improving in China. (5) The administration of justice by law is being established with a legal profession. (6) The Party cadres and government officials are being held accountable to the law.

In 1990, Qi Yuling was accepted by the Commercial School of Jining in Shandong based on her examination. Chen Xiaoqi's father, a local Party secretary stole Qi's entrance examination results and arranged for Chen to be admitted. Years later Chen graduated and got a job in the bank. Qi found out the facts and sued Chen and the school for compensation on grounds of constitutional violation, i.e., deprivation of education opportunity. On August 12, 2001, the People's Supreme Court held for Qi. Qi's case is the first time the PRC Constitution had been successfully invoked and applied by the court. The case opens the door for more constitutional litigation in China. For example, in October of 2003 Zhang Xianzhi was denied employment by the Personnel Affairs Bureau of Wuhu, in East China's Anhui Province because he suffered from Hepatitis B-V. Zhang sued in court claiming employment discrimination under the PRC Constitution. He was vindicated in April 2004.

From the Qi Yuling vs. Chen Xiaoqi et al. case to the White paper on rule of law, it appears that after so many false starts a rule of law regime and constitutional culture is beginning to grow in China, albeit ever so tentatively and slowly.

CHAPTER SEVEN

# Police Reform

## Introduction[1]

Under Deng Xiaoping's economic reform, China has been transformed from a backward state-planned economy and set on the path to a modern economy driven by the market. The economic reform has changed China socially, politically, and culturally.[2] Public Security has been a part of that transformation process. During the last thirty years, the Public Security apparatus has changed its role and functions, core values, leadership, organizational structure and process, management philosophy, and operational procedures and practices.

*Gongan* literally means public peace. In China the police have been referred to as *gongan* and more recently as *jingcha* (police). There are two types of police in China: *minjing* or people's police and *renmiu wuzhuang jingcha budui* or People's Armed Police (PAP).[3] The *Zhongguo gongan baike quanshu* (*Chinese Public Security Encyclopedia*) describes *gongan* as: "The work of maintaining social order, securing public safety, protecting public and private property and citizens' personal rights."

This chapter reviews recent public security reform measures and change processes, focusing on developments in the late 1980s and early 1990s. This was the "radical reform" period that led to the Police Law of 1995. Subsequent developments, not discussed here, are more evolutionary in character.

Chapter 7 is organized into an introduction and five sections. Section 1, "Public Security in China," provides a brief description of PRC police or *gongan*. Section 2, "The Public Security and 'Frame-Breaking' Changes," describes how the PRC police have changed in roles and functions, values and philosophy, structure and process. Section 3, "The Forces Driving Public Security Reform," comes next, while Section 4, "The Direction of Change," addresses the direction of the reform movement. Finally, Section 5, "Some Concluding Thoughts," reflects upon the problems and promises of the PRC police reform movement of the 1990s, concluding with the observation that the PRC police reform movement, in spite of its propitious start and strong momentum, is not likely to last if the attending reasons and proffered justifications for reform fail to reflect the social needs of the people and the political agenda of the leaders.

## Section 1—Public Security in China

### Chinese police system[4]

The Chinese police system consists of five components: the public security police, state security police, prison police, judicial police in people's procuratorates, and judicial police in the people's courts.

The latter four types of police account for only about 14% of the police force. The remaining 86% are the public security police. All five component parts of the overall Chinese police force have the same rank system, uniforms, badges, and symbols. None of these five parts of the police force is subordinate to any other part. Each type of police force performs specifically designed functions, and each has its own organizational structure. Historically, most police functions have been performed by the one force, the public security police.

The situation in the 1980s, especially the influence of the economic reform policy, dictated the need for greater diversification and specialization of some police functions. Hence, some functions of the public security police were transferred to other law enforcement agencies.

### The Public Security Police

The central agency of this police force is the Ministry of Public Security (hereafter MPS). The headquarters of the MPS is in Beijing. The MPS is directly accountable to the State Council.

### The State Security Police

This police organization was established in 1983. It has responsibility to safeguard state security and to prevent foreign espionage, sabotage, and conspiracies. The state security police are under the leadership of the Ministry of State Security, which is also one of the government organs directly accountable to the State Council.

### Prison Police

This is the correctional arm of the overall police system. Such police are stationed in prisons and correctional units and are responsible for supervising convicted offenders who serve their sentences in prisons. However, the supervision of those who serve their sentences in communities falls to the Public Security Police. The Ministry of Justice in China has the function of administering the nation's prison system. Thus, prison police are under the leadership of the Ministry of Justice, another government organ under the State Council.

## Judicial Police

In China, there are two types of judicial police. One is the judicial police attached to various levels of courts who are responsible for maintaining security and order in courts and serving legal documents, some also execute death sentences. The other type is the judicial police attached to various levels of procuratorates who are responsible for escorting suspects on trial and investigating cases under the procuratorates jurisdiction, e.g., police dereliction of duties. Hence, these two types of police are unlike the other three types in that the judicial police are not attached to a specific ministry that has direct access to the State Council.

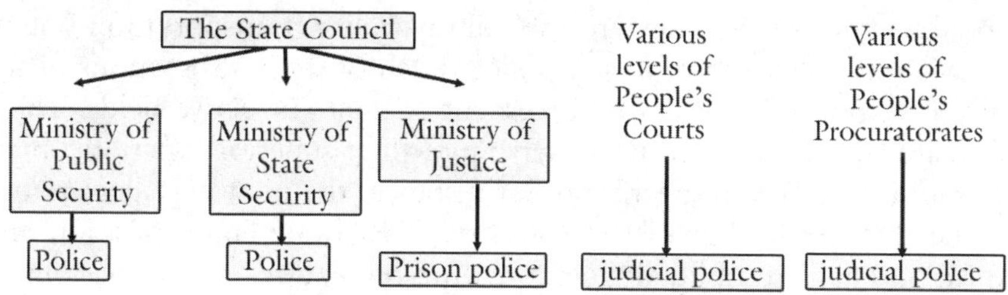


Diagram 1: The four police forces

## Characteristics of the Public Security Police

The public security police are organized according to both a centralized and a decentralized structure. In terms of profession and operation, all public security police fall under the leadership of MPS, but in terms of administration, they fall under the leadership of the corresponding governments.

The MPS exerts centralized leadership over the public security police in drafting regulations and rules for the public security police nationwide, guiding policing operations nationwide, and directing international communication on police matters.

Decentralization is demonstrated in that thirty-one local public security bureaus or departments at the provincial, municipal, and autonomous regional levels have discretion to decide the size of the police force needed in their jurisdiction and the power to determine their own priorities in policing according to their respective local situations. However, such discretionary power must be consistent with MPS instructions.

Each of these local public security bureaus is responsible for its own practices. The appointment and promotion of police officers are up to the local governments, but the local governments must consult the public security police services at the higher level for advice beforehand. Also, the local government is responsible for providing the police force in its jurisdiction with its budget.

## The Organization of MPS

At the top of the organizational hierarchy is the Ministry of Public Security. There are four levels of local public security police services under MPS (see Diagram 2). As stated previously, local police services are under the dual leadership of the local governments and the police services above them. But the internal assignments to police stations are solely under the direct leadership of the police bureaus above.

Besides the regular public security police, there are four other forms of police under MPS. They are the railway police, transportation police, civil aviation police, and forestry police. Each of these subsections of the police is responsible for law enforcement in their respective fields. These police are subject to the dual leadership of their superior functional ministries and the MPS, respectively. For instance, the railway police are under the dual leadership of the Ministry of Railway Transportation and the MPS. They are obliged to enforce the regulations and provisions of the MPS and also report their work to and seek assistance from MPS.

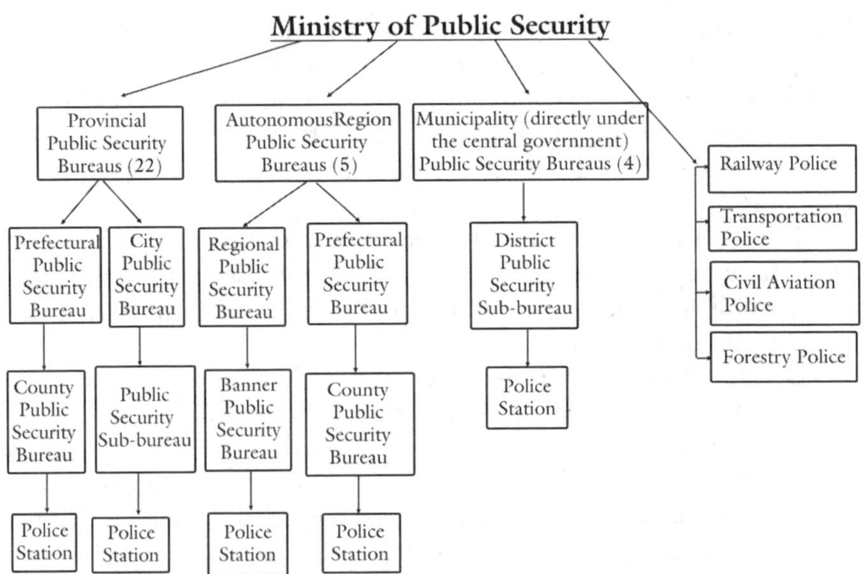


Diagram 2: The Structure of MPS

Another police force in China that needs to be mentioned is the armed police. It was established in 1983. The duties of armed police include patrolling borders, maintaining security and order in border areas, and guarding VIPs and foreign embassies and consulates stationed in China and important institutions, buildings, and facilities as well. The force is under the joint command of the MPS and the Central Military Committee.

Within the MPS, there is another new form of police—the patrol police. Their main function is patrolling the streets to deter crime and apprehend offenders. They also deal with minor offenses, participate in safeguarding major events, and render first-aid in large-scale catastrophes and natural disasters, as well as providing other minor forms of help to the public.

## The Police Rank System

The police rank system was adopted in China in 1992 according to the People's Police Ranking Regulations 1992. In the Chinese police there are five grades with twelve levels of ranks. They are as follows:

General Commissioner (awarded to individuals who hold the posts as ministers of the MPS or the Ministry of State Security);

Deputy General Commissioner (awarded to those who hold the posts as deputy ministers in the ministries previously mentioned, and the rest may be based on equating rank with post);

Commissioner (of first, second, or third grade);

Superintendent (of first, second, or third grade);

Sergeant (of first, second, or third grade);

Constable (of first or second grade).

## Police Functions

Police in China perform a greater variety of functions than any other police in the world. All the functions are performed by specific types of police officers trained and assigned to their respective fields. The functions stipulated in the Police Law 1995 are as follows:

- preventing, stopping, and investigating criminal offenses;
- maintaining social order and preventing activities that jeopardize it;
- keeping traffic safety and order and dealing with traffic accidents;
- organizing and implementing fire prevention and supervision;
- controlling firearms, ammunition, controlled knives, and flammable
- explosive and radioactive materials;

- supervising and administrating the operation of certain types of occupations (such as the industry of engraving seals and entertaining industries as various clubs) and industries stipulated by laws or regulations;
- guarding personnel stipulated by the State, the important institutions and facilities;
- controlling mass rallies, parades, and demonstrations;
- administering the household registration; conferring or revoking nationality; handling matters in regard to entry and exit of the country, stay and travel of aliens in Chinese territory;
- keeping order and security in border areas;
- executing the penalties for offenders sentenced to control, criminal detention, deprivation of political rights, and offenders who serve their sentences outside of prisons; supervising offenders serving suspended sentences and offenders on parole;
- monitoring and administering the security and protection in the computer information network;
- guiding and monitoring security work in state organs, social organizations, and enterprises in addition to order and security in major construction project sites; guiding the Neighborhood Security Committee (NSC) and other mass-line units in maintaining social order and crime prevention;
- performing other duties prescribed by law and regulations.

Within the headquarters of the MPS there are about twenty bureaus or departments under its direct leadership. Each of them is responsible for administering or coordinating a specific police function nationwide. Police bureaus or departments at the provincial, prefectural, and county levels have similar divisions or sections in charge of specific duties.

Table 1: Bureaus and departments within the headquarters

The General Office
Zhengzhibu or Personnel Department
Bureau of Public Order Control
Bureau of Policing Economic Institutions
Bureau of Policing Cultural Institutions
Bureau of Household Administration
Bureau of Control of Entry and Exit
Bureau of Border Control and Frontiers Inspection
Bureau of Criminal Investigation (similar to CID in the West)
Bureau of Fire Prevention and Control
Bureau of Border Control and Frontiers Inspection
Bureau of VIP Security
Bureau of International Cooperation
Bureau of Traffic Control
Bureau of Computer Management and Supervision
Department of Internal Supervision
Department of Legal Studies
Department of Science and Technology
Department of Budget and Accounting

In addition, there are several research institutes directly under the leadership of MPS with nearly 3,000 research and scientific staff.

One of these is the Police Science and Technology Research Institute and Information Center, which not only provides the latest information on police exhibitions and symposia worldwide but also carries out research on police equipment, information management, communications, and the technical prevention of crimes.

Another research institute is the Forensic Science and Police Science Literature Retrieval Center. This Institute provides expert testimony and has the ability to undertake comprehensive analyses and comparisons through its computer services for establishing a scientific basis for development of research projects.

The Traffic Control Research Institute mainly conducts research on traffic control.

The Institute of Public Security (Fourth Research Institute) is the only one in the MPS engaged in research on social science, specifically in the study of basic and applied theories about policing.

Police publications by these institutes that relate to scientific research and social science research include *Police Technology, Forensic Science, China Crime Prevention Products Information*, and *Public Security Studies*, among others.

## Police Powers

The powers of the Chinese police are stipulated in the Police Law (1995) and the The Criminal Procedural Law of China (1979). Various amendments to the latter were made through 1996, primarily empowering the police with authority to arrest, detain, and interrogate suspects under specific circumstances.

Moreover, the Police Law 1995 gives the police priority in cases of emergency while carrying out their duties, such as using public transportatio and going through traffic after identifying themselves.

The Criminal Law stipulates which offenses are defined as crimes that deserve criminal sanctions and which are defined as minor offenses that are dealt with according to the prescriptions in the Regulation Governing Offenses against Public Order of People's Republic of China (RGOPO).

There are three categories of punishments for minor offenses: warning, fine, and administrative detention.

Administrative detention is the most severe of the three. It involves depriving offenders of their freedom for not less than one but not more than fifteen days.

## Section 2—The Public Security and "Frame-breaking" Changes

During the 1990s, the Public Security system in China was in the process of "frame-breaking" changes. As explained by Michael Tushman, these are "revolutionary changes *of* the system as opposed to incremental changes *in* the system." Frame-breaking changes usually imply: (1) a reformed mission; (2) a change in core values; (3) an alteration of power structure and status; (4) a reorganization of structure and process; and (5) a replacement of leaders.[5]

### (1) A reformed mission

Traditionally, the chief missions of the police have been law enforcement, order maintenance, and public service. In the mid-twentieth century, Mao Zedong added a political dimension to this conventional idea of policing. He observed that police work had been a political instrumentality of the state employed to suppress and oppress the enemy class. In a capitalistic state, the interests of the propertied class had been manifested as that of the state's, to be secured by law and protected by the police. In early post-Mao China, the Public Security continued to perform a dual role of political militancy and social service. On the one hand, the Public Security was to be involved in suppressing the enemies of the people (landlords, capitalists, reactionaries, and counterrevolutionaries). On the other hand, the Public Security was also to be devoted to serving the people.

Under Deng Xiaoping, however, the role, mission, and function of the organization have undergone a radical transformation, moving away from most political matters into primarily law enforcement and order maintenance. The organization's mission statement clearly sets law and order as the primary duties. It limits the political function of Public Security to enforcing internal security laws, such as the investigation of counterrevolutionaries.

The newly established Ministry of State Security has assumed much of the sensitive political work involved with national security. The People's Armed Police (*renmin wuzhuang jingcha budui*) have been made responsible for curbing political disorders or civil disturbances. The people's police (*minjing*) are solely responsible for maintaining law and order. This is far different from the 1950s when the Public Security was preoccupied with purging internal political threats, real or imagined. The very first public security organization law, the Police Act of 1957, had set forth the basic missions of the people's police (*minjing*),[6] and these had included as much political suppression as traditional law enforcement.

Recent police work has in large part been defined by public expectations and community needs. The changed nature of police work can be gauged from police response to the public's calls for assistance. In 1993 Shanghai's Public Security introduced an emergency "110" telephone service.[7] In two months, May and June, the station received a total of 39,000 calls. The police handled 4,700 (12%) of those calls. Of the 4,700 requests for assistance, 526 (11.2%) involved criminal cases; 2,550 (54.3%) were public security or order maintenance cases; 1,176 (25.1%) were road traffic cases; 440 (9.4%) were for emergency services; and the rest remained unclassified. The police were involved with order maintenance work for over 50% of the time.

Public security has also become less concerned with providing service and more focused on controlling crime. The economic reform has caused an explosion in criminality. A recent survey of 1,115 counties and cities in eleven provinces all over China showed that 779, or 69.9% of them, enjoyed fairly good public security, while 287 (27%) experienced average public security, and 40 (4.4%) had poor public security.

The relatively low crime rates in China have been better than in most Western countries. However, historical comparison shows that China's crime problem is rapidly getting out of hand and requires swift and decisive countermeasures. More significantly, people are becoming worried and political leaders disturbed. People see crime as a threat to their traditional "good" way of life. Political leaders fear that runaway crime may jeopardize the nascent reform process. If allowed to persist, the crime problem might cast doubts and aspersions on the ability of political leaders and the credibility of the Chinese Communist Party.

The Minister of Public Security, Tao Siju, thus made reducing the crime rate one of the top public security priorities of 1994. He observed that crime was relatively high because the economic reform was bringing about unprecedented social changes: new class tensions, inability of the old comprehensive social control system to cope with the new tensions, decline in individual morality and standards of conduct due to economic and cultural change, inability of public security to effectively deal with the new wave of crime and social problems.

Public security has become less concerned with serving the people in general and more committed to meeting the needs of economic development.

The overriding mission of the public security in the post-Deng reform era is to secure a stable social and political environment for the economic reform to develop and prosper. This goal means providing a secure and stable social, political, and business environment in which investors and entrepreneurs can operate. More importantly, the investors and entrepreneurs must be reassured that their property rights and personal safety are truly respected and adequately protected by law. In practice this requires public security to devote substantial time, energy, and effort to resolving emerging conflicts, preventing newly discovered opportunities for crime, and deterring potential workplace violence. For example, the Minister of Public Security has recently called for better protection of employers by promulgating a "Circular on Taking Practical and Effective Measures to Protect Enterprise Leaders Personal Safety."[8]

The role of public security in enterprises undergoing transformation has often been conflict resolution and order maintenance.[9] In the case of Sichuan province's Santai county public security bureau, for example, this has meant dealing with disgruntled employees, the unemployed, internal theft in businesses, and the need to protect managers and business property.[10]

### (2) A change in core values

Significantly, the core values and entrenched culture of security personnel are changing. They are becoming more materialistic.

In the past, public security performance was evaluated on the basis of ideological enthusiasm, political correctness, and personal virtue. Public security workers were exhorted to serve the public selflessly. They were asked to emulate Lei Feng, who had personified the ideal of public service at its best.[11] The role model of Lei Feng taught selflessness, fearlessness, and altruism.

Recently, the Party and government began rewarding exemplary behavior with material goods.[12] The message was clear: The political leadership no longer expected the people to emulate Lei Feng's selfless devotion. The change was significant for a number of reasons. It showed that Chinese leaders were becoming less ideological and more pragmatic, were relying more on external incentives than internal rewards, and were less interested in shaping character and more intent on conditioning their people's behavior.

In another case in Liaoning province, Tieling city, Yinzhou Public Security substation resorted to increased material incentives to improve morale and attract young recruits. All 239 public security officers at the substation were given a two-bedroom apartment, an in-house telephone, a beeper, and a bicycle. The case demonstrated the willingness of leadership to use material rewards to induce loyalty. It also showed the effectiveness of such material incentives in boosting the self-image of the officers and enhancing the public appeal of police service as a career.[13]

There are a number of reasons accounting for the change in core values from idealism to materialism and hedonism. First, public security as a social institution has been very much affected by prevailing social norms and moral values. Second, public security has been drawing its members from the community, which shapes their disposition and expectations. Third, prevailing economic conditions have determined what public security can do in providing for its members.

These changes in core values have had wide-ranging effects. In a province-wide security bureau chiefs' meeting held in Jilin, for example, the chiefs found that police officers were more and more affected by the individualism, hedonism, and materialism that pervades the larger society. Some officers were using their positions to become bad debt collectors or bodyguards for the rich. Various public security organs were selling public services for a fee. Some were even selling their public authority for bribes, and the worst offenders were using their offices to engage in illegal activities, such as smuggling.[14]

Public security officers have been constantly reminded of their subordinate role to the booming economy.[15] Most of the economic reform could not have been achieved without law and order, but the people who have provided that order have not been given commensurate economic benefits. In 1993, for instance, police officers were made to provide security for a Chinese rock singer in concert. The singer made a huge amount of money for his appearance while the officers were paid merely subsistence wages. They felt exploited and left out.

The police have had to face demanding working conditions, long hours, high occupational risks, and low pay. They have had to deal with reduced social status, battered self-esteem, and, for many, deteriorating physical health and marital problems. All the while, the economy has been booming and other people have been prospering.[16]

The corrupting effect of materialism has been overwhelming and widespread. Within the Public Security ranks it is commonly accepted that the study of political thought has become outdated and irrelevant in the modern-day economy and that money is the measure of an individual's power, ability, and status.[17]

In a bid to forestall the corrosive influence of materialism and commercialism, the Minister of Public Security has spoken out against commercialization of police work and allowing police officers to engage in a second job. It is feared that allowing the police to engage in business would invite a conflict of interest and might lead to corruption.[18]

### (3) An alteration in power structure and status

Frame-breaking changes have involved strategic shifts of power. Decision making in Public Security has been shifting from the old, conservative political cadres to the reform-minded and the professional, and from the Party central government to local governments.

A recent survey of the composition of National People's Congress (NPC) Standing Committee membership showed that between 1975 and 1983 the political background of members had shifted. There were more non-Party and non-red (worker/peasant/military) people entering the elite decision-making body. More significantly, the 1983 members were more educated (96.8% with college level education) and had broader backgrounds (44.6% in management, professions, or teaching).[19]

This trend has grown unabated as evidenced by recent Public Security appointments to the Eight NPC. There were forty-three central and local public security officials appointed: thirty-eight to the NPC and five to the CPPCC. Their ages ranged from thirty to seventy.[20] The group was younger, more broadly representative, and more educated and well prepared by training and working experience than past leaders.

### (4) A reorganization of structure and process

Before the current reform, the Public Security system's organizational structure, administrative process, and operational procedures suffered from two historical disabilities.

First, the system was antiquated and dysfunctional. The system was designed in the 1950s to serve the needs of an administrative state with a communist ideology and planned economy. It had become ill-suited to deal with the new challenges posed by a market economy and capitalistic culture.[21] Specifically, it was insufficient to deal with new types of crime spawned by economic changes, it could not successfully respond to new social and economic realities, and it was built to serve a rigid central command structure rather than being functionally flexible.

Second, the system was poorly organized. The Public Security structure and process were ill-defined, resulting more from historical accidents, political considerations, and administrative convenience than rational planning and informed design. The net effect was an organization with an amorphous role, undifferentiated functions, and contingent process. Public Security officials were looked upon as all-purpose community service agents[22] rather than highly trained professionals. As the border area Supreme Court Chief Justice Lei Jingtian observed, everything involved in the old system was politically related to the Marxist idea of the masses rather than to professional law enforcement.[23] This populist justice model emphasized popular participation and mass mobilization with few legal or bureaucratic constraints.[24]

### (5) Rationalization of public security

The economic reform required the Public Security apparatus to become much more organized, rationalized, and accountable—in effect, more predictable. Increasingly, Public Security had to organize itself along functional lines and govern itself through a hierarchy of command. A modern Weberian bureaucracy came into being.

The MPS is now made up of one General Office and the specialized bureaus, departments, and offices that follow, all organized along professional specialization and functional lines. The role, function, mission, responsibility, jurisdiction, and authority of each respective office are clearly defined:

(1) Economic and Cultural Protection Bureau (*jingji wenhua baoweiju*) is in charge of supervising security work in government institutions, enterprises, associations, universities, and schools.
(2) Public Order Management Bureau (*zhi'an guanli ju*) is in charge of social security poll registration and identification cards issuance.
(3) Frontier Guard Bureau (*bianfang guanli ju*) is in charge of frontier inspection and security management at the border and the control of all points of entry and exit all over the country.
(4) Criminal Investigation Bureau (*xingshi zhencha ju*) is in charge of crime detection and investigation and administers the China Central Bureau of International Criminal Police Organization.
(5) Exit and Entry Management Bureau (*churujing guanli ju*) is in charge of manning the exit and entry points into and out of China and supervises the application and issuance of passports, visas, and resident permits.
(6) Security Guards Bureau (*jingweiju*) is in charge of providing security for state officials, VIPs, and important state meetings and functions.
(7) Computer Management and Supervision Department (*jisuanji guanli jiancha si*) is in charge of supervising telecommunications and computer utilization at the ministry, including providing for computer safety.

(8) Science and Technology Department (*keji si*) is in charge of planning, developing, coordinating, and guiding scientific and technological work at the ministry.
(9) Preliminary Examination Bureau (*yusheju*) is in charge of preliminary examination by public security and management of all detention centers.
(10) Traffic Safety Control Bureau (*jiaotong anquan guanli ju*) is in charge of road traffic safety and control of all roads in the country.
(11) Legal System Bureau (*fazhi ju*) studies Public Security laws and regulations and oversees law-reform matters (abolition, revision, and reformation) and the implementation of laws and regulations.
(12) Foreign Affairs Bureau (*waishi ju*) is in charge of all foreign affairs at the ministry, including working with foreign police agencies, friendly exchange, and technical cooperation.
(13) Planning and Equipment Department (*jihua si*) is in charge of supplying equipment and providing logistical support to public security bodies.
(14) Department of Government Offices Administration (*jiguan shiwu guanli si*) is in charge of providing administrative support and services to the MPS.
(15) Political Department (*zhengzhi bu*) is in charge of ideology, organizational discipline, work style, education and training, and sports events for police.(16) Audit Office (*shencha shi*) is in charge of supervising all revenues and expenditures at the ministry and conducting audits for all organizations and institutions under the ministry.
(17) Office of Management of Fire-Fighting and Material Production (*xiaofang qicai shengchan guanli bangongshi*) is in charge of managing all fire-fighting equipment and other materials manufactured all over the country.

There are four research institutes within the ministry. The First Research Institute (*diyi yanjiu suo*) conducts research on communication devices, computer application systems, TV monitoring systems, security and alarm technology, credential identification techniques, and criminal investigation techniques. The Second Research Institute (*dier yanjiu suo*) engages in forensic investigation and research in criminal techniques. The Third Research Institute (*disan yanjiu suo*) conducts research on computer applications, transmission technology, and safety alarm technology. The Fourth Research Institute (*diyisi yanjiu suo*) conducts research in public security issues and in problems linking China with foreign nations.[25]

Public Security work is increasingly subjected to the rule of law. The *gong'an* was established by the *PRC Constitution* (1982)[26] and organized under the *PRC People's Police Regulation* (Police Act).[27] Police powers are bestowed and circumscribed by the *PRC Arrest and Detention Act* (1979).[28] *Gong'an* operations are guided and regulated by various legislative decrees, administrative rules, policy statements, and official interpretations; chief among which are the *PRC Criminal Law* and *PRC Public Security Regulations.*[29] *Gong'an* actions are limited and confined by the *PRC Constitution*, the *PRC Criminal Procedure Code*, and the *PRC Administrative Hearing Regulations.*[30]

In a move to further institutionalize public security work through law, the Ministry of Public Security, as directed by the CCP Central Committee and the State Council, organized a special team to research and draft an allnew comprehensive *People's Police Law* in 1982. After eleven years and over twenty drafts, the proposed *Zhonghua remin jingcha fa* (Chinese People's Police Law) was finally ready to be submitted to the State Council and the NPC Standing Committee for final review. The draft law was first scheduled for submission on July 29, 1991 but was later withdrawn for further discussion , which took place on January 14–15, 1993, and a hearing was held on March 11, 1993. The draft included seven chapters and thirty-six provisions, including general principles, responsibilities and authorities, management formation, police protection, law enforcement supervision, and police insignia and flags.[31] The first comprehensive People's Police Law of the PRC was finally adopted by the Standing Committee on February 28, 1995.

To improve public accountability, the public security agencies, as state administrative organs, are now held accountable to and are supervised by the Ministry of Supervision, particularly through the Supervision Bureau set up at the Ministry of Public Security. The Ministry of Supervision is responsible for supervising and inspecting the work of the public security to ensure that: (1) state policies, laws; and regulations are properly implemented; (2) corruption is avoided; and (3) public security organs are managed properly and efficiently.[32] In order to promote self-discipline and internal control, the MPS recently published a draft of the "*Renmin jingch a zhiye daode guifan*" (People's Police Professional Ethical Standards).[33] The standards deal with disciplinary issues and other matters of public security, such as loyalty to the Party, love of the people, impartiality, bravery and self-sacrifice, civilized performance, and probity and honesty.

In the past, public security managers had to be politically correct, ideologically pure, and senior in Party stature. Increasingly, other aspects of leadership are being emphasized, including technical knowledge, functional competency, and professional qualifications.

Today's Chinese police managers, like their counterparts elsewhere, run complex bureaucracies with huge staffs and sophisticated equipment. Their duties and responsibilities often include organizational development, strategic policy formulation, personnel management, office administration, operations planning and execution, staff recruitment, training, and discipline, among many others, the implementation of which has to be according to the *Renmin jingcha neiwu tiaoli* (People's Police Internal Service Regulations).[34]

## Section 3—The Forces Driving Public Security Reform

There is now a common conviction that the public security apparatus needs to be overhauled and modernized and, most important of all, invigorated. The people in the street as well as the political leadership at the top have observed that public security has not moved along at the same pace as economic reform and changes in society. The call for reform has come from the national as well as the local governments, the top as well as the bottom of the public security organization, inside as well as outside the criminal justice system. In short, the call for reform has been widespread and deeply felt.

### The national political leaders

The NPC members see the need for drastic, comprehensive, and speedy public security reform. The civilian NPC members were mostly concerned with incompetence, corruption, abuse, and lack of education. NPC members from the public security ranks were mainly concerned with (1) the lack of legal definitions of the police's role, function, responsibility, and authority; (2) the lack of adequate resources for the force; and (3) the need for police accountability.

### The public security leadership

The top public security leadership has consistently spoken out for a more professional police force. Minister of Public Security Tao Siju acknowledged that the public order situation in China had been worsening and crime rising. The people's fear of crime was growing while quality of police officers remained low. He attributed much of the poor performance to the inadequacy of the old system for handling new problems. The current system had been inherited from the 1950s. For example, there was no common recruitment standard to act as quality control, no uniform basic training to guarantee minimum competency, no in-service training to maintain performance skills, and no systematic way to supervise, reward, and discipline officers. He stated that the most difficult task at hand was to change the established thinking, entrenched culture, and fixed habits of the old public security system.[35]

Table 2: Substantive reform proposals by eight NPC police representatives

| Proposals | | Numbers |
|---|---|---|
| (i) | **Police funding, staffing, and resources** | |
| | Increase funding | 4 |
| | Increase establishing and staffing | 2 |
| | Strengthen the PAP | 1 |
| | Improve funding, equipment and establishment for Inner Mongolia | 1 |
| | Increase funding for border forces | 1 |
| | Increase local funding | 2 |
| | Establish budgeting autonomy | 1 |
| | Subtotal | 12 |
| (ii) | **Working equipment, facilities, conditions** | |
| | Improve working conditions | 2 |
| | Improve basic police equipment | 2 |
| | Improve working conditions of PAP at labor reform camps | 2 |
| | Improve PAP's staff living conditions | 1 |
| | Improve PAP's weaponry and fighting capability | 1 |
| | Improve rural police's communication and transportation | 1 |
| | Subtotal | 9 |
| (iii) | **Police welfare** | |
| | Raise police income, benefits and welfare | 6 |
| | Reduce the income gap between locals and PAP troops | 1 |
| | Establish law to protect PAP from job release and transfer | 4 |
| | Subtotal | 11 |

| Proposals | | Numbers |
|---|---|---|
| (iv) | **Police performance** | |
| | Improve police education | 1 |
| | Improve police quality | 4 |
| | Improve police efficiency and effectiveness | 2 |
| | Subtotal | 7 |
| (v) | **Institutional reform** | |
| | Rationalize current security system | 1 |
| | Raise the ranking structure of PAP | 1 |
| | Establish special court and prosecutor, judicial system for PAP | 2 |
| | Overhaul the firefighting system | 1 |
| | Institutionalize PAP's procurement system | 1 |
| | Change rank insignia display | 1 |
| | Subtotal | 7 |
| (vi) | **Legal environment** | |
| | Early release of *People's Police Law* | 9 |
| | Establish law to regulate police duties and responsibilities | 5 |
| | Amend law on social order administration | 1 |
| | Establish law to regulate prosecutors, judges and lawyers, case intake, labor education/reform | 1 |
| | Amend *Criminal Law* and *Criminal Procedure Law* | 1 |
| | Improve economic law system | 1 |
| | Establish law to safeguard PAP's interests | 1 |
| | Subtotal | 19 |
| **Total** | | 65 |

Source: Extracted from political platforms of NPC police representatives as reported in "Renda daibiao, zhengxie daibiao geren dang'an, 1 zhi 7" (NPC and CPPCC Members' Biographical Data, 1 to 7), *Renmin gongan bao*, March 16, 18, 20, 23, 25, 27,1993 and April 1, 1993, 2.

## Police middle managers and administrators

Police middle managers are keen on reforming the police. They are committed to correcting the outdated mindset of the police and making police work more progressive and responsive.[36] The reformers want to anticipate emerging problems and detect latent ones, especially in the face of fast-moving economic reforms. They also want to be able to provide appropriate solutions to grassroots problems. Above all, they want to avoid a return to officialdom, bureaucracy, and red tape, which might make them lose touch with the people.[37]

## Social context for change

Since the beginning of the economic reforms, people's thinking on public security issues has changed in material and substantial ways. Crime has become a major social problem. Public security efficiency and effectiveness have become important political concerns. Corruption and abuse of power among the public security are significant political issues.

Much of the pressure for police reform comes from the consumers of police services: the general public. People complain about the service they receive, the absence of officers when needed, and the lack of initiative by the police.[38] People are so frustrated that they resort to extralegal channels. They can get better, faster, and cheaper services from *gong-guan qigai* (public relations beggars). These "beggars" can resolve commercial disputes, collect bad debts and return stolen vehicles for a fee. The existence of such extralegal services reflects poorly on a public security system on the verge of losing public confidence and support.[39]

## Organizational Setting

After fourteen years of experimenting with reform, the Public Security, as an organization, is now more than ever receptive to the forces of change. A "change" culture is now in place, especially at the urban police departments:

(1) The thinking of the police at the grassroots level has been changing. The old guard is gradually being replaced by a younger breed. New officers are much more innovative, entrepreneurial, and reform minded.

(2) Economic reforms have revolutionized people's thinking, altered their behavior patterns, and redefined social mores , which have created grave adjustment problems for the police for a number of reasons. The changes were too fast, too extensive, too overwhelming, and too radical for the police to handle in the beginning. Fifteen years into the reform process, however, police organs and personnel

have had time to adjust. They have also had time to experiment with new programs and to learn from others, including their counterparts overseas.[40]

(3) Police reform has advanced to a stage where systematic study is not only possible but necessary. Police reformers can now draw upon police research and studies for ideas, concepts, and theory developed over a decade or more. Police reform efforts have generated enough experience and data to allow for more comprehensive analysis, reflective thinking, and methodical theorizing. Police studies are now more policy oriented, forward looking, and concerned with functional issues and underlying causes. In all, the nature of police study has changed in focus, method, and sources of research data.[41]

(4) There are now more books and instructional materials for the training and education of officers. In 1985, the Caicheng published the first public security book *Go'ngan xue gainlun* (*Introduction to the Science of Public Security*), and in 1991, the Public Security University, after four years of preparation, published *Gong'an jichu lilun yanjiu* (*Public Security Theory Research*).[42] These books introduced public security workers to a new perspective and paradigm on modern policing in the reform era.

## Section 4—The Direction of Change

### Change in Management Philosophy

In the wake of economic reform and openness, the Chinese government has tried changing its management philosophy in several significant ways: from micro-management to macro-management; from direct control to indirect control; from administrative means to economic and legal means; from guidance to supervision and services. In this respect, public security organs are adopting modern management principles and reorganizing along rational and scientific lines. This calls for the use of economic incentive and for a division of responsibility, a hierarchy of command, and standardization of work. It ties performance to incentives.

**(1) Applying classical economic principles to public security work**

In the post-Deng era, public security, as with other state-administered enterprises, is expected to compete for survival in the open market. This means that public security has to justify its existence and economize on its operations. In day-to-day terms, it will have to do more—service more people, control more activities, and fight more crime—with less (fewer people, less support, and fewer resources). Public security also must adopt economic principles and applied competitive rules to reform the administrative bureaucracy. In practice, the police must introduce a performance-based merit system and competition to improve work efficiency and effectiveness.

In organizational terms, bringing economic principles to public security organs mean paring down the traditional top-heavy public security command by reducing the staffing ratio between headquarters and field operations, pruning outdated departments and units, and reducing bureaucratic drag by ending formalism and officialdom.

A good example of public security organizational reform is in Liaoning province, Anshan city, in the Lishan public security substation. The guiding policies for organizational reform there were: "jingjian jiguan" (simplify office structure) and "chongshi jiceng" (strengthen the basic level). The Lishan station transferred twenty-seven office staff to the line. This reduced office staff by 7% of the establishment, that is, from 21% to 14%. The original branches and offices of the public security bureau were consolidated into six functional systems: command and dispatch, political work, public security management, case approval, case investigation, and grassroots work. In order to reduce the workload of office staff, the following office functions were reassigned to police substations: disciplinary supervision, industry and enterprise section, dangerous goods and special unit system, joint-defense and Public Security section, and urban migration registration.[43]

In operational terms, applying economic principles to public security work has meant promoting personal responsibility and directly tying material incentives to performance. This has entailed doing away with permanent tenure employment by introducing the contract employment system, matching job requirements with individual skills, implementing an individualized incentive pay system, rewarding officers according to performance, and assessing public security work comprehensively and not on subjective criteria.[44]

The Lishan substation implemented a comprehensive personnel reform by adopting a post-responsibility system and its collateral contract responsibility system. The first step was to assign public security officers to postings based on personal qualification and ability. Public security officers were closely monitored and evaluated. Their performance was subjected to disciplinary supervision—rewards for good performance and discipline for those who failed to achieve. In 1993, eleven leading cadres were disciplined, that is, 2.8% of the force of 385: four were dismissed, one was given a warning, and another six were asked to make improvement within a fixed period.

All Public Security cadres were put on employment contracts. Public Security officers were graded and classified based on performance. There were four levels of performance under the system: the first-class people's police were entitled to first grade pay, prioritized promotion, and early induction into the cadre ranks. Outside training opportunities were given to those with second-class rating. Those who were classified as third class had to improve within a given time. Finally, those who failed to advance in grade within a year were to be dismissed or asked to resign. All officers were placed on floating wages.[45]

**(2) Applying scientific principles to public security work**

*Management by objectives.* In the past, public security work, especially the scope and range of responsibility, had not been well defined. The security committee of the residential neighborhood and the area public security organ were jointly responsible for maintaining law and order in the area. Crime control was everyone's business, which amounted to it becoming no one's concern.

Recently, the public security leadership has introduced the principle of MBO (Management by Objective) to increase efficiency. Objectives and performance have been linked to rewards and incentives to promote the attainment of desired results. Public security leaders believe that management by objective or by result can promote much greater effectiveness and efficiency in police work.[46]

A good example is the criminal investigation work at Jinan's Railroad Public Security Bureau. In the past, detective team leaders were responsible for assigning work and making staff evaluations based on subjective criteria. Simply put, the team leader could do what he wanted with his team, a system that had no clear definition of duties and responsibilities. The system created complacency and irresponsibility and was highly inefficient and ineffective. A change came in 1990, however, when work assignments and performance assessments began to be made on the basis of clearance rates, detection rates, arrest rates, and the number of criminals/cases handled. These statistics became the measure of all performance evaluations including promotion, merit pay, and commendations. The clearly defined objectives provided work focus. The identification of responsibility for individual cases generated performance pressure. The reward created the motivation to achieve. Overall, this system improved efficiency and achieved the desired results.[47]

*Adopting the contract responsibility system.* The MBO is further buttressed by the contract responsibility system. Under the contract responsibility system, the duty to prevent crime and avoid loss is placed squarely upon the people who should, and could, control crime and prevent loss. Contract responsibility means that those who allow crime to happen or loss to occur should pay. For example, Jiangsu province has adopted the *jiti caiwu beidao zeren peichangzhi guiding* (regulation on compensation responsibility for stolen collective goods), which requires people who are deemed responsible for the loss of goods to compensate the collective. The system places the blame and responsibility where it belongs and creates added incentive to prevent crime and reduce loss.[48] Similarly, on July 1, 1993, Shangdong province started a *zhongda anjian fangfan zeren chajiu zhidao* (major crime prevention responsibility system). The system imposed responsibility on those who neglected their duty in keeping their collective, enterprise, or organization from avoidable harm and damages to property.[49]

**(3) Applying a rational principle to public security work**

*Standardization.* The MPS has requested standardization for the police all over China. Standardization includes uniformity in appearance, ranking, organization, work standards, and processes. There are three areas requiring special attention: standardization of working conditions, standardization of working process, and standardization of performance. National standards are to be set by the MPS in consultation and cooperation with the provinces and cities nationwide.[50]

Starting January 1, 1993, the people's police all over China were expected to wear proper uniforms with personal identification and rank insignia,[51] which promoted uniformity and professionalism.[52]

*Standardization of ranking.* In 1992, the Seventh NPC's standing committee passed and promulgated the *Zhonghua renmin gongheguo renmin jingcha jingxian tiaoli* (Regulations on PRC People's Police Ranking). The implementation regulations from the MPS were approved by the State Council in September 1992. The new ranking structure and uniform requirements improved police discipline, conduct, and appearance on the way to a much more regularized force.[53]

On December 12, 1992, Premier Li Peng officiated at the first rank award ceremony for the first group of PRC police commissioners and deputy commissioners. The legal ranking system regularized, rationalized, and legalized the police system along the Weberian line.[54] After a year, the Vice-Minister of Public Security, Jiang Xianjin, reflected on the success of the newly implemented rank system. The new system had been successful in improving discipline by enhancing a sense of professional pride through meritorious promotion and award. In 1992, law violations had fallen by 15%, and disciplinary infractions had dropped by 5.7%. Formal ranking had provided opportunity, through assessment for promotion, to educate and improve officers. It had also improved organizational command and control, promoting efficiency and effectiveness. There were still problems to be resolved, but it was a giant step in the right direction.[55]

## Change in operations

### Introduction of street patrol[56]

Foot patrol was introduced in order to return policing to local control, make policing more relevant and responsive to local needs, and beef up police street presence. The major functions of street patrol are maintaining order, providing services, and preventing crime.[57]

In a national conference on foot patrol on June 26, 1993, the Minister of Public Security, Tao Siju, explained the reasons for implementing foot patrol. Foot patrol was adopted as an innovative measure to combat new public security problems brought about by the economic reform and market development. It was estimated that 100 million peasants had uprooted themselves from their rural households and had drifted around the country for jobs. Twenty million of them had ended up in various towns and cities, which had created many kinds of social problems and crime risks. Foot patrols could help to control these problems and act as an effective deterrent against would-be criminals or troublemakers. The patrols could also offer numerous services and emergency-related duties with the help of the newly established emergency "110" telephone number system. More significantly, the foot patrol could take care of problems before they happened or otherwise react quickly to citizens' calls for help.[58]

The foot patrol control concept originated in Tianjin. The city had had a well-established foot patrol program as early as 1902. More recently, the idea of foot patrols was brought up in a 1984 national public security basic foundation conference when the MPS called for deploying more police onto the street.[59] In 1988, when then Minister of Public Security, Wang Fang, was on an inspection tour in Shanxi, he suggested that the public order administration should be proactive instead of reactive, that is, patrolling in the street instead of staying in the police station waiting for things to happen. In August 1992, the current Minister of

Public Security, Tao Siju, finally gave his blessing to the full and speedy implementation of foot patrol by regular and armed police.[60]

In 1993, following the directive of the Ministry of Public Security, all major metropolitan areas—Beijing, Tianjin, Shanghai, and Guanzhou—adopted various kinds of police foot patrol programs. Tianjin has had its own since September 1992, Shenzhen since July 1992, and Shanghai since December 1992. By June 1993 there were fifty-six foot patrol programs in various cities in China. The Shanghai program was started with a specialized detail costing RMB4.5 million with 4,500 officers.[61] The program in Tianjin was a grassroots operation centered around the local *paichusuo* with the help of the People's Armed Police. The Shenzhen program was the most sophisticated and highly technological. It has been deployed and controlled by a central command and control communication center connected to the various officers via individualized communication equipment.[62]

Some form of a police patrol program was also integrated into the local crime prevention, detection, and control network. Kaifeng Municipal Public Security Bureau in Henan has integrated its police patrol into an interlocking system of crime prevention and control. There are the so-called "two layers and three levels" of protection in the system. The first layer of projection has been provided by the public security patrols. The second layer of protection has been formed with the substation joint-defense public security teams. The first level has provided foot patrol for busy streets. The mobile and riot police patrol the rural areas and high crime spots. The second level is staffed by joint-defense team members who provide both a fixed post and a foot patrol in the neighborhood. The third level of defense is provided by the residential public security committee, which looks after neighbors and watches out for its members and reports to the police on any suspicious activities.[63]

Early results show that the foot patrol experiment is having the intended effect. Crime rates are down and crime reporting is on the increase. In Fuzhou, twenty-two of thirty-eight patrol beats have been without criminal incidence for one year. In Shenzhen the police received 313,128 crime reports during first eleven months of trial operations. In Shanghai the patrol officers cracked 7,830 public security and criminal cases on the spot.[64]

## Section 5—Some Concluding Thoughts

The Chinese public security system is changing in fundamental ways. It is in the process of regenerating itself. The impetus of reform has come from within as well as without the organization. The forces of change have been both economic and social, though political considerations have invariably played a part. The direction of reform has been toward more rationalization, institutionalization, and legalization of police service. That much is clear from the above discussion. Less clear is what the future holds for police reform in China. In this regard, there are two points that are of most concern: the durability of past changes and the direction of future reform. For example, will the police reform process sustain itself? How fast, how deep, and how comprehensive will the reform process be? In what direction and manner will the reform process move in the short and long term? More significantly, what will the public security system "with Chinese characteristics" look like?

The future prospect of police reform, in durability and direction, is contingent on two factors: the maturity of past changes and the dynamics of future reform.

It is difficult, especially in China, to speculate on the future development of the police. However, we can provide some educated guesses by seeking to understand the dynamics of the reform process, especially the reasons for its existence and the principles governing its development. Particularly, why was reform necessary in the first place? What has been the ultimate objective of the reform?

In the early stage of the economic reforms, Public Security put up a heroic fight against reforming itself. A siege mentality developed that blamed everything and everyone for Public Security's own lapse of responsibility in fighting crime and maintaining order. All the traditional social control measures were tried and found wanting. Neither ideological education, nor household control, nor administrative sanctions, nor criminal punishment, nor labor reform were able to arrest the growing crime rates or slow the disintegration of social order. It was at this stage that Public Security started to experiment with various reform measures to address specific problems posed by the economic reform, mainly runaway crime rates and lapses in police performance.

A careful analysis of the public security reform process reveals that the reform has been characterized by six salient features: (1) Public security has undergone reform not because it chose to, but because it had to. (2) The reform measures were taken in reaction to events. (3) The precipitating events were, first, crime and social disorder, and secondarily, police incompetence, corruption, and abuse. (4) The immediate objective of reform measures was the solution to a problem. (5) The ultimate objective of the reform process was to secure economic, social, and political stability. (6) The reform was not driven by a vision of the future, informed by a grand theory, or embodied by an all-encompassing ideology.

From that analysis, police reform in China thus far has been reactionary in nature and practical in application. This reactive approach to reform was justified overtly by reference to Deng's teaching in pragmatism—one should reform by experimenting and only to keep problems from getting out of control. This reactive and pragmatic approach will most likely guide and circumscribe future police reform in China.

Thus, all future PRC police reforms will probably be driven by discreet social, economic, and political needs. All reform measures will be directed at solving the problem at hand in the most expeditious, direct, and limited fashion. There will be few attempts to anticipate or hasten to solve incipient problems. Little effort will be made to devise all-encompassing, integrated solutions to deal with emerging social problems. In short, future reform measures will likely be instrumental, ad hoc, incremental, and piecemeal, with no theoretical connections between them or ideological foundation.

Is the current police reform in the PRC likely to last? This chapter has cited much evidence to support the thesis that the police in China are embarking on a process of "frame breaking changes." There is little doubt that the police are undergoing revolutionary changes, unheard of only a few years ago. There is, however, less evidence on the depth, scope, and momentum of the reform—data critical for rendering an informed and balanced judgment on the vitality and viability of the change process.

In this attempt to investigate police reform in China, it is clear that more is known about government pronouncements, objectives, and actions than about the reforms' effects, failures, and opponents at lower levels. In other words, we know more about the formal and official aspects of the reform, to the exclusion and at the expense of the more important (for our purpose of analysis) unofficial and informal accounts of changes that transpired. An informed and balanced judgment on the future prospect of the current reform process has to wait for more objective information and properly conducted surveys, not to mention an enlightened perspective and seasoned analysis.

At present, police research in China has great potential, but it is still in its infancy!

CHAPTER EIGHT

# Chinese Theory of Community Policing

> The value of criminal records for history is not so much what they uncover about a particular crime as what they reveal about otherwise invisible or opaque realms of human experience.
> Muir & Ruggiero (1994)[1]

> The American city dweller's repertoire of methods for handling problems including one known as "calling the cops.
> Egon Bittner (1970)[2]

> If the people were allowed to manage their affairs for themselves, they could do that with half of the number of policeman who were now employed.
> Halley Steward, MP (1888)[3]

## Section 1—Introduction

Introduced in the 1970s in the United States, community policing (CP) is a philosophy and strategy to involve and engage the public to fight crime and improve quality of life in their own community. The ultimate purpose of CP is to provide for more responsive, responsible, efficient, and effective police service. CP takes many forms, for example, team policing, and is realized in different ways, for example, problem-oriented policing (POP).

CP, as a democratic practice, seeks to actualize Sir Robert Peel's policing principle, "Police are the people, people are the police." CP requires the police to work together with the community in identifying, prioritizing, and dealing with crime, safety, and order issues.

"Mass line policing" (MLP) was practiced in China in the revolutionary areas as early as 1927–1932. The "mass line" (ML) principle was formally introduced by Mao Zedong in 1943.

MLP, as a communist ideology, pursues the ideal of "from the people, to the people." MLP requires the police to listen to the people, ascertain their problems, mobilize and empower the people to solve them.

CP and MLP share much in common. Both seek to actualize democratic policing. Both engage the public to solve community problems. Both look to the community for guidance, support, and supervision.

CP and MLP, however, are not identical. They differ in one major respect—CP relies on the police to fight society's crime. MLP depends on the people to solve their own problems.

This study of first impressions explores the philosophy of CP/MLP in China,[4] as it offers a radically different Chinese theory of CP, "Police power as social resource theory" (PPSRT), to explain such CP/MLP practices.

PPSRT addresses three main questions: Who are the police? What is the relationship of the police to the people? Why do people call the police?

This Chinese theory of CP conceptualizes police power (1) from the perspective of the people, not that of the state; (2) as a function of problem solving, not defined solely by law.

In terms of foundation, PPSRT is a theory of the people, a theory of democratic governance, a theory of empowerment, and a theory of self-help.

This chapter is organized in the following manner. This brief Introduction will be followed by an overview in Section 2 of "What Is Community Policing?" Section 3, "Philosophy of Community Policing in Modern China (PRC)," explores the philosophical differences in policing between East (China) and West. Section 4, "Principles of Mass Line Policing," explores the idea, ideology, and principles behind MLP. Section 5, "Constructing a Chinese Theory of Policing," details the major propositions and defines the basic concepts of the theory. Section 6, "Discussion, Argumentation, Justification," presents the logic and evidence in support of PPSRT. Section 7, "Conclusion," compares MLP with CP.

## Section 2—What Is Community Policing?

In the United States, CP resulted from an overall failure of traditional policing to fight crime and service the people.[5] According to research, random patrol does not deter crime.[6] Incidence-driven policing does not solve community problems. Speedy response has little success in catching criminals.[7] Detectives rarely solve crimes.[8] Traditional policing deals with the symptoms, not roots, of crime and disorder.[9] Legalistic policing prefers to substitute procedural justice over substantive justice.[10] Technocratic policing allows efficiency to stand in the way of effectiveness.[11] Paramilitary policing is too confrontational.[12] Profiling policing is too discriminatory.[13] In the end, people were frustrated and dissatisfied with traditional professional policing. They wanted changes.

At this juncture, researchers were able to show that repairing broken windows reduces crime, well-kept neighborhoods improve the quality of life, and foot patrol reduces fear of crime.[14] Police started to change their policing strategy.[15] Instead of reacting to crime, they started to look at crime as a problem to be solved.[16]

## What is CP?

The seventh of Sir Robert Peel's nine Principles of Policing provides a solid foundation for CP: "To maintain at all times a relationship with the public that gives reality to the historic tradition that the *police are the public and that the public are the police*; the police being only members of the public who are paid to give full time attention to duties which are incumbent on every citizen, in the interest of community welfare and existence" (italics supplied).

There are two mainstream approaches to defining CP, one as a philosophy and the other as a strategy. The philosophical approach described CP as "a new philosophy, based on the concept that police officers and private citizens working together in creative ways can help solve contemporary community problems related to crimes, fear of crime, social and physical disorder, and neighborhood decay."[17]

Alternatively, Bob Trojanowicz described CP as "a philosophy of full-service, personalized policing where the same officer patrols and works in the same area on a permanent basis, from a decentralized place, working in a proactive partnership with citizens to identify and solve problems."[18]

In South Africa the "main objective of CP is to establish and maintain an active partnership between the police and the public through which crime, its causes and other safety-related issues can jointly be determined and appropriate solutions designed and implemented."[19]

Approached this way, CP is democratic governance in action, which is, providing or promoting public participation in policing, from input of ideas[20] to engagement with operations to monitoring of outcomes.

As a strategy, CP has variously been associated with police public relations, team policing, foot patrol, and crime prevention. Whatever the strategy, its aim is the enhancement of human relations, a community-sensitive and user-friendly police service, consultation on the needs of communities, respect for human rights, cultural sensitivity, continuous positive contact with community members, discretion on the part of police officers when they enforce the law, and the establishment of mechanisms to enhance the accountability and transparency of the police.[21]

CP has revolutionized policing in untold ways, some by design, most by default. Thus, while there are continued and unrelenting debates over various aspects—philosophy, strategy, effectiveness—of CP, there is little disagreement that community policing has fundamentally changed the way police organize and operate.

## Section 3—Philosophy of Community Policing in Modern China (PRC)

The PRC has taken a different approach, at least up until very recently, in defining police-community roles and functions in fighting crime and keeping order. In the PRC view, "Our public security work ... is not to have matters monopolized by the professional state agencies. It is to be handled by the mass.... *The mass line principle ... is to transform public security work to be the work of the whole people...*" (italics supplied).[22]

### The burden of the ubiquitous past

Historically, social control in China was decentralized and organized around natural communal and intimate groups, for example, family and clan, with governmental endorsement and support.[23] Emperors ruled the state by and through officials, who in turn governed the people by and through the family heads and community leaders.[24] Such decentralized, grassroots social control practices were informed by Confucian teachings.

Functional social control in China was supplied informally and extrajudicially, which resulted from deliberate state policy built on traditional Chinese cultural practices. In theory the local magistrates' offices were supposed to be in total control of all matters large and small in rural China, but in practice broad police powers were delegated or conceded to the local community and the family.

PRC crime control policy and practices are very much influenced by this historical Chinese (Confucian) pattern. Traditionally, Chinese ideas on social regulation and crime control were based on the following premises: the local nature of crime control; prevention as the bedrock of crime control; effective crime control by integration of families, community, and the state; the multifaceted nature of effective crime control; and the necessity for dealing with root social causes of crime.

Consistent with the above Confucian ideas and ideals, crime prevention and social control in traditional China were realized through indigenous groups: starting with the family, which provided the education and discipline for character building; the neighbors, who provided the supervision and sanction against deviance; and the community, which set the moral tone and customary norms to guide conduct. Finally, the state acted as the social control agent of last resort by providing punishment for crimes and economic maintenance and social welfare to prevent civil disorder. The Chinese definitely subordinated the freedom of the individual to the well-being of the group.

## The influence of an all-consuming present

The philosophy of PRC policing, conceptually and operationally, is determined by Communist political ideology. The PRC leadership from Mao to Deng to Jiang stated that the people are the masters of their own destiny. What constitutes ML and how committed Deng, and especially Jiang, were to the notion of ML are questions that must be addressed. How Mao's idea of ML might be interpreted and applied to policing in the 1990s and in the future, given Deng's concern with pragmatism and Jiang's emphasis on technocratic solutions to social ills, should not be lightly dismissed. However, the central thesis of this chapter—that the local people, by tradition and philosophy, are very much involved in policing themselves—is beyond challenge.

Reliance on the masses was a hallmark of early PRC history and Mao practiced this doctrine by using individual voluntarism and mass mobilization to move the country ahead in conducting the people's business.

In historical and cultural context, voluntarism in the service of a larger cause, such as saving the country or righting a wrong, has a long and venerable history in China. The popular admonitions, "guojia xingwang, pifu youze" ("The rise and fall of an empire is the responsibility of the individual.") and "xian tienxia ziyou er you, hou tienxia zi le er le" ("One should worry about the world's problem before all others, enjoy the world's pleasure after all others.") speaks to this philosophical ideal and fairly sums up the sentiment. Though the admonitions have more application to scholars and gentry, they were nevertheless sought-after ideals for the common people. For example, clan rules promote honorable conduct, including rendering voluntary assistance to the needed. Finally, voluntarism in aid of others (charity) and in support of higher cause (honor) was deemed virtuous conduct that should be pursued for its own sake. Thus when the KMT government decided to declare economic war on the British for indiscriminate shooting of peaceful demonstrators in Shamian Canton (June 23, 1925), the KMT enlisted the volunteer help of the people to enforce the Guangdong-Hong Kong Strike.[25]

In political context, in the early years of the PRC, mass struggle and self-criticism, not legal norms and judicial process, were used in ordering society. This means that the Party should work and live among the people in order to understand their problems. Translated into work style, the police should be on a first-name basis with the people and work alongside them as close as a family.

It is significant to note that the Chinese democratic principle, "From the mass to the mass," diverges substantially from the American, "By the people and for the people." The Chinese will have the people ruling themselves. Americans would have the people ruled by a government, acting on behalf of the people.

More recently, under the leadership of Peng Zhen and later Qiao Qi, "power to the people" is realized through more systematic and organized means—structured political representation and enforced legal protection. When the idea of ML was applied to justice administration, popular, informal, and societal justice were preferred over formal, judicial, and legal justice. Informal justice involved the masses in the settling of dispute through conflict mediation. Popular justice engaged the mass in the dispensation of justice by public denunciation, among other methods. For example in 1950 and 1951, the mass was involved in dispensing revolutionary justice during the land reform movements. In later years in judicial work, court trial proceedings were integrated with mass debates, effectively bringing the courts to the people. Mass trials were held in public, not to assure a fair trial but to educate the people, raise their consciousness, and empower them.

In terms of policing, ML formed the basis of "people's policing" whereby the local people are supposed to be self-policed. It is more appropriate to refer to ML policing in the earlier days of the PRC as people's policing. The whole of the people, as an exploited and oppressed class, were mobilized to impose their political will. Since 1979, "people's policing" has become "community policing," in which the local people are encouraged to take part in managing their own affairs.

In the context of fighting against political crimes, the people's participation was deemed indispensable. Thus, in the suppression of counterrevolutionaries, the police were supposed to understand the people's point of view, trust the people's instinct, mobilize the people's energy, and rely on the people's support. The police merely played a supplemental facilitating role in helping people achieve social control and justice. In all, the people were considered the lifeblood and backbone of the police. According to Mao, the public should impose law and order themselves and, only when the need arises, seek consultation and help from the police.

Practically, this means that the police must see things from the people's perspective, seek their support, and be amenable to their supervision. Any policing detached and isolated from the people would not be effective in finding local problems and detecting criminals. Hence, one of the more serious mistakes that could be committed by the police would be alienation from the mass.

## Section 4—The Principles of Mass Line Policing

### The "renmin jingcha" ("people's police")

The PRC police were named "renmin jingcha" or "people's police" at the first National Public Security Meeting in October 1949. As an occupational title, "renmin jingcha" captures the basic nature and essential characteristics of the police in Communist China; the police are at one with, belong to, and are dependent upon the people.[26] The police and the people are "blood brothers" from the same family, perfectly aligned in political ideology, class interests, and personal outlook. The U.S. viewpoint is different. It is not necessary for the police and the public to be one and the same in constitution, interest, and outlook. It is important for the police to consult and represent the people under the law.

### Mass line policing (MLP)

ML is the basic tenet of governance of the CCP.[27] James R. Townsend observed, "The theory of the mass line is probably the strongest part of the legacy [of Maoist populism]. It is now deeply implanted in CCP ideology, and it would be difficult to reject it without altering the ideology as a whole."

The ML is at once an ideological postulate, a revolutionary perspective, a mission statement, a leadership style, an organizational method, and an operational principle for the police. As such, MLP has direct application for how police are led, how they are organized, and how they operate.

Functionally, a ML perspective allows the masses to see where their true and long-term interests lie. It effectively liberates the people from the straitjacket of false consciousness in a capitalistic society. It allows the masses to gain political consciousness by having them analyze their own social, economic, and political circumstances from their own vantage point. In so doing, the ML recognizes that no one understands the plight of the people except for themselves.

Operationally, the ML was the method of revolutionary leadership adopted by the CCP to educate and mobilize the people in class struggle on the way to the final establishment of a communist state. It consisted of three recurring steps: gathering scattered ideas of the masses; processing the ideas; and using the ideas to lead—with education, propaganda, and mobilization—the masses to struggle against class enemies. The method is commonly referred to as "from the mass, to the mass."

## History of MLP

The principle of ML as a practice in China has a long history and dates back to the earliest days of the CCP in the Yenan era.[28] As a practice worldwide, it is traceable to Lenin and even to Marx. The theory of ML as a political ideology and a revolutionary leadership style was first espoused by Mao.

Although it is said that Mao was the chief proponent of China's ML, Li Shaoqi is the ultimate theorist and chief strategist who explored and refined the intricacies of the ML. According to Liu, in order to carry out ML, the Party needed to adopt four "mass standpoints." They were serving the people, total accountability to the people, having faith in the people to emancipate themselves, and learning from the people.

There were critical differences between Liu and Mao, especially when the ML was put into practice. Liu tended to equate the ML with selfless service, and Mao demanded much more—learning from the mass and leadership over the mass.

## The foundation of ML

ML is based on the understanding that the masses create history by living the reality. Marx and later Mao credit the masses with the ability to create knowledge and the right to take initiative to change the world in their own image and according to their own interests.[29]

In this regard, Mao pointed out that the people are the masters of their own destiny. "The people, and the people alone, are the moving force in the making of world history."[30] The reason was simple—only the people have the necessary creativity and energy to get things done in their own interest.

The people are also very motivated. "The masses have a potentially inexhaustible enthusiasm for socialism."[31] There are, however, many who do not want to get involved. They are too complacent about the present or too fearful of the future.

In addition, the masses do not always see the whole picture. Their information is scattered, partial, and unsystematic. Their understanding of matters is often subjective, incomplete, and distorted. More specifically, the masses are confined and restricted by their life circumstances and thus have limited access to the true nature of class society and real appreciation of their standing in the class struggle.

The masses' views need to be concentrated and reconstituted—collected, analyzed, and synthesized—to form the whole truth.

The role of a revolutionary leader is to gather disparate ideas and process them into concentrated truth, according to Marx's theory of historical materialism and Hegel's method of dialectics. Mao observed this to be democracy in action.

In seeking to distill and construct the truth, leaders abide by certain general principles. They seek the long-term rather than the short-term interests of the masses and the interests of the whole over that of any of its parts. They do not hesitate to take *political power* through force of arms. They make use of compromises and alliances. Finally, they rely on advanced workers to overcome intermediate and backward workers.

When the processed ideas are ready, the leaders will return those ideas to the masses through study, education, propaganda, and mobilization processes.

From its inception until now, the ML philosophy affects everything the police do, in principle if not in practice.

## Mao's theory of contradiction

Mao did not propose a theory of policing. His thinking on crime and punishment is, however, instructive on how police should behave toward the people and their enemies.

Mao's ideas on crime and punishment are part of his larger political thought on class struggle and proletarian dictatorship. The clearest exposition of Mao's thinking on this subject is in a speech at the Eleventh Session (Enlarged) of the Supreme State Conference, entitled: "On the Correct Handling of Contradictions" on June 18, 1957.[32]

Contradiction in the context of crime and punishment is manifested as conflicts of ideas or ideals or competition in values and interests, which are ultimately settled through the use of law and punishment. Unresolved personal disputes will lead inevitably to disrupted social relationships manifested as crime.[33]

The relevancy of Mao's ideas on contradiction, as they relate to CP, is clear. First, CP presupposes the existence of a self-regulating community that is willing and able to defend its own interests. Second, by its very nature, the CP style of policing only works internally, not externally.

### Acting upon "people's police," doctrine of "contradiction," and MLP

According to Mao's thinking on people's police, MLP, and contradiction, the police are friends of the people and dictators toward the enemy. Friends talk among themselves (nonantagonistic relationship). Enemies fight against each other (antagonistic relationship).

In terms of working with the people, the police should follow the Lei Feng spirit and be guided by MLP. As people's police, the police live with the people, sharing their dreams and understanding their circumstances. The role of the police is to serve the people—to be at one with the people, listen to them, see things from their standpoint, and help them realize their dreams and fulfill their needs.

MLP instructs that the police "should go to the masses and learn from them, synthesize their experience into better, articulated principles and methods, then do propaganda among the masses, and call upon them to put these principles and methods into practice so as to solve their problems and help them achieve liberation and happiness."[34]

The police should always have the best interests of the people in mind. "Production by the masses, the interests of the masses, the experiences and feelings of the masses—to these the leading cadres should pay constant attention."[35]

Mao was quick, however, to caution against commandism. "If we tried to go on the offensive when the masses are not yet awakened, that would be adventurism. If we insisted on leading the masses to do anything against their will, we would certainly fail. If we did not advance when the masses demand advance, that would be Right opportunism."[36] The biggest mistake the police could make in working with the people would be to substitute their own ideas for those of the people.

## Section 5—Constructing a Chinese Theory of Policing

This study of first impression explores the philosophy of MLP in China[37] and offers a radically different Chinese theory of policing, "Police power as social resource theory" (PPSRT), to explain such MLP practices.

The PPSRT addresses three main questions: Who are the police? What is the relationship of the police to the people? Why do people call the police?

This Chinese theory of policing conceptualizes police power from the perspective of the people, not that of the state; and as a function of problem solving, not defined solely by law.

In terms of foundation, PPSRT is a theory of the people, democratic governance, empowerment, and self-help.

## PPSRT

PPSRT advances seven propositions. Together they inform us who the police are and what they do, in the eyes of the people. These propositions are scientific is nature. This means that they are subject to empirical validation, or negation.

Proposition 1: People confront problems routinely as a life course, some of them are called crime.

Proposition 2: Criminal acts cause multiple problems for the victim and others.

Proposition 3: People call the police because they do not have the necessary resources to deal with their problems, crime and non-crime.

Proposition 4: Police power is a kind of emergency social resource made available to the people to solve their problems.

Proposition 5: The more resources at the disposal of the people, the fewer problems the people will be confronted with.

Proposition 6: The more resources at the disposal of the people, the less they have to call on the police when problems happen.

Proposition 7: The more resources at the disposal of the police, the more effective they are in solving people's problems.

## Definitions

Problem is defined as: "An unrealized expectation of wants or needs due to resource deprivation."

Resource is defined as "Things of all kinds, including power, time, materials, skills, culture, ideas, and knowledge, that can satisfy one's wants and needs."

Police is defined as: "A depository of social resources. Police are an all purpose emergency problem solver authorized to use coercive resources to solve problems in a domestic situation and during peaceful times."

## Theoretical framework

Building on the earlier discussion of ideas about people's police, principles of MLP, and the doctrine on contradiction, this section offers a new approach to understanding MLP in China. MLP can best be explained by PPSRT, a theory that views police as a social resource for solving people's problems (including crime) through self-help.

Chinese theory of MLP starts with a basic observation that informs this theory throughout—in a state run by the people, we must understand how the people conceive of the nature of crime and the role of the police; in the words of Mao, "from the mass, to the mass."

From the perspective of the state, crime is a legal violation. From the perspective of the people, crime is a set of life experiences and a multifaceted personal problem. In law, a battery is an unconsented touching. To the people, a battery is broken bones and loss of income.

From the perspective of the state, police power is a political resource to secure control, maintain order,[38] and command obedience.[39] It is defined coercively, structured legally, organized bureaucratically, and imposed unilaterally.

From the people's perspective, police power is a social resource made available by the state and drawn upon by the community or its citizens to handle personal and communal problems of an emergency or crisis nature. More significantly, in the eyes of the people, police power is not reconstructed in a political image, structured by law, or organized with reference to police needs,[40] but dictated by the people and negotiated to fit the personal circumstances and situational needs that the problem calls to mind.

The PPSRT argues that the definition and availability of police power as a political resource happen at a structural-macro level, for example, legislative process and policy debate, and the initiation, distribution, and disposition of police power as a social resource happens at the personal-situational-micro level, for example, reporting crime and preferring charges.

## Policing from the people's perspective

The superiority of looking at police roles and functions from the public's perspective can be justified on a number of grounds.

First, PPSRT calls for looking at problems from the people's perspective, as a matter of birthright and process of maturation. It empowers people to meet their own personal needs, supplying them with the necessary resources on demand and as required.

Second, PPSRT corrects the lopsided relationship between the police and the people by returning the people to center stage, and putting people in control of their own problems[41] through the process of communalization, socialization or personalization of crime, that is, looking at crime as a communal, social, and personal problem, not legal violations.

Third, PPSRT marks a shift of focus from state-centered CP to people-oriented policing. Although CP calls for the police to listen to and serve the needs of the community as a collective in order to enhance its political legitimacy, organizational credibility, and operational efficiency, PPSRT asks the police to be responsible and accountable to people individually and collectively.

Fourth, PPSRT gives social meaning and lends emotional content to police-people activities, which is what policing is all about—dealing with personal issues, human problems, and relationship difficulties of one form or another. In so doing, it socializes and humanizes the police-people interface, making police business truly a people's business.

Fifth, PPSRT liberates the police from the sterile confines of the law and the stifling restraints of bureaucracy. It gets away from "one size fits all" strategy and practices.

Sixth, PPSRT recognizes that police work should be as diverse and complex as people's problem; that is, policing changes with time, place, people, context, circumstances, and situations.

Seventh, and most important, PPSRT allows the people to be heard. For all too long, the public has been an *object* of policing when in fact they are, and should be, the *subject* of policing. Instead of being policed, they are engaged in problem solving.

The legal anthropologist has contributed much, through the study of "trouble cases," to our understanding of how indigenous people of other cultures settle disputes and deal with problems. Such research reveals that the problems of everyday life look and feel very differently from the inside than from the outside.[42] The lesson to be drawn from such studies is that legal classifications of a problem, for example, murder or rape, do not usually capture the problem as experienced by the parties involved. The nature of a problem must be deciphered by the parties involved who are anchored within a multifaceted social milieu, locked into an enduring and patterned relationship, captured by an all-embracing and diversified local custom, and moved along by situational dynamics and personal interactions.[43]

The theory as proposed—people solving their own problems with state resources—is consistent with the civil society movement,[44] the privatization of police trend,[45] and the Alternative Dispute Resolution initiative.[46] The theory, if ever fully realized, allows people to be the master of their own affairs. They have the right to dictate and control the extent and manner of the state's involvement in their life choices.

## Policing as empowerment

When the state police power is imposed by state officials to enforce the law or invoked by the public to deal with a problem, it automatically transforms the nature and affects the handling of the situation at hand.

When the public call the police, it gives the state the opportunity to transform a private/personal matter into a public/legal one. This amounts to the bureaucratization/legalization/professionalization of a communal or private or personal problem. The change transforms a communal or personal problem into one that is recognizable by the police and actionable in court.

The criminal law will only recognize a citizen's complaint for prosecution if the elements of a crime can be proven in a court of law beyond a reasonable doubt: (1) a conduct (actus reus); (2) a criminal intent (mens rea); (3) a harm; (4) causation; (5) a law against it. In being captured by law, a communal or personal problem loses much of its meaning derived from the social milieu, communal setting, interpersonal relationship, historical context, and situational dynamics of which it is an integral part.

Before the police intervene, a personal dispute between two office lovers ending in a street fight at night registers a rupture of a personal relationship, derailment of a marriage plan, disruption of office work, and damage to a career prospect, not to mention hurt ego, tested confidence, and loss of opportunities. When the police are called, the street fight becomes a "public nuisance," and the lovers are turned into "complainant" and "defendant."

In the process of transformation/conversion, the communal or personal problem loses much of the original meaning it held for the actors directly involved and others afflicted, for example, the sons, daughters, and neighbors of a "criminal." More significantly, what matters most to the actors involved—emotion—and to the people affected—relationship—is of least concern to the state.

For example, criminal law does not recognize an honorable motive as a justification or excuse for illegal action. Intentional killing of one depraved criminal to save a million innocent people is as wrong before the law as killing a million innocent people to satisfy one's depraved mind. It is still prosecuted and punished as murder all the same. Likewise, in the eyes of the law, killing a person to relieve his pain is no less of a crime than the cold-blooded killing of a person for no reason at all.[47] Under criminal law, intent to kill—and not motive to kill—is considered what's important. However, communal and personal morality has always been concerned with motivation; why a person kills is as important, if not more important, than the fact that someone intentionally killed.[48]

Criminal law assumes that people are rational, a fact not borne out by experience or validated by empirical evidence. Criminal law builds upon the foundation of utilitarianism[49] and denies the emotions of everyday life. Thus, killing emotionally is no less guilty than killing intentionally, unless it can be said that the emotion overwhelms the individual. Likewise, jurors are instructed not to use their emotions in deliberation lest it influence the outcome of the case. In both situations, the core values of a person are denied in favor of rational administration of the law.

Canadian criminologist Birthe Jorgensen examined sixteen hours of police calls—820 telephone conversations, 210 dispatches, and 53 request reports—in a large suburban police station in central Canada. He clearly observed that legal and administrative considerations came before the citizen's concerns.[50]

Legalization of a problem also shifted the ownership and arena of dealing with the problem from the people to the state. For example, once a family problem is acted upon by the police, the parties involved cannot reclaim ownership of the problem until such time as the police have determined it is no longer in their interest to proceed with the case.

There are formal and informal ways the parties can influence the legal process and outcome, for example, by refusing to testify or becoming adverse witnesses, but they have to do so within the law; that is, people can be forced to testify under a contempt order. The police and prosecutor have long respected the rights of victims not to prosecute. Otherwise, the law makes it possible to mount a private prosecution if the police or state refuses to move forward.[51]

More recently, the victim's rights movement has successfully reformed the law to allow victims to participate in the sentencing of the offenders, and reintegration shame theorists have made it possible for victims to play a key role in having some control over the disposition of cases. All this argues for a prominent role and active involvement for the people in the management of their own business and problems.

PPSRT hopes to address this observed state-police dominance of private and personal matters by empowering the public to deal with their own problems.

The theory also serves to redefine the role of and relationship between the police and the people. Under this theory, the police are an agent of the people, and police power is a resource for the people to use, held in trust by the police. This arrangement empowers people as it gives them much more control over their own affairs. In so doing, the public will be actualizing one of the central tenets of democratic policing, that is, people policing themselves. For example, the state can make a law clearly stating the kinds of cases or circumstances under which the citizen has a right to expect police service and conditions upon which the police powers can be used. Such a law should spell out the right of the public to determine whether to warn, summon, arrest, or prosecute an individual causing a problem for the complainant. The public may also be allowed to use the range of acceptable remedies and punishments deemed acceptable in resolving a "troubled case" under the supervision of the police.

## Policing as self-help

As structured, PPSRT gives credence to community policing in that it openly acknowledges in theoretical terms and explicates in concrete detail why and how the public should play a key role in the deployment and disposition of police power as a social resource in search of a solution to their own problems.[52] To that extent, this is a theory about "self-help,"[53] "private ordering," and "personalized justice."

This theoretical approach—looking at police services from the public's perspective and as personal/community problems—is anticipated by the work of Cumming, Cumming and Edell; Goldstein; and Bittner, though all three of them did not carry their analysis far enough in addressing the central proposition of this theory—that people should be empowered to solve their own problems.

Cumming and her colleagues properly discovered the "support" function of the police but failed to discuss its theoretical and operational import in terms of people's policing.[54]

Goldstein properly identified the "community problem solving" functions of the police but stopped short of recognizing that the public has an inherent *right* to demand police power to solve their own problems.[55]

Bittner properly demonstrated that the police bring with them the "capacity and authority" of using coercive force to solve situational problems of all kinds without also realizing that in actuality the police possess a range of other resources that made them valuable to the public for problem solving, the most important of which is that of legitimacy.

These scholars have contributed significantly to the research on people-problem oriented policing, but none of them envisions a reconceptualization of the roles (problem solving) and relationships (people driven)[56] of the police to the people.

## Cumming, Cumming, and Edell on police service role

Cumming and her colleagues were some of the very first to discover the dual roles of the police, that is, as a control vs. supportive agent. "Finally, besides latent support, the policeman often gives direct help to people in certain kinds of trouble." After analyzing 801 calls over eighty-two hours, Cumming and her colleagues found that over 50% of the police calls sought help of one sort or another. The research team concluded that the police, instead of enforcing law or fighting crime, were asked by the people to help solve their problems. This research is important because it breaks with the traditional conception of police in openly recognizing the social role and service nature of police work.

The specific social services that the police render are less important, for this study, than the fact that a police officer is not solely a political controller, law enforcer, or crime fighter. The police have an important and indispensable social service role to play. They help people to solve their problems of all kinds, as "philosopher, guide and friend".

Like so many other research projects to follow, this research failed to draw upon the empirical findings to articulate a police theory calling for a new understanding of police roles, focusing on problem solving. This task was left to Goldstein.

## Goldstein on police non-legal functions[57]

In a seminal article, Goldstein observes and laments that there is a "tendency in policing to become preoccupied with means over ends."[58] By that, Goldstein means that traditionally police in America have structured their activities around law enforcement and crime control when they should have been orientating themselves to the "substance" of policing, which is, solving crime and related problems of the community. In so doing, he was one of the first to reorient the police function from reactive crime fighting to proactive problem solving in the community. He called for a shift in police strategy and activities to "problem oriented policing," which has since been the organizing principle guiding police reform in the 1980s. "The police must give more substance to community policing by getting more involved in analyzing and responding to specific problems citizens bring to their attention."

This invitation for the police to shift their role and function from dealing with crimes to solving community problems, challenges the police to look at the nature, extent, and remedy for community problems beyond the narrow confines of the traditional role of police as law enforcers and crime fighters.

In so doing, the police no longer fight crime and enforce law but engage in community problem solving.

PPSRT, while agreeing somewhat with Goldstein's POP approach, differs from POP in a number of important ways.

First, Goldstein's POP theory is in the main a theory about solving "community problems" as revealed by individual calls for assistance; for example, repeated calls about robberies in a neighborhood tell the police that this is a criminal "hot spot." Goldstein argues that the police should not be driven by law, focused on crime, or reacting to incidents. Instead, police work should have more pragmatic concerns in dealing with citizens' qua community's problems. By that, Goldstein means that police should not be organized only to fight crime reactively but also to take the initiative to deal with community problems giving rise to crime and disorder.

Although it is true that Goldstein's theory would readily accommodate the use of police to solve victim-personal problems, this is not the original intent of the theory.

Theory this distinction is important for several reasons. First, Goldstein is less concerned about dealing with individuals' problems that make up and radiate from the crime itself than he is with dealing with community problems giving rise to the crime. More bluntly, Goldstein looks at individual problems reported to the police as indicators of larger problems in the community, but not as problems worthy of police attention. In so doing, POP ignores the plight of the victims of crime and their call for help.

PPSRT argues that both communal and personal levels of problems are important; but from the perspective of the people (victims), the problems of the individual are more important. That is why people called the police in the first place: to seek help on crime and related problems.

Second, Goldstein's theory is a "police" theory. Goldstein's main contribution is in having the police looking at the larger picture beyond the immediate crime. He asks the police to investigate into the problems lurking behind crime and disorder in the community. PPSRT is a pure "people" theory of policing. It asks the police to look at crime, disorder, and other problems from the perspective of the people. In so doing, a problem for the public is automatically considered a problem for the police.

Third, Goldstein expects the police to solve community problems with the help of the community. PPSRT envisions people solving their own problems with or without the help the police. More important, the police are only one of the many resources potentially available.

Fourth, Goldstein wants the police to have more expansive police power to solve crime problems. PPSRT wants to empower citizens to solve their own problems, again, with or without the help of others. Although PPSRT does not object to police having more power to serve the public, such power should only be activated and used with the people's consent and under their direction and control.

Fifth, under Goldstein's formulation, police problem solving will lead to more police penetration into the community's life. Under PPSRT the police will be playing a lesser and lesser role in the community, as people become better and better at taking care of their own problems. Goldstein's theory allows the police to enter the people's life at will in search of a solution. PPSRT will allow the public to control the police once they are called for assistance. In short, Goldstein wants to enlarge the state's role while PPSRT wants to create more civil society space.

Table 1: POP vs. PPSRT: A comparison

| Problem orientation And Police vs. citizens role | POP | PPSRT |
|---|---|---|
| Nature of problem | Violation of law | Violation of expectation |
| Definition of problem | Define by law | Define by the people |

| Ownership of problem | Police | People |
|---|---|---|
| Solution to problem | Police provide solution to problem | People draw upon resources to solve problem |
| Means to solve problem | More police (staff, legal, coercive) resources | More community resources of every kind (legal, social, economical, political, cultural) |
| Role of police | State control agent | Police as depository of social resources |
| Role of citizen | Citizens help the police to fight crime | Citizens help themselves to solve problems |

### Bittner on police as a coercive resource

In an equally important and provocative article, Bittner convincingly argues that "the role of the police is to address all sorts of human problems insofar as their solutions do or may possibly require the use of force at the point of their occurrence."[59] More specifically, police are "best understood as a mechanism for the distribution of non-negotiable coercive force employed in accordance with the dictates of an intuitive grasp of situational exigencies."[60]

Bittner came to this definition of the role of the American police after observing how police work in the field in one U.S. state. He observed that the police are the only social institution legally empowered to use force to settle problems in our society in peacetime.

Bittner argues that in most cases police force is not needed and never will be used. However, that does not mean that force *might not* be necessary, as a last resort. To Bittner it is not the actuality or even the probability of using force that defines the role of police; it is the possibility (no matter how slim) and potentiality for the use of force that justifies the definition of the role of the police.

More pertinent for our analysis, Bittner postulates that everyone expects the police possibly to use force to solve problems when they call the police.

Bittner and I agree on one thing: that people call police as a resource to solve their problems. I do not agree with Bittner, however, that all or even a majority of people call the police because of the police's "capacity and authority" to use force. I postulate that people call police because it is a useful social resource to solve their personal problems. The most important resource the police have to offer is not coercion but legitimacy.

My disagreement with Bittner is based on the following arguments:

The public calls the police for a variety of reasons, not all of them requiring the use of force. In fact, most of the problems for which the public calls the police defy the use of force for a satisfactory resolution. For example, when the police are called to help locate a lost relative, the public does not expect the police to use force because force is of no use. Bittner is stretching his logic in order to make a point.

According to PPSRT, people call the police to solve their personal problems because they do not have (or unwilling to use) the personal or community resources to deal with the problem at hand. That is to say, if people have the necessary resources to solve the problem, they will not call the police. Because personal or community resources to deal with a given problem are not evenly distributed, some people will call the police for help while others will not. If the same problem could be solved by citizens without force, it is far-fetched to claim that people who call the police on the same kind of problem do so because the police have a "capacity and authority" to use force as a "contingency," however remote. In most matters that call for police involvement, forceful intervention is inappropriate or even counterproductive.

In some cases, people call police precisely because they do not want force to be used. For example, people may call police as arbitrators in a family dispute in order to avoid the use of force.

According to PPSRT, whether a citizen is seeking the police "capacity and authority" to use force certainly depends on whether the citizen has the "capacity and authority" to use force *relative* to the police, thereby making the police "capacity and authority" superfluous. In cases where the citizen has the "capacity and authority" to use force, for example, arresting and turning a thief over to the police, he has no need to invoke the police for its "capacity and authority" to use force but only to process the person through the next stage of the criminal justice system. For example, if citizens are equipped with guns, they can and will defend themselves against criminals without calling the police.

Most people call the police because of other authority the police possess besides the use of force. For example, people see police as a moral authority representing the people and the state, or a "legitimacy resource." As such, they follow police instructions voluntarily and instinctively, and expect others to do so. Similarly, in Imperial China, the instruction of the father was instantly obeyed, less so because he could use force to exact compliance than because of his elevated social status and ultimate moral authority. Within the Roman Catholic Church, the admonition of the Pope is never challenged because he possesses supreme religious stature and moral authority. The whole point here is that force is only one of the many resources used by the police to put things in order, and arguably the least effective resource.

Finally, and perhaps most important, Bittner's formulation assumes that all people in all cultures at all times look at the coercive role of the police with the same expectations. This presupposition runs counter to the first lesson learned about policing and society. How people of a given society in a certain era conceive of the police and their relationship with society must, of necessity, depend on the cultural understanding of that society about the role, functions, and relationship of the police to the public. Among some tribes in prehistoric times, for example, priests would perform policing functions, and they were readily obeyed without the threat or use of force.

POP that fashions individual self-help promotes moral and individual justice over and above legal or universal justice. Instead of asking whether there is a crime, the question is asked which law can be used to solve the problem? Applying "individual justice" to criminal cases, although not the norm within the Anglo-American criminal justice system, is not entirely unheard of. The juvenile justice system, for example, is based on the individual justice approach, where the juvenile is not treated as a criminal but as a person with a problem in need of help. "The principle of individualized justice is more inclusive than the principle of the offense. It contains many more criteria in its framework of relevance. ...The principle of individualized justice suggests that disposition is to be guided by a *full understanding* of the client's personal and social character and by his 'individual needs.'"[61]

### Crime problem as a function of resource deprivation

When people call the police, they do so because they need help to solve a problem. A problem arises as a result of unmet expectations due to resource deficit. Expectations can be met by deploying proper resources. For example, a simple theft is a problem because it breaches a number of expectations: The victim does not expect to be violated; the victim does not expect to lose money; the victim does not expect to have to walk to work, and so on. Alternatively, problems can be solved by lowering of expectation. Many people do not call the police to report a crime precisely because they do not think the police are willing or able to help, or simply not worth their while to do so.

The victim might not need to call the police, however, if he has resources to meet those expectations even after the theft. For example, if the victim is rich, he might be protected by security guards. If he has insurance, he can claim coverage. If he is the "Godfather", he is inclined to settle the score himself. Alternatively, when an employee steals money from the bank, she is fired, and not turned over to the police. Here the bank has a different set of expectations. The problem is how to avoid adverse publicity, not getting an untrustworthy employee punished.

The most appropriate ways to deal with crime as a personal or social problem are: first, to identify what problems are confronted by the people; and second, to afford the people the necessary resources to prevent or resolve such problems.

This is exactly what Chinese emperors did; they avoided crime through enrichment (material resources) and education (mental resources) of the people.

## Role of government—the police as suppliers of resources

In Imperial China, problems of "crime" and issues with "punishment" were considered philosophically as integrated governance issues. The philosophy of good governance has one objective: how to perfect the emperor's rule approximating the mandate of heaven. Good governance requires the moral leadership and benevolent rule of the emperor, manifested as stern discipline for intellectuals, ethical education for the public, sound economic policy, and paternalistic social programs, all presented as universal principles and best practices of a good government.

Guan Zhong [62] was appointed prime minister of the state of *Qi* in 685 B.C. He was known for his enlightened reform policy in strengthening the state and improving the livelihood of the people. Guan Zhong's major approach to enforcing law, maintaining order, and preventing crime was by providing for the material well-being of the people. According to him, the effective governance of people starts with the provision of physical security and material well-being. In this regard, Guan Zhong made clear: "When citizens are rich, they will settle peacefully at home and pay attention to the family; if they settle peacefully at home and pay attention to the family, they will be respectful of authority and fearful of crime; if they are respectful of authority and fearful of crime, they are susceptible to rule."[63]

In order to govern well, the state must inculcate the people with four dispositions: *li*, *yi*, *lian*, and *qi*. Specifically, people who know etiquette ("li") will not transgress norms; thus people will not undermine authority. People who know honesty ("yi") will not ask for more than deserve; thus people will not act dishonestly. People who know honor ("lian") will not cover up bad deeds; thus people will not indulge in illegality and immorality. People who know shame ("qi") will not tolerate injustice; thus people will stand evil conduct. The best governmental policy is to remove people's anxiety, poverty, needs, and evil. Conversely, the worst policy is to use punishment and coercion, because punishment can never effectively remove desire, and coercion has a tendency to breed resentment and rebellion.

This brief discussion on Chinese history and philosophy makes clear that the best way to fight crime and disorder is to secure the people from needs (materials resources) and educate the people to think (intellectual resources) and behave morally (moral resources). Once people are empowered materially, intellectually, and morally, they are less inclined to commit crimes. That is the reason that crime rates in China have historically been so low.

## Section 6—Discussion, Argumentation, Justification

### A democratic theory of policing

For a long time, police have been seen in the image of the state, not the people. This has led Marl Findlay and Ugljesa Zcekic to observe, "Because of the traditional and on-going claim of the state over police power and function it is not possible to develop an understanding of various policing styles without considering their connection to (or removal from) state-centered or 'official' policing."[64]

State-centered policing has marginalized indigenous and private social controls in favor of public and formal ones.

There are many reasons why a state conception of police power came into prominence and retained its dominance through time.

First, historically, police were originally established by the ruler to secure imperial control.[65]

Second, police power has been closely aligned with the security and well-being of the state.[66]

Third, until very recently, state control through state power has been unquestioned and unquestionable. It was unquestioned because the state's right to govern was considered to have derived from heaven and follow natural law. It was unquestionable because the state did not allow its power to be challenged. People were conditioned into unreflective submission and instinctual acceptance. John Austin appropriately called this "habits of obedience."[67]

Fourth, the state promotes and perpetrates an "emotional-moral" construction of state/police power, largely framed within the ideological terrain of that society's hegemonic group to legitimize its rule and facilitate its control.[68] Karl Marx observed the justice process being distorted under the superstructure[69] and Peter Manning described police image being transformed through "dramatic performance."[70]

With respect to community control, the principle behind it is citizen self-government. There are a number of ways to instill community control in the police, including establishing neighborhood police forces to placing control of police in the hands of local elected officials, organizing "trade unions" of those who are being policed to hear grievances and force changes on the police, and finally seeking "transformation of the police. All these measures seek to establish a de facto community control over the police by informal means."[71] None of these community control measures, however, places control of the police at the individual level and in the hands of the affected citizen, that is, the person calling for police service.[72] PPSRT makes citizens control of police powers a reality.

The rationale and justification for citizen involvement and participation in the criminal justice process is that of citizens' rights and responsibilities. The case for democratization of the criminal justice process is most eloquently stated by Todd R. Clear and David R. Karp:

> The shift toward citizen participation (in state criminal justice) is grounded in two important insights. First, formal social control by police and the courts is a thin layer in a much thicker foundation of institutions and cultural practices that produce social order.... Second, the shift toward citizen participation is grounded in the basic recognition that community members are citizens of a democratic society. Each community member is to be treated with dignity and respect and provided with the autonomy necessary for creating competent, self-reliant, civilly oriented self. This commitment to individuals extends to crime victims as well as to offenders. At the same time, it is assumed that citizens in a democracy must actively work toward the welfare of the whole society and not just look out for themselves. Thus, they are morally obligated to fulfill whatever tasks are necessary to sustain a good society. Our past failures, in part, result from a false assumption that the onus of public safety falls entirely on the criminal justice system.73 (Italian supplied)

This theory explicitly draws a distinction between two forms of policing: democratic and nondemocratic. Within democratic policing, there is a need to draw a further distinction between state and people policing.

Mr. Justice Stephens has made the differences clear between democratic and non-democratic principle of governance (policing):

> Two different views may be taken of the relationship between rulers and their subjects. If the ruler is regarded as the superior of their subject, as being by the nature of his disposition presumably wise and good, the rightful ruler and guide of the whole population, it must necessarily follow that it is wrong to censure him openly, and, even if he is mistaken, his mistakes should be pointed out with utmost respect, and that, whether mistaken or not, no censure should be cast on him likely or designed to diminish his authority. If on the other hand, the ruler is regarded as the agent and servant, and the subject as the wise and good master, who is obliged to delegate his power to the so-called ruler because, being a multitude, he cannot use it himself, it must be evident that his sentiment must be reversed. Every member of the public who censures the ruler for the time being exercises in his own person the right which belongs to the whole of which he forms a part. He is finding fault with his own servant.[74]

As a democratic theory of policing, PPSRT does not explain the police or paternalistic state. In a police state, government officials, from the chief of state to the police officer, are supposed to know what is best for the state and the people. There is an unshakable conviction that there is one set of dominant values—elimination of vice, eradication of corruption, and upholding of justice—and there is one best way—elimination of dissent and suppression of radicals—to achieve it.

Usually the exercise of power in a police state is justified on public welfare and paternalistic grounds. Thus Polizeistaat ("police state"), far from being an oppressive state with unlimited and arbitrary police power, is a benevolent authority working tirelessly to promote the welfare of the people. In the *German Encyclopedia*, a police state is conceived as

> A state which emphasizes welfare and law and order in the widest sense of the word. It assumed the right to unrestricted interference in the private affairs of its subjects, especially with their property and liberty in order to expand general welfare and for protection of public security and order. Owing to its close control of culture and the economy and the restrictions it placed on individual liberty, it was vehemently attacked by the emerging liberal bourgeois movement.[75]

Theoretically, democratic policing in the form of people's policing recognizes as a first principle the people's fundamental right to choose. Simply put, people should have control over their life choices free from government imposition and influence, that is to say, a right to privacy.

Practically speaking, democratic policing postulates that the richness, complexity, and nuances of subjective feelings and personal experience, emotion and all, of the affected individual, are beyond the comprehension and reach of the state. In other words, people know best.

As used here, democratic policing means three things. First, police power is held in trust for the general public. Second, trust power is to be exercised in a responsible manner, without fear or favor. Third, the police are acting as agents of the people and not of the state.

Under a theory of democratic policing, at a minimum, the police are required to take the people's point of view and interest into account before making a decision and taking action. At the maximum, the police should act as agents of the people, having their actions determined and controlled by the people.

There is an inherent tension between considering police power as a public trust and having the police acting as an agent of the people. The trust theory requires the police to act universally with due regard to all the people's interest, uniformly and indiscriminately—following universal justice principles. The police agency theory requires the police to act on behalf of a specific citizen in promoting his welfare or alleviating his problem—following the individual justice principle.

Table 2: Public perspective and private interest as a function of degree of democratic policing:

| **Police political development** | **Perspective** | **Interests** |
|---|---|---|
| Non-democratic policing—imperial policing | State perspective dominates | State interest control |
| Emerging democratic policing—professional policing | State perspective dominates<br><br>State perspective informed by public perspective | State interest control<br><br>State interests accommodate private interests when not incompatible with state interests |

| | | |
|---|---|---|
| Maturing democratic policing—community policing | State perspective dominates<br><br>State adopts public perspective | State interest control<br><br>State interests give way to private interests |
| Progressive democratic policing—people's policing | People's perspective dominates, as reflecting community perspective and as informed by state perspective | Private interests control as overwritten by state interests on fundamental issues |

The particularistic interest of the citizen, being more self-centered and concrete, often runs counter to the collective interest of the people, being more encompassing and abstract. The police power as social resource theory asks that the police respect the will of the citizen who calls the police unless there are good reasons not to do so (e.g. violation of human rights and constitutional law).[76]

The democratic theory of policing is a prescriptive theory to the extent it requires the police to shift from a police power held in trust theory to a police acting as agents of the people theory.

The democratic theory of policing is a descriptive theory to the extent that, notwithstanding existing traditional conceptions of police as law enforcement agents, all empirical evidence points to the fact that citizens calling the police have much influence on when and where police power is invoked. As one researcher puts it, "The pattern of police compliance with complainants gives police work a radically democratic character."[77]

The democratic nature of police activities is structured by the administrative and social organization of policing. In this regard, Donald Black has pointed out that police power is socially organized according to democratic principles because:

Every citizen can invoke police service at will and without much cost. Most police work is reactionary in nature and driven by public demand.

The people, not the police, are the true gatekeepers of the criminal justice system by making the decision to call the police.

Police work is heavily information based. The police must rely entirely on the public (complainants and witnesses) to provide the necessary information to mount investigations, make arrests, and secure convictions.

The police routinely defer to the preference and judgment of the public in taking action against law violators, for example, whether or not a complainant will press charges.

### A theory of policing, recognizing individual agency, personality, and humanity

Existing literature on policing shows that until recently police treated the public as an appendage of the criminal justice system, always in the background and never to be heard. Police complaints are treated as case files. Crime victims are considered as material witnesses. Overall, the police are more concerned with enforcing the law and making arrests than attending to people's problems and concerns.

PPSRT argues that the police should recognize the agency, personality, and humanity of individual citizens. It also argues for the promotion of individual choice as a matter of personal privacy, protected by the constitution.

Philosophically, people's policing recognizes the centrality of the individual's experience in defining his/her own identity and existence. It accepts without question the interest and capacity of the individual to conduct his/her life and attend to his/her own affairs. In more common terms, each one has to live his/her own life on his/her own terms and in his/her own way.

More pragmatically, people's policing, in inviting and empowering the people to solve their own problems, improves upon the efficiency and effectiveness of policing in a number of ways:

First, the people who are the closest to the problem are in the best position to understand its background, context and impact. This is an understanding argument.

Second, only the people who have experienced the problem can appreciate the emotions involved. This is an appreciation argument.[78]

Third, only the person who lived with the problem is entitled to judge.[79] This is an ownership argument.

Fourth, the affected people are in the best position to provide for an effective solution to the problem. This is a remedy argument.

Fifth, the affected person is more motivated to work out a good solution. This is motivation argument.

Overall, the police are less willing, able, and cost-effective than the people in dealing with their own problems.

In more theoretical terms, if police power is a limited resource, it is essential to make use of it in the most effective and economical manner.

Should people's problem be solved by the state? Professor F.A. Hayek states the question thus:

> The question is whether for this purpose it is better for the holder of coercive power to confine himself in general to creating conditions under which the knowledge and initiative of individuals is given the best scope so that they can plan most successfully; or whether a rational utilization of our resources requires central direction[80] and organization according to some consciously constructed "blueprint."

Politically, as a matter of privacy of choice, individuals should have the unencumbered right to make critical decisions pertaining to life, property, and liberty. Current police practice does not recognize the importance of self-determination in problem solving.

The best example to illustrate the importance of private choice in the utilization of police power is that of a rape victim. For all too long, crime victims in general and rape victims in particular have been made an incidental but necessary appendage of the criminal justice system. The rape victim's active assistance is required to prosecute the rapist successfully. However, beyond such meager engagement, the rape victim is left to deal with her own personal and emotional problems. Throughout the criminal justice process, the rape victim is never recognized as a person in her own right but only as a complainant and a witness.

## A theory of policing from the people's perspective

The theory promises to explain the reality of policing at the street level as it reconceptualizes the role and function of police from the perspective of the people.

To say that PPSRT is a theory of policing at the street level is to suggest that the study of police role, functions, and conduct must start with understanding policing in the street, that is, empirically and sociologically, not positively and legally.

To say that PPSRT is a theory from the perspective of the people is to say that, in a democracy, the police must be defined and understood from the perspective of the people who are using police power as service.

What happen with state perspective of police come into conflict with the people's view? For example, a survey of the United States shows that only one state provides for police service in its constitution or laws.

Table 3: Types of police roles specified in state law

| Role | Number of States | Percentage of States |
|---|---|---|
| Peacekeeper (PK) | 3 | 6 |
| Law Enforcement (LE) | 22 | 44 |
| Service (S) | 0 | 0 |
| PK/LE/S | 0 | 0 |
| PK/LE | 24 | 48 |
| PK/S | 0 | 0 |
| LE/S | 1 | 2 |
| Total | 50 | 100 |

Adapted from "Table 3: Types of Police Roles Specified in State Law," Velmer S. Burton, Jr., James Frank, Robert H. Langworthy, and Troy Barker, "The Prescribed Roles of Police in a Free Society: Analyzing State Legal Codes," *Justice Quarterly* 10 (4):683–695 (1993).

This observed disparity in police role and function raises the issue of "impossible mandate"[81] and poses challenges to the legitimacy of the police. The conflicting roles of the police can be reconciled if police work is not looked at entirely and exclusively from the police's perspective, but is also considered from the people's perspective. In doing this, I am taking seriously Flanagan's invitation to allow the public's expectation of the police to influence the actual performance of the police in the street.[82]

In concrete terms, PPSRT argues that from the people's perspective all requests for police assistance are in reality requests for police to solve a community or personal problem. Viewed in this light, what are known as police activities of various kinds are, in actuality, community and personal problems of one form or another. Thus a "problem oriented" approach to police work at a personal level lends conceptual unity and, in turn, theoretical integration to a variety of police functions. In so doing, the theory individualizes, personalizes, contextualizes, and particularizes what have long been considered simple police/legal problems.

The failure to look at policing from the people's perspective will have serious consequences, from lack of legitimacy to denial of service to engagement in self-help. The conflicts between value judgments and cognitive assumptions embedded in law vs. culture have long been recognized. For example, for Friedrich Carl von Savigny, law should give expression to the "spirit" (*Volksgeist*) of the people.[83]

The reduction of law to a written form and a product of legislative processes, transforms a customary law based on "the relations of individuals arising out of chance circumstances" into "an aspect of political power."[84] Researchers have shown that people, especially ethnic minorities, are less inclined to invoke the law if the value of the law does not conform to their own cultural attitude toward law.[85]

The theory as proposed—citizens solving their own problems with state resources—is consistent with the privatization of policing movement, civil society trends, community policing developments, and consumer choice initiatives. Privatization of policing relegates traditional police responsibilities to private security agencies, thereby allowing the public to have the fullest control over the delivery of police service. The civil society movement calls for private citizens and NGOs to take care of their own social control problems. The community policing development asks citizens to participate in policing the community. The consumer choice initiative, as part of a larger performance culture in government, requires the police to be responsive to citizens' needs.

Consistent with these movements and trends, PPSRT, if ever fully realized, will allow the public to be the master of their own affairs. They will have the right to dictate and control the extent and manner of the state's involvement in their life choices. More specifically, the public will be given de jure control of state police power in dealing with their own problems as they see fit.

## A theory of policing about self-help

PPSRT explains why and how the people should play a key role in the deployment of police power as a social resource to solve their problems. To that extent, this is a theory about individual self-help, private ordering, and personalized justice as a manifestation or reaffirmation of responsible or autonomous citizenship.

This theory, in proposing people's self-help to solve (crime) problems, departs from past police practices. People are not supposed to help themselves to deal personally with crime, law, and order problems. Those who do are described in pejorative terms (e.g., as vigilantes). The people are both denied the power to defend themselves (e.g., handguns are regulated), and are subject to strict liability if they do (e.g., they will be held accountable for the unreasonable use of force). In the end and with much reluctance, people are forced to seek out the police for help and are subjected to the dictates of the police

It is the observation of this chapter that, though the police dominate and control the people over service delivery of police power, law, and order, there is increasing and ample evidence to suggest that it has not been altogether successful.

Do people really want "self-help"? The argument over the need for state policing vs. people's policing turns on this issue. The best answer comes from looking at why people are reluctant to call the police when they are in trouble.

It has often been argued that the public fail to call the police because they are ignorant of the requirement of the law or dismissive of the useful role of the police. The remedy often suggested is more and better public education. The state fails to realize or refuses to accept, though, that no amount of public education and legal sanction can change people's basic instinct and common sense view of the world, about what a crime is, and what police should do. More pertinent, most people want to solve their own problems in their own way and on their own terms.

In this regard, the state has failed consistently to recognize that the people's supposed "ignorance" of the law is actually a quite natural and logical view of the disutility of the law, e.g., to the people justice delay is justice denied. More to the point, in solving problems, people are not interested in upholding state law and pursuing universal justice in the abstract. They are only concerned with pursuing self-interest and personal morality in concrete terms. In this way, all crimes and emergencies requiring police attention are individual problems denominated in personal terms as reflecting broader cultural and social influences and concrete interpersonal and situational determinants.

## A theory of police as a social resource

The understanding of police roles and functions must start with understanding man in society, particularly why people chose collective rather than individual existence. Alternatively, what the society, and in turn the police, can do for an individual when he cannot do for himself.

"A society is a group of unequal beings organized to meet common needs."[86] People as biological humans with various endowments and divergent purposes get together as a natural collective to harness group capacity in achieving a common goal—facilitating social intercourse, providing for mutual security, and increasing productivity (i.e., providing for the needs of all members).

Audrey says, "The just society, as I see it, is one in which sufficient order protect members, whatever their diverse endowments, and sufficient disorder provides every individual with full opportunity to develop his genetic endowment, whatever that many be."[87]

In conclusion, it is interesting to compare Hobbes with the Chinese image of the world, in accounting communal cooperation and collective life. To Hobbs, a strong central state is necessary to prevent people from killing each other. Thus, people live together not because they want to, but because they have to for survival. On the other hand, the Chinese view promotes banding together for the mutual benefit of all.

Collective society provides for security in three senses: security from external attack, internal disorder, and natural emergencies. The collective can be better able to provide for the security of all because a corporate entity has more resources than individuals do. It must also be remembered that the concept of the importance of the individual distinct from the collective, as discussed here, was not widely accepted or even imagined before the fourteenth century

The group, as an integration of all the individuals into a holistic entity, thinks, feels, and acts in unison. What harms the individual also threatens the group. The evidence in support of this thesis is overwhelming and needs no elaborate support. The group and not the individual is the social, political, and economic organizational unit, as evidenced, for example, by the blood feud and moral solidarity. It led Kant to observe that crime is a violation of society and must be avenged.

This observation is of great theoretical import in our struggle to come to terms with the understanding of police and policing in pre-modern days. First, inasmuch as the individual does not survive the collective, there is no separate and distinct harm when one member of the collective is attacked from without. The referent group, to which the individual belongs, not the individual himself, must be avenged. When the individual is attacked from without, the collective can raise an army. When the individual is attacked from within, the collective can call the police.

It was Graham Sumner who observed, "If we put together all we have learnt from anthropology and ethnography about primitive men and primitive society we perceive that the first task of life is to love [i.e. to survive] ... Need was the first experience and it was followed by some blundering effort to satisfy it."[88]

Thus, from the very beginning, the human race has been understandably obsessed with survival. In order to survive, people have to get together to solve problems, large and small, which structures the social relationship within the collective. More specifically, in the primitive world, people discover strength, security, and welfare in numbers. They find that intercourse, security, and productivity can be better enhanced and secured by collective effort rather than individual action.[89] Two things stand out. First, everyone in the collective is committed to helping one another get over difficulties. Everyone is his brother's keeper. Everyone is a mediator, police officer, and soldier as they move from one role to another unconsciously and as called upon by the situation at hand.

Second, every kind of power and resource is brought to bear on a problem indiscriminately, and later in an integrated and holistic manner. Organization and justification for the use of power come much later. The problem defines the solution, not the other way around. Wicked people, sick people, and criminals are treated alike with reference to the need for preservation, protection, and advancement of community interests. They are a disruption to and deviance from a firmly established and clearly delineated normative order and must be dealt with accordingly. People are concerned with result (removing danger) and not process (correct vs. incorrect ways). This places modern-day police power—an all embracing social resource to solve emerging problems—in historical context, providing clues to its true understanding.

In the modern world, in the name of effectiveness, efficiency, and morality, police are institutionalized, specialized, and professionalized. Police power is classified, organized, and structured. A reification process takes place. Roles and functions of policing are defined with respect to what police do, de jure or de facto, as intended or by effect. Likewise, police power is defined with reference to what police should possess when they go about their duties. This definition of police roles and powers departs substantially from and takes us conceptually far away from our original and natural understanding of what police power is all about in collective life (i.e., the embodiment of aggregate social resources in the management and solving of day to day emergencies and crises confronted by the people individually).

Viewed in this light, police power is an institutionalized and specialized social resource to assist the individual members of a collective to achieve personal security.

Police organizations are set up to deal with personal security and emergency issues because they have the ideological, legal, administrative, coercive, organizational, informational, and technological means bestowed by the government for serving the people. The police officer is both a provider and gatekeeper of valuable and critical social resources.

The public's personal view of police is simple. The public lives in a social and cultural world unto themselves. The meaning of police must be found in the social milieu, cultural context, and personal experience of the person calling the police. For example, most citizens have very little knowledge of the law and look at problems differently than a police officer. Studies have shown that people are ignorant of the law.[90]

The empirical evidence indicates and this theory postulates that the people do not like to engage the police and invoke their power to solve problems, except as a last resort.

Alternatively, the public prefers to invoke the personal resources of family, clan, guild, or friends to help with a problem.

Why then do people report problems to the police? It is because their personal or associated resources are insufficient for dealing with the problem. In other words, they believe that they have no alternative.

PPSRT argues, additionally, that when a person cannot solve his problem and the police are not able to help, he/she will resort to illegal means.

At a more theoretical level, this formulation of police roles and functions, in breaking with traditional wisdom, requires the strongest justifications. Theoretically, the issue is why the state should be responsible for making power resources available to help the citizen solve his problem. On the practical side, if the state is ever responsible, to what extent and under what circumstances is it responsible?

The idea that the state should make available state police power as a social resource to the public can be justified philosophically, politically, legally, socially, historically, and empirically.

Philosophically, in order to survive and reproduce itself, the state must teach its people to cooperate and adopt moral principles of reciprocity.[91]

Politically, the state has an affirmative duty to help its citizens take care of their problems in the most minimal way (i.e., by helping the citizens to help themselves, specifically by providing citizens with sufficient resources). This formulation of the state's role in the police context differs from the current police role in the following regards: (1) Theoretically, the police have a role to protect but not assist citizens. The police do not have a legal duty to do both, but in practice, they do both. (2) Legally, police power is a resource at the disposal of the state by and through police officers in the street. The public has no legal control over police power.

The Social Contract, as a justification for the state, argues that people give up liberty for security. State police power as a social resource argues for an expansive definition of security, which includes the state providing resources to take care of people's problems when they are in need suddenly due to circumstances beyond their control. In this way, the state may be conceived of as the ultimate insurer of our pressing needs.

Legally, the availability of law as a resource for management of personal problems has a long and well-established intellectual history. One of the major functions of civil law is for the public to use the law for personal ends. For example, social workers always use law as a resource to solve their clients' problems.

The state police power as a social resource calls for returning of the power of self-determination to the people. Instead of the conventional wisdom that the citizen's problem is transformed into a police problem once the police are called, the theory calls for citizens to play a more active role in determining how police powers should be used consistent with the law.[92]

Historically, Peel's "new police" were proposed as a crime prevention and order maintenance force, but it turned out that the police provided more service to the people than first anticipated. As one noted British historian observed, "They [the working class] may not necessarily have liked the police, but the political rhetoric was that the police were there to serve and to protect everyone, and it was perfectly valid to utilise that service."[93]

More significantly, consistent with our theory of police power as resource, the police were used by the people to solve personal and community problems from locating missing persons to contacting people living abroad to providing for child discipline.

Local police forces even engaged in providing for welfare services for the less advantaged and establishing charitable funds to assist the poor. "In the 1870s and early 1880s two superintendents in the Lancashire Constabulary, apparently independently, established soup kitchens for the poor children in their divisions, supplied them with clothes and even arranged summer excursions.... Police collect money on sport days to be used to purchase new tools for the colliers who had lost theirs in disaster."[94]

From 1838 to 1857, Horncastle, a small town in Lincolnshire, was allowed to run its own police force under the Lighting and Watching Act of 1833. The Act required detailed record keeping, including fortnightly meetings of "Inspectors" and collection of police notebooks. A close reading of the records finds that the townspeople were concerned about problems of one sort or another, but not about significant crime. Those problems included everything from disposal of sewage to the care of animals.

## Section 7—Conclusion

The whole purpose of this chapter is to introduce a new way of thinking about CP, making policing a people's business and a problem-solving exercise. This novel method of CP is encapsulated in a new theory of policing: PPSRT.

The core principle that drives this research is China's MLP, captured by Mao's statement, "The people, and the people alone, are the moving force in the making of world history."[95]

In the case of Mao's policing, the political principle of ML formed the basis of "people's policing," whereby the local people are supposed to police themselves.

Under Mao, MLP preached that in the context of fighting against political crimes and later all social crimes, the people's participation was indispensable to winning the "people's war."[96] Thus, in the suppression of counterrevolutionaries, the police were supposed to understand, trust, mobilize, and rely on the people."[97] The police played a supplemental, not central, role. In all, the people were considered the lifeblood and backbone of the police.

Practically and operationally, this means that the police must see things from the people's perspective, seek their support, and be amenable to their supervision.[98] Any policing detached and isolated from the people would not be effective in finding local problems and detecting criminals.

There are many reasons for engaging the people in MLP. First, the people have the right as a ruling class to participate in their own governance. This is akin to the idea and ideal of localism in the United States, where all the powers of the central government come from the people. "Legislators enact many laws but do not attempt to reach those countless matters of local concern necessarily left wholly or partly to those who govern at the local level."[99]

Second, the people have the responsibility to fight crime. In the PRC people's rights and responsibilities are complementary. The PRC Constitution (1982) Article 33 provides that "Citizens enjoy rights guaranteed by the Constitution and law but they must also fulfill their constitutional and legal responsibility." This is akin to the notion of "communitarianism" in the United States, which is defined as "a mindset that says the whole community needs to take responsibility for itself. People need to actively participate, not just give their opinions ... but instead give time, energy, and money."[100]

Third, the people are in the best position to see that "people's justice" is done, including making decisions on who to police, what to police, and how to police. Mao supplied the rationale for MLP in his "Report on an Investigation of the Peasant Movement in Hunan." He wrote, "The peasants are clear sighted. Who is bad and who is not quite vicious, who deserves severe punishment and who deserves to be let off lightly—the peasants keep clear accounts and very seldom has the punishment exceeded the crime."[101] This is akin to the idea in the U.S. that the community notion of order and justice prevails over the rule of law.[102]

Fourth, the people were deemed to be more motivated, thus more vigilant, as an oppressed class to detect counterrevolutionaries.[103] This is akin to the idea that citizens of a state, as with employees of an organization, naturally seek responsibility if they are allowed to "own" a problem.

Fifth, the people are in the best position, being more able, efficient, and effective in conducting the people's business. Criminals and counterrevolutionaries live in the mass. They cannot long survive within the mass without being exposed. This is akin to the notion in the U.S. that the people are the best source of intelligence for the police.[104]

Sixth, the police could not be everywhere at the same time and in any one place all the time. This is especially the case in the sparsely populated border and rural areas.[105] It is unlikely that the police could be informed of illegal activities if it were not for the people.[106]

In comparing and contrasting CP and MLP, it must be noted that there are substantial differences between the two in theory and practice.

MLP is the embodiment of a political ideology— communism. The ultimate objective of communism is to transform the society from a capitalistic to a communist one, through raising the consciousness of the "mass." As such, MLP is an end unto itself. Practice of MLP is practicing communism.

CP, in contrast, is a policing philosophy. Its ultimate objective is to improve the efficiency and effectiveness of the police by working with the people. As such, it is a means to an end. The practice of CP simply improves policing.

The tougher debate is whether MLP and CP are conceptually distinguishable, when CP also serves the people in a democratic society. More significantly, in practical terms a clear distinction between MLP and CP cannot be drawn when, for all intents and purposes, policing cannot be effective without the volunteer participation and active engagement of the people in reporting crime, supplying intelligence, and giving evidence. Viewed in this light, the conceptual discussion may be too academic to be of relevance and too refined to make a difference. However, the distinction is an important one. When it is said that MLP is an inseparable part of a larger and all-encompassing ideological framework of communism, it implies a number of things:

First, MLP is not a stand-alone philosophy, theory, concept, strategy, policy, or practice, all of which have been ascribed to CP. In fact, separate from its roots and cut away from its cloth, MLP has no meaning. MLP is the embodiment of communism. The suggestion that since MLP is communism in action just like CP is democracy in action, and thus there is no discernible difference between the two, fails to capture the essence of MLP and its relationship with communism. MLP is not something a police officer thinks or does, though invariably communists think and act consistently with ML principles.

Second, MLP is a dynamic process, just as communism is. Communism is a never ending process of regeneration, renewal, and refinement, always arriving but never having arrived. This is particularly so when society is in the process of moving toward communism, a stage where China is now, called the "primary stage of socialism." During the primary stage, MLP takes on different missions, objects, and measures. In the early days of the revolution, MLP sought to protect the Party from domestic counterrevolutionaries and external enemies. It called for mass mobilization for violent struggles against class enemies of all kinds. In the primary stage of socialism, the MLP focuses on securing democratic dictatorship of the people with rule by law under established processes. MLP is now concerned with dealing with contradictions among friends more than struggles with class enemies.

The CP principle is a static philosophy capable of generating many strategies and creative applications. However the core principle, that policing works best when the community is engaged and involved, does not change. In this regard, CP is applicable in democratic as well as communist countries, in urban areas as well as small towns, with uniform policing as well as detective investigation.

Third, with arrival of communism, the "masses" are to be the masters of their own destiny. There is no need for a separate organized police organ to provide for policing in a communist state. Before that, MLP is policing by the mass.

Table 4: Comparing traditional theoretical orientation vs. proposed theoretical orientation

| Dimension of Police Power | Traditional Theoretical Orientation | Theoretical Premises | Proposed Theoretical Orientation | Theoretical Premises |
|---|---|---|---|---|
| Ideological base | State | Power as instrumentality of State | Democratic | Power as a resource of the people |
| Perspective | Police | Police professional perspective | Public | Public personal perspective |
| Vantage Point | Top Down | Power is created and imposed from a center | Bottom Up | Power rendered and shared by the people |
| Orientation | Past | Mechanical solidarity<br>Punitive law<br>Public justice<br>Defendant's rights | Future | Organic solidarity<br>Restitution law<br>Private justice<br>Victim's welfare |
| Method | Consensus | People are more alike than different | Critical | People are more different than alike |
| Dimension | Unitary | Power as control | Pluralistic | Power as resource |
| Defined by | Law | Power justified by legal rule | Problem | Power justified by situational needs |
| Structured by | Bureaucracy | Rational rule | Culture | Historical—cultural—customary norms |
| Function | Coercion | Non-contingent and non-negotiable force to suppress | Resource | Contingent and negotiable resource to resolve |
| Purpose | Control | Monopolistic/Central/Political/Ideological | Empowerment | Pluralistic/Local/Social/Personal |
| Availability | Supply | Determined by interests | Demand | Determined by morality |
| Application | Executed | Imposed by police | Self-help | Sought out by the public |

## Epilogue

Mao's MLP was espoused some fifty years ago. Since then China has undergone substantial changes, especially in the reform era (1979 to now).

This is especially the case with communism as an ideology.[107] With the demise of communism, what will happen to the MLP? For one good reason, this theory serves to keep MLP alive, long after the disappearance of communism as an ideology. Mao's MLP is a more scientific way of looking at state craft, policing included.

# NOTES

## Chapter One

1. Lening Zhang, Steven F. Messner, and Jianhong Liu, "A Critical Review of Recent Literature on Crime and Criminal Justice in China: Research Findings, Challenges, and Prospects (Introduction)," *Crime, Law and Social Change* 50(3): 125–130 (2008); Mengyan Dai, "Policing in the People's Republic of China: A Review of Recent Literature," *Crime, Law and Social Change* 50(3): 221–227 (2008). Jianhong Liu, "Developing Comparative Criminology and the Case of China," *International Journal of Offender Therapy and Comparative Criminology* 51: 3–8 (2007).
2. Jianhong Liu, Lening Zhang, and Steven F. Messner, *Crime and Social Control in a Changing China* (Westport, CT: Greenwood Press, 2001), vii.
3. Howard L. Boorman, "The Study of Contemporary Chinese Politics: Some Remarks on Retarded Development," *World Politics* 12: 585–599 (1960).
4. Crime and Social Control in a Changing China, op. cit., note 2, *supra*.
5. Mark Sidel, "The Re-Emergence of China Studies in Vietnam," *China Quarterly* (*CQ*) 142: 521–540 (1995).
6. Willem Adriaan Bonger, *Criminality and Economic Conditions*, trans. Henry Pomeroy Horton (New York: Little, Brown, and_Co., 1916), xiii.
7. See Chapter Two "The Idea of Police," infra.
8. See Chapter Eight "Chinese Theory of Community Policing," infra.
9. T'ung-Tsu Chu, *Law and Society in Traditional China* (Paris: Mouton & Co., 1965).
10. Jia Yuying, *Zhongguo gudai jiancha zhidu fazhang shi* (A developmental history of traditional China supervision system) (Beijing: Renmin chubanshe, 2004), 3.
11. William P. Alford, "Law, Law, What Law?: Why Western Scholars of Chinese History and Society Have Not Had More to Say about Its Law," *Modern China* (*MC*) 23 (4): 398–419 (1997).
12. Cyrus H. Peake, "Recent Studies on Chinese Law," *Political Science Quarterly* 52 (1): 117–138 (1937).
13. G.F. Hudson, *Europe and China* (London, Edward Arnold: 1931).
14. Peake, "Recent Studies on Chinese Law," op. cit., note 12, *supra*.
15. Ta Tsing leu lee, being the fundamental laws, and a selection from the supplementary statutes, of the penal code of China (London: T. Cadell & W. Davies, 1810).
16. Robert M. Marsh, "Weber's Misunderstanding of Traditional Chinese Law," *American Journal of Sociology* 106 (2): 281–302 (2000).
17. Peake, "Recent Studies on Chinese Law," 121. op. cit., note 12, *supra*.
18. Ibid., 125.
19. Ibid.
20. Ibid., 126.

21. Shang Yang, *The Book of Lord Shang. A Classic of the Chinese School of Law.* Translated from the Chinese with Introduction and Notes by Dr. J.J.L. Duyvendak (London: Arthur Probsthain, 1928).
22. "Law, Law, What Law?" op. cit., note 11, *supra.*
23. Michael R. Dutton, *Policing and Punishment in China: From Patriarchy to 'the People'* (Cambridge, U.K.: Cambridge University Press, 1992).
24. Michael R. Dutton, *Discipline and Punishment: The Birth of Prison* (Harmondsworth, U.K.: Peregrine Books, 1979).
25. Dutton, Policing and Punishment in China, 5. op. cit., note 23, supra.
26. C. Wright Mills, *The Sociological Imagination* (New York: Oxford University Press, 1959 [1976]).
27. A. R. Radcliffe-Brown, Structure and Function in Primitive Society: Essays and Addresses (London: Cohen and West, 1952), 3.
28. Hanchao Liu, "The Art of History: A Conversation with Jonathan Spence," *The Chinese Historical Review* 11 (2):133–154, 142 (2004).
29. Homer H. Dubs, "'Nature' in the Teaching of Confucius," *Journal of the American Oriental Society* 50: 233–237 (1930).
30. Tao-Wei Hu, "The Chinese Version of the Law of Nature," *International Journal of Ethics* 38 (1): 27–43 (1927).
31. "The Practice of Law as an Obstacle to Justice: Chinese Lawyers at Work," *Law & Society Review* 40:1 (2006).
32. "Why Do They Not Comply with the Law? Illegality and Semi-Legality among Rural-Urban Migrant Entrepreneurs in Beijing," *Law & Society Review* 39 (3): 527–62 (2005).
33. "Law, Law, What Law?" op. cit., note 11, *supra.*
34. Elizabeth J. Perry, "Trends in the Study of Chinese Politics: State-Society Relations," *CQ* 139: 704–713 (1994).
35. Gordon White, "Democratization and Economic Reform in China," *The Australian Journal of Chinese Affairs* 31: 73–92 (1994).
36. Lucian W. Pye, "Review: Social Science Theories in Search of Chinese Realities," *CQ* 132: 1161–1170 (1992).
37. Philip C. C. Huang, "County Archives and the Study of Local Social History: Report on a Year's Research in China," *MC* 8 (1): 133–143 (1982).
38. Philip C. C. Huang, "Theory and the Study of Modern Chinese History: Four Traps and a Question," *MC* 24 (2): 183–208.
39. Tao Tao Liu and David Faure, *Unity and Diversity: Local Cultures and Identities in China* (Hong Kong: Hong Kong University Press, 1996).
40. Seung-hwan Lee, "Asian Values: The Magic Charm," *Asian Values and the Future of the Confucian Culture* 12 (1): 45–61 (2000).
41. Lucian W. Pye, "On Chinese Pragmatism in the 1980s," *CQ* 106: 207–234 (1986).
42. Linda Chelan Li, "The 'Rule of Law' Policy in Guangdong," *CQ* 161: 199–220 (2000).

43. Julia Kwong, "The 1986 Student Demonstrations in China: A Democratic Movement?" *AS* 28 (9): 970–985. (1988).
44. Jie Chen, "Comparing Mass and Elite Subjective Orientations in Urban China," *The Public Opinion Quarterly* 63(2): 193–219 (1999).
45. Linda Chelan Li, "The 'Rule of Law' Policy in Guangdong: Continuity or Departure? Meaning, Significance and Processes," *CQ* 161: 199–220 (2000).
46. Kevin J. O'Brien and Lianjiang Li, "Accommodating 'Democracy' in a One-Party State: Introducing Village Elections in China," *CQ* 162: 465–489 (2000).
47. Peter Howard Corne, "Creation and Application of Law in the PRC," 50 *American Journal of Comparative Law* 369 (2002).
48. "All areas resolutely implement the spirit of National Public Security Bureau Chiefs Meetings" ("Gedi guanche luoshi quanguo gongan-ting-ju zhang huiyi jingshen") *China Police Daily* Online Jan. 11, 2002.
49. Gary G. Hamilton, "Patriarchalism in Imperial China and Western Europe: A Revision of Weber's Sociology of Domination," *Theory and Society* 13 (3): 393–425, 405 (1984).
50. Tian Rushua and Zheng Baitong, "Avoiding Five Misused of Terms in Police and Justice Documents," *PSUJ* 54: 75–79 (1995).
51. Yang Hongping, "The Roles of Publishing Article by Academic Magazines by Police Colleges" ("Gongan gaoxiao xuebao de yonggao yuanze"), *PSUJ* 1: 103-105 (1999).
52. Zhang Jing, "Getting Out of Problems Areas in Public Security Legal News reporting" ("Jiuchu Gongan fazhi baodao de wuqu"), *PSUJ* 54: 79–81 (1995).
53. Li Jianhe, "Thinking about 'A Topic of General Interest' in Comparative Police Discipline," *PSUJ* 101: 43–48 (2002).
54. Kang Daimin, *Discourse on Broad Concept of Public Security* (Beijing: Qunzhong chubanshe, 2001).
55. Boorman, "Study of Contemporary Chinese Politics," 585–599, op. cit., note 3, *supra*
56. Joan Liu, "Finding Chinese Law on the Internet," *GlobaLex* http://www.nyulawglobal.org/globalex/China.htm
57. Jerome Alan Cohen, "New Developments in the Study of Chinese Law: Introduction," *The Journal of Asian Studies* 27 (3): 475–483 (1968).
58. Ministry of Public Security, "Notice regarding prohibiting foreign journalists from illegal reporting activities ("Guanyu jizhi weiguo jizhe feifa caifang hudong de tongzhi") (April 22, 1994).
59. Ole Bruun, Soren Poulsen, Hatla Thelle, MC Research Danish Experience (University of Copenhagen, 1991) Center for East and Southeast Asian Studies, 18–29.
60. Zhang Chao "Discussion of framework of opening of police work" ("Lun jongwu gongkai zhidu goujian"), *PSUJ* 99: 97–105 (2002).
61. The author has published with *PSUJ*, and appointed as an international editor with *Zhejiang Police Journal* (2007 to current). He is one of the very few foreign scholars appointed as an editor.

62. *Gongan Yanjiu*, 78 (1): 8 (2000).
63. Zhou Zhaoping and Zhang Xiaolin, "A Summary of Symposium of Reconstruction of Police Disciplines in China," *PSUJ* 95:106–111 (2002).
64. The Editorial Office, "To Enhance the Research of Public Security Theories and Guide the Practice of Public Security Work," *Gongan Yanjiu* 72: 6–7 (2000).
65. *Gongan Yanjiu* 78 (1): 8 (2000).
66. *Gongan Yanjiu* 79 (2): 77–79 (2000).
67. Zheng Ling "A Brief Discussion of Development and Use of Public Security Literature" ("Qiantan Gongan wexian de gai liyong,"), *PSUJ* 55: 78–81 (1995), 39.
68. "Top Legislator on Implementation of Criminal Procedure Law," *People's Daily*, Monday, November 20, 2000.
69. Kam C. Wong, "Police Legitimacy Crisis and Police Law Reform in China II," *International Journal of Police Science and Management* 7 (1): 1-14 (2005).
70. Kam C. Wong, "Sheltering for Examination: Law, Policy, and Practice," in *Occasional Papers/Reprints Series in Contemporary Asian Studies*, University of Maryland, School of Law (Sept. 1997), 53.
71. Wan Shenzi, Li Zhenyu, Zhang Caigui, and Zhang Lincun, "The Issue about Police Participating—Non-Policing Activities" ("Guanyu gongan minjing canyu fei jingwu huodong de tiaocha"), *Gongan Yanjiu* 69 (1): 21–24 (2000), 22R.
72. Ding Shijie and Fung Liping, *Public Security Applied Writings* ("Gongan Yingyong Xiezuo") (Beijing: Zhongguo renmin Gongan daxu chubanse, 2002), Chapter 1: Public security officials documents ("Gongan jiguan xingzheng gongwen").
73. "Methods of Dealing with Documents of State Administrative Agencies" ("Guojia xingzheng jiguan gongwen chuli banfa") (Promulgated by State Council on February 18, 1987. Amended on November 21, 1993 and August 24, 2001.)
74. Ibid.
75. *Pinyin Chinese English Dictionary* (Hong Kong, Commercial Press, 2005) *PYCED*, 477R.
76. Administrative records, Article 9 (1) (1993).
77. *PYCED*, 822L.
78. Administrative records, Article 9 (2) (1993).
79. *PYCED*, 373R.
80. Administrative records, Article 9 (3) (1993).
81. Security applied writings, 52–53. op. cit., note 72, *supra*.
82. *PYCED*, 902L.
83. Ministry of Public Security, "Notice regarding stern execution of inspection of vehicle registration" ("Guanyu yange jixing hefa cheliang paizheng guiding deng wenti tongzhi").
84. Ji Wei Wei, "Analysis on Calculation of Quotation in Journal of Jiansu Police Officer College," *Journal of Jiansu Police Officer College* 89: 181–188 (2003).
85. Eduard Vermeer, "New County Histories: A Research Note on Their Compilation and value" *MC* 18 (4): 438–467 (1992).
86. "Draft Decision on the Compilation of New County Histories" (1981), 443.

87. Accessible at http://cache.tianya.cn/index.htm?vitem=158
88. Kam C. Wong, Police Stories: Voices from Within (2009). A book manuscript in progress.
89. Kam C. Wong, Police Reform in China: Issues, Problems and Promises (2009). Work in progress.
90. Lucian W. Pye, "On Chinese Pragmatism in the 1980s," *CQ* No. 106: 207–234 (1986).
91. Mathieu Deflem, "Policing International Society: Views from the United States." Review essay on 'Cops Across Borders,' by Ethan A. Nadelmann and 'Crime and Law Enforcement in the Global Village,' edited by William F. McDonald. *Police Forum* 7(3): 6–8 (1997)..
92. "Law, Law, What Law?" op. cit., note 11, *supra*.
93. Philip C. C. Huang, "Biculturality in Modern China and in Chinese Studies," *MC* 26 (1): 3–31 (2000).
94. Chen Yuanxiao, "Ponder over the Sustained Development and Improvement of Policing," *Gongan Yanjiu* 78: 22–26 (2001)
95. *Philip C. C. Huang*, "The Paradigmatic Crisis in Chinese Studies: Paradoxes in Social and Economic History," *MC* 17 (3): 299–341 (1991).

## Chapter Two

1. Zhu Shaohou, *History of Traditional Public Order System in China* (Zhongguo gudai zhian zhidu) (Henan: Henan daxue chubanshe, 1998), 2.
2. David Bayley, *Patterns of Policing: A Comparative International Analysis* (New Brunswick, NJ: Rutgers University Press, 1985).
3. James Q. Wilson, *Varieties of Police Behavior* (Cambridge, Mass.: Harvard University Press, 1968).
4. "On practice," Mao Tsetung, *Five Essays on Philosophy* (Peking: Foreign Language Press, 1977), 1–22.
5. David Bayley, *Forces of Order: Policing Modern Japan*, 2d ed. (Berkeley, CA: University of California Press, 1991).
6. Victor Shaw, *Social Control in China: A Study of Chinese Work Units* (Westport: Greenwood Press, 1996), 19–25.
7. Fei Chengkang, *The Family and Clan Rules in China* (Zhongguo de jiafa zhugui) (Shanghai: Shanghai shehui kexue chubanshe, 1998).
8. Hon Yanlung and Su Yigong, *Contemporary Police History* I (Zhongguo jindai jingchashi) (Beijing: Shehuikexue chubanshe 1999). (Hereinafter: *Contemporary Police History* (1999.)
9. Kam C. Wong, "The Philosophy of Community Policing in China," *Police Quarterly* 4 (2): 186–214 (2001).
10. Liu De, "Preface One." In Mu Yumin, *Beijing Police: A Hundred Years* (Beijing Jingcha Bainian) (Beijing: Zhongguo renmin gongan daxue chubanshe, 2004).
11. Mo Fengyun, "Look Back to Find the Future, Review the Old to Know the New" (Jian wang zhilai, wengu zhixin), *Public Security Studies* vol. 6:5-8 (1989).

12. *Record of Historians: The Self-Preface of Shi Taigong* (Shi Ji. Shi Taigong Zhixu).
13. Zhang Jinfan and Wang Chao, *History of Chinese Political System* (Zhongguo zhengzhi zhidu shi) (Beijing: Zhongguo zhengfa daxue chubanshe 1987).
14. Pu Jian, *Traditional Administration and Legislation in China* (Zhongguo gudai xingzheng lifa) (Beijing: Beijing daxue chubanshe, 1990).
15. *Overview view of Research on Chinese Legal and Institutional history* (Zhongguo falu zhidu shi tonglan) (Tianjin: Tianjin jiaoyu chubanshe, 1989).
16. Sidney David Gamble and John Stewart Burgess, *Peking: A Social Survey Conducted under the Auspices of the Princeton* (New York: George H. Doran Co., 1921), 303–323.
17. *Contemporary Police History* (1999), 18, op. cit., note 8, *supra.*
18. Men Juntian, *Bao Jia system in China* (Shanghai: Commercial Press, 1936).
19. *Contemporary Police History* (1999), op. cit., note 8, *supra.*
20. Frederic Wakeman, Jr., "American Police Advisers and the Nationalist Chinese Secret Service, 1930–1937," *Modern China* 18(2):107–137 (1992); Frederic Wakeman, Jr., "Policing Modern Shanghai," *The China Quarterly* 115: 408–440 (1988); especially "Origin of Shanghai Police," 409.
21. *Contemporary Police History* (1999), 4, op. cit., note 8, *supra.*
22. Frederic Wakeman, Jr., "Policing Modern Shanghai," *The China Quarterly* 115 408–440 (1988).
23. *Contemporary Police History* (1999), 4, op. cit., note 8, *supra.*
24. Ibid. 6.
25. "Reflection and Thinking About Our Nation's Public Security Investigation" (Dui woguo Gongan shi yanjiu de huigu yu shikao), *PSUJ* 152–157 (2004).
26. Editorial staff, "Public Security Higher Education Journals Must Serve the Needs of Contemporary Public Security Struggle needs" (Gongan gaoxiao xuebao yaowei Gongan xianxi douzheng fuwu), *PSUJ* 1: 1–2 (1993).
27. Personal communication with Professor Mei of MPS, January 2008.
28. Michelle Yeh, "The 'Cult of Poetry' in Contemporary China," *The Journal of Asian Studies* 55 (1): 51–80 (1996).
29. Zheng Zhongwu, "Exploring the Historical Origins and Development of Police I, II, III, IV" ("Jingshi yuan liu shitan") *PSUJ* 3: 100-103 (1998); 4:100-103; 4: 84–87 (1998); 5: 108-111 (1998); 6: 87–90 (1998).
30. F. Engels, *The Origin of the Family, Private Property, and the State* (1884).
31. "Exploring the Historical Origins and Development of Police I," op. cit., note 29, *supra.*
32. G. MacCormack, "Hsiang Hsing and Hua Hsiang: The Problem of 'Symbolic' Punishments in Early China," *Revue internationale des droits de l'antiquité*, 2002, 297–325. http://www.ulg.ac.be/vinitor/rida/2002/maccormack.pdf
33. Zheng's assumption of human nature and state of nature resembled that of Jean-Jacques Rosseau, *Social Contact* (1762).
34. Li Kunsheng, "Thinking over the 'Police Theory' and the Construction of Its Academic System," *PSUJ* 4:109–120 (2001).

35. Guo Yuheng, *Chinese History of Public Security* (*Zhongguo baojia zhidu*) (Zhongguo zhian shi) (1997), 250 ff.
36. *Contemporary Police History* (1999), "Preface," op. cit., note 8, *supra*, 1.
37. Yang Hongping, "The Roles of Publishing Article by Academic Magazines by Police Colleges," (Gongan gaoxiao xuebao de yonggao yuanze) [Author's note: Better translated as "Principles governing publication of articles at public security colleges"], *PSUJ* 1: 103–105 (1999).
38. Ma Li "Understanding and rRealizing Public Security Academic Journal Quality Control" (Gongan xueshu qikan zhilian kongzhi de rengshi yu shijian), *PSUJ* 3: 107–109 (1997); Jia Yongsheng, "Personal Views about the Well—Running of the Academic Magazines of Public Security Colleges" (Banhao gongan gao deng yuanxiao xuebao zhi wojian), *PSUJ* 3:101–102 (1997); Xu Yeli, "Regarding reflection on editing by scholars," *PSUJ* 2: 106–109 (1997).
39. The Editorial Department, "The Vocation of Police Journals: Giving Energetic Publicity to the Theme of Spiritual Civilization Construction," *PSUJ* 1: 1–2 (1997).
40. Mao Zedong, *Selected Works on Media work* ("Xinwen gongzuo wenxuan") (Beijing: Xinhua chubanshe,1983).
41. Xu Zhengqiang, "The Characteristics of Professional Academic Journals and Quality of Editors" (Zhuanye xing xueshu qikan de teshi yu bianji suzhi), *PSUJ* 3: 99-102 (2000).
42. Michael Bond, *Beyond the Chinese Face. Insights from Psychology* (Oxford: Oxford University Press, 1992).
43. Hao Xiajun and Mao Lei, *Comparison between China and West in 500 Years* (Bijing: Xinhua chubanshe, 1996).
44. Liu Tingsheng (ed.), *Treatise on Early Qin Public Security Ideas* (Xian Qin zhian sixiang lungao) (Beijing: Wenhi chubanshe, 2000).
45. Thomas Metzger, "The Western Concept of the Civil Society in the Context of Chinese History," Stanford CA: Hoover Institute (n.d.).
46. "Synthetic Reason, Aesthetic Order, and the Grammar of Virtue," *Journal of the Indian Council of Philosophical Research* 18 (4): 13–28 (2001).
47. See "II. The Intellectuals and Confucian Ethics." In pages 36–39, Kam C. Wong, "The Behavior of Qing Dynasty Speech Crime Law in China: A Cross-Cultural Application of Black's Theory of Law." Dissertation, School of Criminal Justice, University at Albany, State University of New York (1998).
48. Philip J. Ivanhoe, *Confucian Moral Self Cultivation* (Indianaplis, IN: Hackett Pub Co; 2nd edition) (March 1, 2000).
49. Ge Fang et al., "Social Moral Reasoning in Chinese children: A Developmental Study," *Psychology in School* 40(1): 125–138 (2003).
50. Fareed Zakaria "Culture Is Destiny; A Conversation with Lee Kuan Yew," *Foreign Affairs* March/April, 1994.
51. Jianhong Liu, Lening Zhang and Steven F. Messner, *Crime and Social Control in a Changing China* (Westport: Greenwood Press, 2001).
52. Cecilia Chan, "The Cultural Dilemmas in Dispute Resolution: The Chinese Experience," Conference of Enforcing Equal Opportunity in Hong Kong, Hong

Kong University, June 14, 2003. http://www.hku.hk/ccpl/pub/conferences/documents/14062003a-CeciliaChan.pdf

53. Donald C. Clarke, "Dispute Resolution in China," *Journal of Chinese Law* 5(2): 245-267 (1991).
54. John R. Watt, *The District Magistrate in Late Imperial China* (New York: Columbia University Press, 1972).
55. Bradley W. Reed, "Money and Justice: Clerks, Runners, and the Magistrate's Court in Late Imperial Sichuan," *Modern China* 21(3): 345–83 (1995).
56. Chen Yu and Mao Wei, "The Three Social Stratum and Legal Practice in Chinese Characters" (*Rulin waishi* zhong de sange jieceng yu falu shijian), *Journal of Jiangsu Police Officer College* 17(2), 109–119 (1997), 116R.
57. Donald Black, *The Behavior of Law* (New York: Academic Press, 1976).
58. "Jingcha wenhua de yanjiu qi dian—Jingcha dingyi" (translated from "Where to Begin, Images and Expectations, Thinking About the Police," *PSUJ* 6: 40–41 (1997).
59. Hugh Collins, *Marxism and Law* (Oxford: Oxford University Press, 1984), 17–34.
60. Zhongguo shehui kexue yuan, faxue yanjiu yuan (ed.), *Zhongguo jingcha zhidu jianlun* (A Brief History of Police System in China) (Beijing: Qunzhong chubanshe, 1985), 2.
61. Brian Chapman, *Police State* (London: Macmillan, 1970), 13.
62. *Black's Law Dictionary*, abridged 5th ed. (St. Paul, MN.: West Publication Co., 1983), 30L.
63. Charles Reith, *The Blind Eye of History: A Study of the Origins of Present Police Era* (Montclair, N J.: Peterson Smith, 1974), 21.
64. David Bayley, *Patterns of Policing* (New Brunswick, N J.: Rutgers University Press, 1985), 7.
65. Xu Fake, *Zhongguo Jingcha Fa Lun* (A Treatise on Chinese Police Law) (Hunan: Hunan Chubanshe, 1997), 3.
66. *Ci Yuan* (Source of Words) (辭源) (Beijing: Commercial Press 1983).
67. Li Kungsheng, "On Concept of Police" (Lun Jingcha de gainian), *PSUJ* 11(3):9 (1995).
68. Xie Min, "Establishment of Modern Chinese Police System in Late Qing Dynasty" (Qing shiqi de zhongguo jindai jingcha zhidu jianshe), *Journal of Jiangsu Police Officer College* 4:161–165 (July 2003).
69. Liu Xiaochuan, *Jingcha Shiyong Zhishi Quanshu* (Compendium of Police Practical Knowledge) (Beijing: Zhongguo gongan daxue chubanshe, 1995), 66.
70. *Contemporary police history* (1999), op. cit., note 8, *supra*, 234–5.
71. Zao Yanlung & Su Ligong, *Zongguo jindai jingcha shi* (Police History of Contemporary China) (Beijing: Shehuishe wenxian chubanshe, 1991).
72. *Hayu Dachidian* (Beijng: Hayu Dachidian Chubanshe, 1994), 417L.
73. Yuan Xiaohong, "Police administration thinking of Huang Sunxian" (Huang Zunxian jingzheng sixiang shulue), *PSUJ* 1: 95–6 (1999).
74. *Zhongguo gongan baike quanshu* (China Public Security Encyclopedia) (Jinlin: Jilin chubanshe 1989), 2024R.

75. MPS, "Regulations on People's Police Basic Unit Political Instructor Work" (Trial) (Renmin jingcha jiceng danwei zhengzhi zhidao yuan gongzuo tiaoli [shixing]) (May 5, 1984).
76. Hegel Mark Neocleous, "The Police of Political Economy" (1998).
77. Frederick Engels, *The Origin of the Family, Private Property and the State* (1884).
78. *Zhongguo jindai jingcha zhidu*, Chapter 1, 40–47.
79. Ji Sulan, "Massline Under the Party Leadership is Important Historical Experience of Public Security Work" (Dangwei lingdao xia de qunzhong luxiang shi zhongguo gongzuo de zhongyao lishi jingyan), *PSUJ* 49: 12–15 (1994).
80. Hou Junhua, Li Mozhen, Zhong Min, and Pan Jiagui, *Secret Police Files of Jiang Jieshi (Jiang Jieshi mimi jingcha dangan)* (Beijing: Qunzhong chubanshe, 1994), 35–43.
81. *Jingcha shiyong cuanshu* editorial committee, *Jingcha shiyong quanshu* (Compendium of Police Practice Knowledge) (Beijing: Renmin gongan daxue chubanshe, 1986), 71.
82. Ji Sulan, op. cit., note 79, *supra*.
83. Ibid. See also Intelligence Resource Program http://www.fas.org/irp/world/china/mss/history.htm
84. Ibid.
85. See *Zhongguo gongan baike quanshu* (China Public Security Encyclopedia) (Jinlin: Jilin chubanshe 1989), 205L.
86. Kang Daimin, "Police studies? Public security studies?" (Jingcha xue? Gonganxue?), *Public Security Education* 4: 20–22, 1998.
87. See *Zhongguo gongan baike quanshu* (China Public Security Encyclopedia) (Jinlin: Jilin chubanshe 1989), 205L.
88. *The Pinyin Chinese Dictionary* (Hong Kong: The Commercial Press, 1995), 234L.
89. Wang Hongshi, "The Title of Public Security: Origin and Existence," *Journal of Jiangsu Police Officer College*, 19 (1): 98–103 (2004).
90. Charles Reith, 20, op. cit, note 63, *supra*.
91. The Great Learning, Chapter IX: 4. James Legge (trans.), *The Four Books* (Hong Kong: Culture Book, 1981), 23.
92. Kam C. Wong, "Community Policing in China: Philosophy, Law and Practice," *International Journal of the Sociology of Law* 29:127–148 (2001).
93. "The Ideas of Regulating Officials Reflected in 'the Rules for Acting as Officials' of the *Qin* Dynasty Bamboo Documents," Zhang Jinfan, *Zhongguo Falushi Lun* (Treatise on Chinese Legal History) (Beijing: Falu Chubanshe, 1983), 96–111.
94. Liu Wang Hui-chen, *The Traditional Chinese Clan Rules* (Locust Valley, N.Y.: J.J. Augustin Incorporated Publisher, 1959).
95. Michael Dutton, *Policing and Punishment in China* (Cambridge: Cambridge University Press, 1992), 3.
96. Pu Jian, *Zhongguo Gudai Xingzheng Lifa* (Traditional Chinese Administrative Legislation) (Beijing: Beijing daxue chubanshe, 1990), 12.
97. Pu Jian, *Zhongguo Gudai Xingzheng Lifa* (Traditional Chinese Administrative Legislation) (Beijing: Beijing daxue chubanshe, 1990), 12.

98. Liu Xiaochuan, *Jingcha Shiyong Zhishi Quanshu* (Compendium of Police Practical Knowledge) (Beijing: Zhongguo gongan daxue chubanshe, 1995), 5.
99. *Zhongguo Gudai Xingzheng Lifa,* 81, op. cit., note 96, *supra.*
100. Liu Xiaochuan, *Jingcha Shiyong Zhishi Quanshu* (Compendium of Police Practical Knowledge) (Beijing: Zhongguo gongan daxue chubanshe, 1995), 5.
101. *Zhongguo Gudai Xingzheng Lifa,* 81, op. cit., note 96, *supra.*
102. Liu Xiaochuan, 5, op. cit., note 97, *supra.*
103. *Zhongguo Gudai Xingzheng Lifa*, 50–52, op. cit., note 96, *supra.*
104. Guo Chengwei, *Shehui Fanzui yu Zhonghe Zhili* (Crime in Society and Comprehensive management), 35–36.
105. *Zhongguo Gudai Xingzheng Lifa*, op. cit., note 96, *supra.*
106. "Zhouli.Daishikou" (The Rites of Zhou. Grand Justice Official). Gao Shaoxian, *Zhongguo Lidai Faxue Mingpian Zushi* (Annotation of Famous Jurisprudence Literatures from Chinese Historical Periods) (Beijing: Zhongguo renmin gongan daxue chubanshe, 1993), 29–33.
107. "Shangshu. Luxing," 24–28.
108. David Bayley, *Patterns of Policing: A Comparative International Analysis* (New Brunswick, NJ: Rutgers University Press, 1985), 14.
109. *Zhongguo Gudai Xingzheng Lifa*, 50–52, op. cit., note 96, *supra..*
110. Ibid., 98.
111. Shang Yang (390 to 388 B.C.), "Shang Yang de Fazhi Lilun he Bianfa Shijian" (Shang Yang's Theory of Rule by Law and Practice of Legal Reform) in Liu Hainian and Yang Yi-fang, *Zhongguo Gudai Falu-shi Zhishi* (Knowledge in Chinese Legal History) (Helungjiang: Helungjiang renmin chubanshe, 1984), 75–81.
112. Guo Chengwei, *Shehui Fanzui yu Zhonghe Zhili* (Crime in society and comprehensive management), 50.
113. Wu Shuchen, *Zhongguo Zhuantong Falu Wenhua* (Chinese Traditional Legal Culture) (Beijing: Beijing daixue chubanshe, 1990), Chapter 4, 258–345.
114. Guo Chengwei, *Shehui Fanzui yu Zhonghe Zhili* (Crime in Society and Comprehensive Management), 80.
115. *Zhongguo Gudai Xingzheng Lifa,* 81, op. cit., note 96, *supra.*
116. Dutton, *Policing and Punishment in China* (Cambridge: Cambridge University Press, 1992).
117. "Zhongguo fengjian shidai jaincha zhidu de bianqian" (The Evolution of the Feudal Supervision System in China) in Liu Hai-nian and Yang Yi-fang, *Zhongguo Gudai Falu-shi Zhishi* (Knowledge in Chinese Legal History), 176–182.
118. "Qin Shi Huang falu xixiang de zhuyao neirong" (The Primary Content of Qin Shi Huang's Legal Thoughts) in Liu Hai-nian and Yang Yi-fang, *Zhongguo Gudai Falu-shi Zhishi* (Knowledge in Chinese Legal History) (Helungjian: Helungjiang renmin chubanshe, 1984), 223–228.

## Chapter Three

1. Han Yanlong, *Zhongguo jindai jingcha zhidu* ("Contemporary Police System") (Beijing: Zhongguo renmin gongan daxue, 1993), 710.

2. Editorial Committee, *Dangdai zhongguo gongan gongzuo* (Contemporary Chinese Police Work) (Beijing: Dangdai Zhongguo Chubanshe, 1995).
3. "Strategy in China's Revolutionary War" (Dec. 1936) in *Selected Works of Mao Tse-Tung* vol. 1 (Peking: Foreign Languages Press, 1965), 179–254.
4. Patricia E. Griffin, *The Chinese Communist Treatment of Counter-Revolutionaries 1924-1949* (N.J.: Princeton University Press, 1976), 3.
5. *History of Chinese Labor Movement* (Beijing: Gongren chubanshe, 1994), vols. 1-5.
6. *CCP Party History ArchiveAmaterials* (Beijing: Zhonggong dangshi chubanshe, 1992). vol. 1—current.
7. *Chinese Revolutionary Legal History* (Upper volume) (Beijing: Zhongguo shehui kexue chubanshe, 1987).
8. *A Brief History of Chinese Policing* (Beijing: Renmin gongan daxue, 1989).
9. (University of California Press, 1995).
10. *Contemporary Chinese Police History* (Beijing: Zhongguo renmin gongan daxue, 1993).
11. (Chichester, U.K.: Harvester Press, 1977).
12. "The Canton Province-Hong Kong Strike Committee Pickets" ("The Sheng-Guang bagong weiyuanhui jiucha dui").
13. The pinyin for Canton is "Guangdong" and will be used interchangably.
14. *Zhongguo gongren yundong shihuo* vol. 2, 168.
15. *Wu-San-Shi yundong he Sheng-Gang bagong* (The May 30th Movement and Canton-Hong Kong Strike) (Jiangsu: Jiangsu guji chubanshe, 1985), 333–341.
16. Zhang Xipo and Han Yanlong, *Zhongguo geming fazhishi* (Chinese Revolutionary Legal History) (1921–1949), upper volume (Beijing: Zhongguo shehui kexue chubanshe, 1987), 283–289.
17. Ibid.
18. Ibid., 284.
19. "The Canton-Hong Kong Strike," in Jean Chesneaux, *The Chinese Labor Movement* (Stanford, California: Stanford University Press, 1968), 291–318, 292–293.
20. "The Canton-Hong Kong Strike," 293.
21. "Guangdong sheng zhengfu yubei huiyi" (Canton Provincial Government Preparatory Meeting) (July 2, 1925, Thursday).
22. "Zhonghua minguo guomin zhengfu zuzhifa" (Organic Law of Chinese National Government) was promulgated on July 1, 1925.
23. Chu Tung-tsu, *Local Government under the Ching* (Cambridge, Mass.: Harvard University Press, 1962); Van der Sprenkel, *Legal Institutions in Manchu China* (London: Athlone Press, 1962).
24. *Sheng-Gang dabagong ziliao*, 576–579, 576.
25. "Guo Min Zhengfu dui bagong weiyuanhui pafa tongdian yuyi mianfei xunling gao" (July 8, 1925 (when drafted) Zhonghua minguo guomin zhengfu xinling, di wu hao). ("Guangdong National Government's Directive Ordering that the Guangdong-Hong Kong Strikers' Union Headquarters Be Allowed to Send Circulars with Telegram Free of Charge") (Chinese National government

instruction, no. 5) in *Wu-San-Shi yundong he Sheng-Gang bagong* (The May 30th Movement and Canton-Hong Kong Strike) (Jiangsu guji chubanshe, 1985), 262.

26. Quotation from *Sheng-Gang gongren dabagong ziliao* ("Materials on Canton-Hong Kong Big Workers' Strike") (Guangdong: Guangdong gongren chubanshe, 1980), 7187.
27. "Zhengfu wei weichi cizhong zhengyi xingwei, bing cuqi jinxing sushou dongda qijian ..." and authorized the strike.
28. "Guomin zhengfu guangyu fengsuo Xiang-Gang ji Xin- Jie kouan gonghan gao" ("Guangzhou National Government Secretariat's Official Letter Concerning Blockading the Ports of Hong Kong and Xin-Jie kouan") (July 13, 1925), 7264.
29. Published in *Gongren zilu*, No. 227, February 9, 1926. Reprinted in *Sheng-Gang dabagong ziliao*, 310.
30. Published in *Gongren zilu*, No. 89, September 21, 1925. Reprinted in *Sheng-Gang dabagong ziliao*, 310.
31. Published in *Gongren zilu*, No. 267, March 22, 1926. Reprinted in *Sheng-Gang dabagong ziliao*, 313–314.
32. Tang Zhongxia, "Sheng-Gang dabagong," in *Sheng-Gang dabagong ziliao*, 23–53, 51.
33. *Sheng-Gang dabagong ziliao*, 48.
34. Published in *Gongren zilu*, No. 227, February 9, 1926. Reprinted in *Sheng-Gang dabagong ziliao*, 310.
35. Published in *Gongren zilu*, No. 227, February 9, 1926. Reprinted in *Sheng-Gang dabagong ziliao*, 298–299.
36. "The jiucha dui organic law." Published in *Gongren zilu* , No. 254. March 9, 1926. Reprinted in Sheng-*Gang dabagong ziliao*, 234–235. (Organic Law.)
37. "Official Letter of the Guangzhou National Government's Military Committee Concerning Blockading Qianshan, Wanzi and Other Places in Guangdong." ("Guomin zhengfu junshi weiyuanhui guanyu jiaqiang fengsuo Qian Shan, Wan Zi deng chu gong han") (October 5, 1925), in *Wu-San-Shi yundong he Sheng-Gang bagong* (The May 30th Movement and Canton-Hong Kong Strike) (Jiangsu: Jiangsu guji chubanshe, 1985), 314.
38. "Dispatch from the Baoan (Guangdong) Peasant Association Requesting that Unscrupulous Merchants, Local Tyrants and Evil Gentry Who Had Sabotaged the Strike Be Punished" ("Yue Baoan yuan nongmin xiehui deng wei jianshang tuhao lieshen yunlingshi deng jieji Gangying pohuai bagong daiydian") (November 14, 1925).
39. "Guangdong-Hongkong Strikers' Union Headquarters Report on the Activities of British Spies" (October 9, 1925) ("Sheng-Gang bagong weiyuanhui baogao Yingren jinxing tewu huodong han").
40. "Guangdong-Hongkong Strikers' Union Headquarters' Message Reporting on the Secret Transportation of Military Equipment by the Hong Kong Authorities" ("Sheng-Gang bagong weiyuanhui baogao Yingdi touyun junxie bingpai tewu jinxing huodong han") (October 9, 1925).

41. "Guangzhou National Government's Order Authorizing the Eastern Expeditionary Army to Suppress the Unscrupulous Merchants Who Were Smuggling Grain to Hong Kong" ("Guomin zhengfu guanyu Dan jianshang oujie difang junjing yun yanghuo ji jieji Xiang Gang liangshi yanxing jieji ling") (November 25, 1925).
42. Published in *Gongren zilu*, No. 254, 255, March 9 and 10, 1926. Reprinted in Sheng-*Gang dabagong ziliao*, 237–236.
43. Published in *Gongren zilu*, No. 262, 265, 267; March 17, 20, 22, 1926. Reprinted in Sheng-*Gang dabagong ziliao*, 244–247.
44. *Zhongguo gongren yundong shihua*, vol. 3, 194.
45. "Guo Min Zhengfu dui bagong weiyuanhui pafa tongdian yuyi mianfei xunling gao" (July 8, 1925), "Zhonghua minguo guomin zhengfu xinling, di wu hao" ("Guangdong National Government's Directive Ordering that the Guangdong-Hong Kong Strikers' Union Headquarters Be Allowed to Send Circular Telegrams Free of Charge") ("Chinese National government instruction, no. 5") in *Wu-San-Shi yundong he Sheng-Gang bagong* (The May 30th Movement and Canton-Hong Kong Strike) (Jiangsu guji chubanshe, 1985), 262-263.
46. *Zhongguo gongren yundong shihua*, vol. 2, 194.
47. Ibid., vol. 3, 197–199.
48. "Guomin zhengfu guanyu weichi Shenggang bagong weiyuanhuo ge jueyian xunlin" (July 8, 1925), "Zhonghua minguo guomin zhengfu xinling, di san hao" (Guangzhou National Government's Directive Authorizing the Guangdong Provincial Government to Carry out Its Decision to Support the Guangdong-Hong Kong Strikers' Union Headquarters) (Chinese National government instruction, no. 3) in *Wu-San-Shi yundong he Sheng-Gang bagong* (The May 30th Movement and Canton-Hong Kong Strike) (Jiangsu guji chubanshe, 1985), 260-261.
49. :Sheng-Gang bagong weiyuanhui guanyu shencha Lin Heji pohuai baogong an jingguo han" (July 19, 1925). (Guangdong-Hongkong Strikers' Union Headquarters' Message Concerning the Trial of Lin Heji (Who Had Sabotaged the Strike), Ibid. 265–267.

## Chapter Four

1. Chapter 2: "Kangri zhanzheng shiqi de renmin jingcha" ("People's Police during the War against the Japanese") in Li Junhu, *Gongan baowei gongzuo* ("Public Security Defense work") (Shanxi: Shanxi renmin chubanshe, 1989).
2. Li Yiqing, "Dang de zhengce shi gongan gongzuo shengli zi ben" ("Party Policy is the Foundation of Public Security Work Success"). Ibid., 357–360.
3. Editorial committee, *Zhongguo renmin jingcha jianshi* ("A Brief History of Chinese People's Police") (Beijing: Jingguan jiaoyu chubanshe, 1989).
4. Li Yiqing, op. cit., note 2, *supra*.
5. "Police" and "public security" are used interchangeably.
6. Chinese Public Security University Editorial Board, *Jingcha Shiyong Zhishi Quanshu* (Compendium of Police Applied Knowledge) (Beijing: Zhongguo Renmin Gongan Daixue Chubanshe, 1995), 15.

7. Chapter 9: "Reds" in Frederic Wakeman, Jr., *Policing Shanghai 1927–1937* (Berkeley: University of California Press, 1995), 132–161.
8. Benjamin I. Schwartz, *Chinese Communism and the Rise of Mao* (Cambridge, Mass.: Harvard University Press, 1951).
9. Frederic Wakeman, Jr., *Policing in Shanghai 1927-1937* (Berkeley: University of California Press, 1995), 135.
10. Ibid., 134.
11. Shanghai municipality promulgated the "Shanghai shi gonganju jingcha jingshi fuwu xiji'" (October 1930).
12. "Xian qu fangong ziwei zuzhi tiaoli" (December 1938).
13. "Shanghai shi jinji zhian tiaoli" (April 1949).
14. Cheng Pengsheng, *Shanghai fazhi fazhan zhanlue yanjiu* ("Research into the Strategy of Shanghai Legal System Development") (shanghai: Fudan Faxue chubanshe, 1991), 63.
15. *Zhongguo gongren yundong shi* (A History of The Chinese Labor Movement) (Guangzhou: Guandong renmin chubanshe, 1998, 6 volumes), volume I, 1.
16. *Zhonguo renmin jingcha jianshi*, *supra*, note 3. 4.
17. "Gongan zhengzhi gongzuo" ("Public Security Political Work") in Editorial Committee, *Zhongguo guoqing daci dian* (A Dictionary of China's State of the Union), 242–243.
18. "Guanyu guojia anquan jiguan xingshi gongan jiguan de zhencha, jubu, yushen, he zhixing dibuquan de juding" (1983). In "Guojia anquan bu" in Editorial committee, *Zhongguo gongan baike quanshu* (China Police Encyclopedia) (Changchu, Jilin, Jilin Chubanshe, 1995), 1183.
19. Li Junhu, *Gongan baowei gongzuo* (Public Security Defense Work) (Shangxi: Shanxi renmin chubanshe, 1989), 8–9.
20. "Zhongguo gongchandang Shan, Gan, Ning bianqu weiyuanhui, Shan Gan, Ning bianqu zhengfu, Goumin gemingjun dibalu jun, houfang liushouchu guanyu dongyuan zhuangding de xunling" (ci zi di 121 hao).
21. "Shan-Gan-Ning bianqu zhengfu mingling-guanyu bianqu xingzheng zuzhi de pianzhi."
22. Yang and Fang, *Shan-Gan-Ning bianqu fazhi shi gao* ("Historical Records of Shan-Gan-Ning Border Area Legal System"), (Beijing: Falu chubanshe, 1986), 42–55.
23. "Tai guanfan, haowu zhongxin, tai haogao maoyuan, zhiyao duo jiang jingcha suochang de gan jingcha jiugou."
24. Liu Jiuxiang, "Liaoxian de gongan baowei gongzuo" ("The Public Security Work of Liao County"), *Gongan baowei gongzuo*, *supra*, note 2, 370–379.
25. *Shan, Gan, Ning bianqu zhengfu wenjian xuanpian* ("A collection of Shan, Gan, Ning Border Area Government Documents"), vol. 1 (Beijing: Dangan chubanshe, 1986), 7.
26. *Shan-Gan-Ning bianqu fazhi shi gao* ("Historical records of Shan-Gan-Ning border area legal system") (Falu chubanshe, 1986), 14.
27. Yan Li, *Gongan paichusuo yewu quanshu* (Zhongguo renmin gongan daixue, 1994), 2.

28. "Shan, Gan, Ning border area government organization regulations" (passed by the Shan-Gan-Ning border area senate on February, 1939, promulgated on April 4, 1939). See *Shan, Gan, Ning bianqu zhengfu wenjian xuanpian* ("A Collection of Shan, Gan, Ning border Area Government Documents"), vol. 1 (Beijing: Dangan chubanshe, 1986), 212–216.
29. "Shan-Gan-Ning bianqu xianzhengfu zhuzi tiaoli' (passed by the second border area senate on November 1941) in Han Yanlong and Chang Zhaoru (ed.), *Zhongguo xinminzhu zhuyi gemin shiqi genjudi fazhi wexian xuanbian* ("Collection of Historical Documents of Chinese New Democratic Revolution Base Area Period") (Beijing: Zhongguo shehui kexueyuan chubanshe, 1981) vol. 2, 218–221.
30. In *Shan-Gan-Ning bianqu zhengfu wenjian xuanpain* (Collection of government documents from Shan-Gan-Ning border area), vol. 11 (Dangan chubanshe, 1991), 301–305.
31. "Shan-Gan-Ning bianqu weijing tiaoli (caoan)."
32. "Shan, Gan, Ning bainqu jingcha gongzuo guize."
33. "Shan-Gan-Ning bianqu zhengfu ming ling" [min zi 74 hao] *Shan, Gan, Ning bianqu zhengfu wenjian xuanpian* ("Collection of Shan, Gan, Ning border area government documents") (Beijing: Dangan chubanshe, 1991) vol. 11, 18–9.
34. "Shan-Gan-Ning bianqu weijing tiaoli (caoan)."
35. "Shan-Gan-Ning bianqu zhengfu zanxing zuzhi guicheng" (passed on April 9, 1949 by the joint meeting of Shan-Gan-Ning border area senate, standing committee, Shan-Gan-Ning border area government committee) in Yanlong and Chang Zhaoru (ed.), *Zhongguo xinminzhu zhuyi gemin shiqi genjudi fazhi wexian xuanbian* (Collection of historical documents of Chinsese new democratic revolution base area period) (Beijing: Zhongguo shehui kexueyuan chubanshe, 1981), vol. 2, RK-1 Czgx 19009, 466–470.
36. *Shan, Gan, Ning bianqu zhengfu wenjian xuanpian* ("A collection of Shan, Gan, Ning border area government documents"), vol. 1 (Beijing: Dangan chubanshe, 1986), 28, as reported in *Xin zhonghua bao* (New Chinese News) of October 14, 1937.
37. *Zhongguo renmin jingcha jianshi*, *supra*, note 3, 52.
38. *Zhongguo renmin jingcha jianshi*, *supra*, note 3.
39. "Shan-Gan-Ning bianqu shizheng ganling" proposed by Communist Party border area Central Department ("zhonggong bianqu zhongyanju") and approved by the Communist Party, Political Bureau on May 1, 1941.
40. "Shan-Gan-Ning bianqu disanjie dierci zhengfu weiyuanhuo jueyi" (1946).
41. "The report of Liu acting chairman at the joint meeting: Regarding last year's government work" ("Lui dai zhuxi zai lianxi hui shang guanyu yi nian lai zhengfu gongzuo de baogao") (1949).

## Chapter Five

1. John W. Lewis and Xue Litai, "Social Change and Political Reform in China: Meeting the Challenge of Success," *China Quarterly* 176: 926–942 (2003).
2. Chapter 7, infra.

3. Interview, Ex-PRC Police Instructor, Chinese University of Hong Kong, Nov. 1998.
4. William J. Mathias, "Higher Education and the Police," in Arthur Niederhoffer and Abraham S. Blumberg (eds.), *The Ambivalent Force,* 2[nd] ed. (Hinsdale, Ill.: The Dryden Press 1976), 377–384.
5. Robert E. Worden, "A Badge and a Baccalaureate: Policies, Hypotheses, and Further Evidence," *Justice Quarterly* 7: 565–592 (1990).
6. David Geary, "College Educated Cops—Three Years Later," *Police Chief,* 37(4): 62–72 (August 1970).
7. Charles B. Saunders, *Upgrading the American Police* (Washington, D.C.: Brookings Institution, 1970).
8. L. Sherman and the National Advisory Commission on Higher Education for Police Officers, *The Quality of Police Education* (San Francisco: Jossey-Bass, 1978), 30–33.
9. Gerald W. Lynch, "Why Officers Needs a College Education," *Higher Education and National Affairs* (September 20, 1986), 11.
10. Larry D. Soderquist, "Upgrading the Service," *Police Chief* 36 (8): 101–118 (August 1969).
11. C. Lewis, "Transitions in Police Education," *Queensland Police Union Journal,* Sept. 19-26 (1992), 21. D. Carter, A. Sapp, and D. Stephens, *The State of Police Education: Policy Direction for the 21st Century* (Washington, D.C.: Police Executive Forum, 1989), 9–15.
12. D. Carter, A. Sapp, and D. Stephens, *The State of Police Education: Policy Direction for the 21st Century* (Washington, D.C.: Police Executive Forum, 1989), 47; Lee H. Bowker, "A Theory of Educational Needs of Law Enforcement Officers," *Journal of Contemporary Criminal Justice* 1: 17–24 (1980).
13. Kenneth Peak, *Policing America* (NJ: Prentice-Hall, 1997), 87.
14. Egon Bittner, *The Functions of Police in Modern Society* (Rockville, Maryland: U.S. Government Printing Office, 1970).
15. Stanley K. Shernock, "The Effects of College Education on Professional Attitudes Among Police," *Journal of Criminal Justice Education* 3 (1): 71–92 (1992).
16. Victor Kappeler, Allen D. Sapp, and David Carter, "Police Officer Higher Education. Citizen Complaints and Departmental Rule Violation," *American Journal of Police* 11: 37–54 (1992).
17. A. Dalley, "University versus Non-university Graduated Policemen: A Study of Police Attitudes," *Journal of Police Science and Administration* 3:348–368 (1977).
18. Robert Trojanowitcz and T. Nicholson, "A Comparison of Behavioral Styles of College Graduate Police Officers vs. Non-College Going Police Officers," *The Police Chief* 43: 56-59 (August 1976).
19. David Mahony and Tim Prenzler, "Police Studies, the University, and the Police Service: An Australian Study," *Journal of Criminal Justice Education* 2 (2): 283–304 (1996).
20. D. Bradley, "Escaping Plato's Cave: The Possible Future of Police Education," in P. Moir and H. Eijkman (eds.), *Policing Australia* (South Melbourne: Macmillan, 1992), 13.

21. Gerald Lynch, "Cops and College," *America* 274–5 (April 4, 1987).
22. G. Fitzgerald, *Report of a Commission of Inquiry Pursuant to Orders in Council* (Brisbane: Goprint, 1989).
23. E.J. Delattre, *Character and Cops in Policing* (D.C., Washington: American Enterprise for Public Policy Research), 1989.
24. Dennis C. Smith and Elinor Ostrom, "The Effects of Training and Education on Police Attitudes and Performance: A Preliminary Analysis," In Herbert Jacobs, *The Potential for Reform of Criminal Justice* (Beverley Hills, CA: Sage, 1974).
25. National Advisory Commission on Criminal Justice Standards and Goals, *Report on the Police* (Washington, D.C.: U.S. Government Printing Office, 1973), 369.
26. "Identification of Educational Needs," Law Enforcement Administration Assistant, *The National Advisory Commission on Criminal Justice Standards and Goals* (1973), 378.
27. Charles W. Tenney, Jr., "Education, Jr. "Education of Law Enforcement," *Trial* (October–November 1969), 19.
28. R. A. Myren, Remarks at a conference on police education, Police Foundation, Washington, D.C., March 1976.
29. E. Cummings, I. Cummings, and L. Edell, "Policeman as Philosopher, Guide and Friend," *Social Problems* 12: 276–286 (1965).
30. Michael Banton, *Policeman in the Community* (London: Tavistock Publications, Ltd., 1964), 6–7.
31. J.Q. Wilson, *Varieties of Police Behavior: The Management of Law and Disorder in Eight Communities* (Cambridge, Mass.: Harvard University Press, 1968).
32. Jerome H. Skolnick, *The Politics of Protest* (New York: Ballantine Books, 1969).
33. *National Advisory Commission on Civil Disorders Report of National Advisory Commission on Civil Disorders* (Kerner Report) (Washington, D.C.: U.S. Government Printing Office, 1968), 157.
34. Anothony Platt and Lynn Cooper, *Policing America* (Englewood Cliffs, N.J.: Prentice-Hall, 1974), 10.
35. Peter Manning, "The Police and Crime: Crime and the Police," *Sociologische Gids*, Maurice Punch, ed. (May 1, 1978).
36. Jerome H. Skolnick and David Bayley, *The New Blue Line* (N.Y.: Free Press, 1986), 3–6.
37. Wickersham Commission (1931).
38. Hon Yanlung and Su Yigong, *Contemporary Police History* (Three volumes) (Zhongguo jindai jingchashi) (Beijing: Shehuikexue chubanshe 1999), 241.
39. Ibid., 255.
40. Li Jiangje, "Lun zhian kexue jianshe" (Discussion on Public Security Students Establishment) *Gongan Jiaoyu* (Public Security Education) 74:36 (2001)
41. Li Wenneng, "Luli tigao jiaoyu zhiliang, shi gongan zui zhongyao di renwu" (Work Hard to Promote Education Quality, Is the Most Important Task Facing public Security Education) *Gongan Jiaoyu* (Public Security Education) 42: 6–7 (1997).
42. Cheng Shengjun, "Shishi kejiao qiangjing zhanlue, tigao gongan duiwu de zhengti zhisu" ("Implement the Strategy of Scientific Education to Strengthen Policing,

Enhance the Overall Quality of the Entire Security Force," *Gongan Jiaoyu* (Public Security Education) 42:2 (1997).
43. Editorial Committee, *Jingcha shiyong zhishi quanshu* (Comprehensive Handbook of Police Practical Business) (Beijing: Zhongguo gongan daxue chubanshe, 1995).
44. Liu Fu Xian, *Gongan Jiaoyu Xue* (Public Security Education Study) (Beijing: Jingguan chubanshe, 1998), 37.
45. See item 3 "Guanyu jiaoyu gongzhu de zhishi." Ibid.
46. Donald Munro, *The Concept of Man in Early China* (CA.: Stanford, Calif. Stanford University Press, 1969).
47. Cited in Julian Baum, "New-Old Role Model: Peking Propagandists Bring Back Their '60s Hero: Lei Feng." *The Christian Science Monitor* March 6, 1987.
48. Erik Eckholm, "Beijing Journal: At a Trying Time, China Revives Mao's Model Man," *The New York Times*, April 16, 1998; Section A, 4.
49. Douglas Sloan, "The Teaching of Ethics in American Undergraduate Curriculum, 1876–1976," in Donald Callahan and Sissela Bok (eds.), *Ethics Teaching in Higher Education* (New York: Plenum Press, 1980), 2.
50. "Personal Recollections of Charles William Eliot," *Harvard Graduates' Magazine* 32:342 (1924).
51. *Report on Some Problems of Personnel in the Faculty of Arts and Sciences* (Cambridge, Mass.: Harvard University Press, 1939), 77.
52. Derek Bok, *Beyond the Ivory Tower* (Cambridge, Mass.: Harvard University Press, 1982),119.
53. Joycelyn M. Pollock, "Ethics and the Criminal Justice Curriculum," *Journal of Criminal Justice Education* 4 (2): 377–390 (1993).
54. Jeffrie. Murphy, *Punishment and Rehabilitation* (Belmont, CA: Wadsworth, 1992), 4.
55. Lawrence. Sherman, *The Teachings of Ethics in Criminology and Criminal Justice* (Washington, D.C.: Joint Commission on Criminology and Criminal Justice Education and Standards, 1981); *Ethics in Criminal Justice Education* (New York: Hasting Centre, 1982).
56. "Teaching the Applied Ethics in Criminal Justice Ethics Cours,." in F. Schmallegers (ed.), *Ethics in Criminal Justice* (Bristol, Ind.: Wyndham Hall, 1990), 148–164.
57. Joycelyn M. Pollock, op. cit, note 53, *supra*.
58. Fu Xian Liu, *Gongan Jiaoyu Xue* (Public Security Education Study) (Beijing: Jingguan chubanshe, 1998). Lawrence W. Sherman, *The Quality of Police Education* (San Francisco, CA: Jossey-Bass Publishers, 1978).
59. Wang Yanju, "Preliminary Probe into The Study on The System of Public Security Discipline" ("Gongan xueke tixi yanjiu chulun"), *Journal of Chinese Public Security University* (Gongan Daxue Xue Bao) ("PSUJ") 19 (1): 1–5 (2003).
60. Wang Cui-yuan, "Probe into Several Problems on Basic Theory of Public Order Discipline" ("Zhi-anxue rugan jichu lilun wenti cai tantu"), *PSUJ* 107: 116–121 (1/2004), 116L.

61. Chen Shouyi, "A Review of Thirty Years of Legal Studies in New China," *Journal of Chinese Law* 2: 181–200 (1988); M. Sidel, "Recent and Noteworthy Legal Works Published in China," *Journal of Chinese Law* 1: 251–269 (1987).
62. Xiong Yixin, "Summary of "National Conference on New Century Public Security Studies Academic Discipline Building" ("Quanguo xinshiqi zhian xue xueke jianshe yantu hui" zhongshu"), *PSUJ* 96: 115–119 (2002).
63. Wang Cui-yuan, op. cit., note 60, *supra.*
64. "Regarding research subject of discipline" ("Guanyi xueke de yanjiu duixiang"). Ibid.
65. Xiong Yixin, op. cit., note 62, *supra.*, 115L.
66. ("guilu") *PYCED* 255L
67. Xiong Yixin, "Summary of "National conference on new century public security studies academic discipline building" ("Quanguo xinshij zhian xue xueke jianshe yantu hui" zhongshu"), *PSUJ*, 96: 115–119 (2002), 115R.
68. Zhao Xiuping "The Current Status and Analysis of Criminal Investigation Technical Education at Public Education Higher Education Institutes" ("Gongan gaodeng yuanxiao xingshi jishu jiaoxue xianzhuang de fexi"), *Public Security Education* (Gongan Jiaoyu) 98: 40–44 (2003).
69. *Methodology:* Date of research: 2002. Research focus: Assessing the adequacy and effect of criminal investigation technical education at public education higher education institutes. Sample frame: All senior students at three national and provincial criminal investigation colleges (one MPS, one provincial—degree, one provincial—professional). *National:* Chinese Criminal Investigation Police College (sponsored by MPS) Zhongguo Xingjing Xueyuan (Gonganbu). *Provincial college:* Jiansu Police Officer College ("Jiangsu Jingguan xueyuan") (sponsored by Jiansu province). *Provincial professional college:* Shandong Public Security Professional College" zhuanke xueyuan ("Shandong Gongan zhuanke xueyuan") (sponsored by Shangdong province). *Sample size:* 266. *Response rate:* 260 (97.7%). *Survey instrument:* "Questionnaire on the current status and analysis of criminal investigation technical education at public education higher education institutes" ("Gongan gaodeng yuanxiao xingshi jishu jiaoxue xianzhuang tiazhong wenjuan"). *Individual interviews:* Faculty 20, Students 25. Ibid.
70. Ibid.
71. Zhou Zhongwei, "Perplexed and Thinking about Two Essential Factors in the Elementary Education of Public Security" ("Guanyu Gongan jichu jiaoyu liangdai yaosu de huhuo tu sikao"), *PSUJ* 96: 111 – 115 (2/2002), 112L.
72. Barry Keenan, "Revitalizing Liberal Learning the Chinese Way: Fostering Motivation and Teacher-student relationships," *Change* 30 (6): 38–42 (November/December 1998).
73. Lucian W. Pye, "On Chinese Pragmatism in the 1980s," *The China Quarterly* 16: 207–234 (1986).
74. Pan Maoyuan, "The Basic Regularities of Education and Their Application in Higher Education Research and Practice," *Chinese Education and Society* 40 (3): 45–63 (May/June 2007).

## Chapter Six

1. Note, "Concepts of Law in the Chinese Anti-Crime Campaigns," 98 *Harv, L. Rev.* 1890 (1985); James D. Seymore and Mark Finday, "Show Trials in China: After Tiananmen Square," 16 *Journal of Law and Society* 352–59 (1989); "Human Rights and the Law in the PRC" in Victor C. Falkenheim (ed.), *Chinese Politics from Mao to Deng* (N.ew York: Paragon House, 1989), 271–299.
2. "Quanguo jiancha jiguan diyici 'qinquan' duzhi anjian zhencha gongzuo huiyi," *Law Yearbook of China* (1991), 802.
3. "Quanguo jiancha jiguan dierci 'qinquan' duzhi anjian zhencha gongzuo huiyi," *Law Yearbook of China* (1992).
4. Yang Yichen, Chief Procuratorate: "*Zui gao renmin jianchayuan gongzuo baogao*" (The Supreme People's Procuratorate Work Report) (1 April 1988 the 7th NPC, first meeting). *Zhongguo jiancha nianjian* (1990) (Procuratorial Yearbook of China (1990), 21–28.
5. "Zuigao renmin jianchayuan gongzuo baogao" (At second meeting of 10[th] NPC, March 10, 2004). *Procuratorial Yearbook* (Beijing: Zhongguo jiancha chubanshe, 2005), 5–8.
6. National Commission on Law observance and Enforcement: *Report on Lawlessness in Law Enforcement* (Washington, D.C.: United States Government Printing Office, 1931).
7. Carl E. Pope and Lee E. Ross, "Race, Crime, and Justice: The Aftermath of Rodney King," *The Criminologist* 17 (1992): 1–10.
8. *The Challenge of Crime in a Free Society* (Washington, D.C.: United States Government Printing Office, 1967).
9. New York City Knapp Commission (1969–1972), Commission to Investigate Allegations of Police Corruption and the City's Anticorruption Procedures (New York City; Witman Knapp, Chairman), Commission Report (1972).
10. Robert J. McCormack, "Confronting Police Corruption: Organizational Initiatives for Internal Control," in *Managing Police Corruption: International Perspectives,* eds. Richard H. Ward and Robert McCormack (Chicago: Office of International Criminal Justice, University of Illinois at Chicago, 1987), 151–165.
11. William C. Heffernan and Richard W. Lovely, "Evaluating the Fourth Amendment Exclusionary Rule: The Problem of Police Compliance with the Law," *University of Michigan Journal of Law Reform* 24(2):311–369 (1991).
12. Kam C. Wong, "Federalization of Local Criminal Procedures: A Study of Conflict in Values and Process," *International Journal of the Sociology of Law* 29(3): 203–235 (2001).
13. Thomas E. Reed and William D. Beckerman, "The Value of Equality in the Rule of Law," *International Journal of Criminology and Penology* 6(4):363–371 (1978).
14. William A. Westley, *Violence and the Police: A Sociological Study of Law, Custom, and Morality* (Cambridge, Mass.: MIT Press), 11.
15. Jerome H. Skolnick, *Justice without Trial* (New York: Wiley, 1966).
16. Jonathan Rubenstein, *City Police* (New York:Farrar, Straus, and Giroux, 1973), 127–128.

17. "April 1, 1999—Businessman held despite court's ruling" in Human Rights Chronology: China, Hong Kong, Tibet. March–April 1999.
18. Kam C. Wong, "Sheltering for Examination: Law, Policy, and Practice," *Occasional Chapters/Reprints Series in Contemporary Asian Studies*, University of Maryland, School of Law, 9/1997.
19. Interviewed with Peter So, a Hong Kong businessman, who was detained by Chinese public security over a custom dispute from December 16, 2004 to May 28, 2007. I interviewed him in San Francisco on September 5-6, 2008. So was detained on December 16, 2004, arrested on January 21, 2005, and charged on April 17, 2006. His charge was "withdrawn" by the Public Prosecutor on May 18, 2007. In So's long confinement every aspect of his legal rights under PRC Constitution and PRC Criminal Law were violated, e.g., he was detained much longer than authorized by law, he was not given an opportunity to speak privately with his lawyer, he was not notified of the charges during initial investigative detention. See People's Republic of China, Beijing No. 2 Intermediate People's Court Criminal Award. (2006) Er-Zhong-Xing-Chu No. 484. (On file with Author.)
20. Zhu, Ni, "A Case Study of Legal Transplant: The Possibility of Efficient Breach in China" *Georgetown Journal of International Law*, 36, 1145–1172, 1146, (2005).
21. Donald Clarke, "Power and Politics in the Chinese Court Systems: The Enforcement of Civil Judgments," *Columbia Journal Of Asian Law* 10(1): 1– 92 (1996).
22. Zhang Xian Chu, "A Law Unto," *Hong Kong Lawyer* March 1998. (Judges are not independent, incompetent, and corrupt.) sunzi1.lib.hku.hk/hkjo/view/15/1501429.pdf; Joseph Kahn, "Dispute Leaves U.S. Executive in the Chinese Legal Netherworld," *New York. Times*, Nov. 1, 2005, at A1.
23. Don Lee, "Return to China Is Risky for U.S. Citizens." *Los Angeles Times,* May 2005.
24. Xue Chun-bo, "A Brief Comment on Significance of Sticking Current Leading System of Public Security Organ," *Journal of Quizhou Police Officer Vocational College* 14(2): 75–78 (2002).
25. Kam C. Wong, "Police Powers and Control in the People's Republic of China: A case study of *shouron shencha*," *Columbia Journal Of Asian Law* 10 (3): 367–390 (1996).
26. Lawrence M. Friedman, *The Legal System: A Social Science Perspective* (New York: Russell Sage Foundation, 1975), 15.
27. Harold Bermen, *Law and Revolution* (Cambridge, Mass.: Harvard University Press, 1982).
28. H.L.A. Hart, *The Concept of Law* (Oxford: Clarendon Press, 1961).
29. J. Bentham, *A Fragment on Government*, in 1 Work 221, 230 (Bowring ed., 1895) (preface, 16th para).
30. John Rawls, *A Theory of Justice* (Cambridge, Mass.: The Belknap Press of Harvard University Press, 1971).

31. James D. Seymore, "Human Rights and The Law in the PRC," in Victor C. Falkenheim (ed.), *Chinese Politics from Mao to Deng* (1989), 272.
32. Readers' Comments. Posted by zzyzx January 23, 2007. Susan Jake, "The Time Magazine Office of Letters and Visits," *Times—China Blog* January 23, 2007 5:39. http://time-blog.com/china_blog/2007/01/the_time_magazine_office_of_le_1.html
33. "Complaints against Judiciary Decrease Despite Exposures of Unjust Trials." *China Daily Online.* March 11, 2006. (http://english.peopledaily.com.cn/200603/11/eng20060311 _ 249897.html
34. Ningnan County Party and Government Xinfang Responsibility System [Zhonggong ningnan xian wei ningnan xian renmin zhengfu guanyu luoshi xinfang gongzuo zeren zhi he zeren zhuijiu zhi de shishi yijian], issued February 27, 2006. See Congressional-Executive Commission on China, 2006 Annual Report, "VII. Development of the Rule of Law and Institutions of Democratic Governance, VII(c) Access to Justice," note 100.
35. Minxin Pei, "Citizens v. Mandarins: Administrative Litigation in China," *The China Quarterly* 152: 832–862 (1997).
36. Administrative Procedure Law of the People's Republic of China (Adopted on April 4, 1989).
37. Minxin Pei, "Citizens v. Mandarins: Administrative Litigation in China," *The China Quarterly* 152: 832–862 (1997), Table 1, 836; Table 2: "Regional Distribution of ALC Accepted by Court in 1994," 838.
38. Chen Zhiming, *Chen Zhiming fanshi shinian gaige* (Chen Zhiming Reflecting Upon Ten Years of Reform) (Beijing: Dangdai yuekan chubanshe, 1992), 67–70.
39. Victor Li, *Law without Lawyers* (Boulder, Colo.: Westview Press, 1978), 13.
40. John King Fairbank, *The United States and China* (4th ed.) (Cambridge, Mass.: Harvard University Press, 1979).
41. Brain McKnight, *Law and Order in Sung* (Cambridge: Cambridge University Press, 1992).
42. David Y.F. Ho, "Chinese Patterns of Socialization: A Critical Review" in Michael H. Bond (ed.), *The Psychology of the Chinese People* (Hong Kong: Oxford University Press, 1986), 1–37.
43. Liang Zhiping, "Explicating 'Law'": A Comparative Perspective of Chinese and Western Legal Culture," *Journal of Chinese Law* 3:55–94, 55–63 (1989).
44. Chapter 1 to William Jones *The Great Qing Code* (New York: Oxford University Press, 1994).
45. Li, op. cit., note 39, *supra.*
46. Jones, op. cit., note 44, *supra.*
47. Michael Dutton, *Policing and Punishment in China* (Cambridge: Cambridge University Press, 1991), 3.
48. James Brady, *Justice and Politics in People's China* (London: Academic Press, 1982), especially Chapter 4: "Popular Revolution and the Creation of People's Justice," 55–69.

49. Mao Zedong, "On the Correct Handling of Contradictions among the People," in *Selected Works of Mao Zedong*, vol. 5 (Beijing: Foreign Languages Press, 1977).
50. Albert Blaustein, *Fundamental Legal Documents of Communist China* (New Jersey: Fred B. Rothman & Co., 1962), xv.
51. "How to Be a Good Communist," (July, 1939, delivered as a lecture at the Institute of Marxism-Leninism in Yanan.) in *Selected Work of Liu Shaqi* vol. 1 (Beijing: Foreign Languages Press, 1984), 107–156.
52. Shao-chuan Leng, "The Role of Law in the PRC as Reflecting Mao Tse-tung's Influence," *Journal of Criminal Law and Criminology* 68:356–575 (1977).
53. Note, "Concepts of Law in the Chinese Anti-Crime Campaigns," *Harvard Law Reiew* 98:1890 (1985).
54. B. Swartz, "On Attitudes toward Law in China," in M. Katz (ed.), *Government under Law and the Individual* (Washington, D.C.: American Council of Learned Society), 27–9.
55. H. Collins, *Marxism and Law* (Oxford: Clarendon Press, 1982).
56. "Progress in China's Human Rights Cause," in 2003 Information Office of the State Council of the People's Republic of China (March 2004, Beijing), PRC.
57. Qiao Congqi, "Zhongguo zichan jieji de renquan yu fazhi lilun" (A theory of Chinese Capitalist Class Human Rights and Legal System), *Zhongwai faxue* 3: 50–57 (1992).
58. Chen Yunsheng, *Minzhu xianzheng xinchao* (*New Tide in Democratic Constitutional Politics*) (Beijing: Renmin chubanshe, 1988), esp. Chapter 7: "A few issues of theory and practice on strengthening our country's constitutional supervision," 200–289.
59. Stefan T. Possony, "The Maoist Constitution of 1975," in *The. New* Constitution *of Communist China: Comparative Analyses* (Taipei: Institute of International Relations, 1976).
60. Kuan Hsinchi, "Socialist Constitutions in Comparative Perspective," *Chinese Law and Government* XVI (2–3): 2–44 (1983).
61. Peng Zheng, one of the two (besides Dong Biwu) most prominent legalists within the Communist ranks, disagreed with such an analysis.
62. *Selected Works of Mao Tse-Tung* vol. 1 (Beijing: Foreign Languages Press, 1977), 28.
63. Donald J. Munroe, *The Concept of Man in Contemporary China* (Ann Arbor: University of Michigan Press, 1977), 9–13.
64. Ibid., 16–7.
65. Chapter 4: "The Function of Government," 84–196.
66. Ibid.

## Chapter Seven

1. This chapter is adapted from "Policing in PRC – Road to Reform in the 1990s," *British Journal of Criminology* 42:281–236 (2002).
2. Charles Burton, *Political and Social Change in China since 1978* (New York: Greenwood Press, 1990).

3. Tai Ming Cheung, "Guarding China's Domestic Front Line: The People's Armed Police and China's Stability," *The China Quarterly* 146: 525–547 (1996).
4. The rest of this section is transposed with some revisions from "Crime and Policing in China" by Li Xiancui, Associate Research Fellow, Institute of Public Security, Ministry of Public Security, People's Republic of China; and Visiting Scholar, Justice Studies, Queensland University of Technology. Presented at Australian Institute of Criminology, September 7, 1998.
5. Michael Tushman et al., "Convergence and Upheaval: Managing the Unsteady Pace of Organizational Evolution," *California Management Review* (Fall, 1986), reprinted in *The Strategic Process* (New Jersey: Prentice-Hall, 1992), 416.
6. *Zhonghua renmin gongheguo renmin jingcha tiaoli* (PRC People's Police Regulation) (1957).
7. "Shanghai '110' baojing fuwuti" (Shanghai 110 Police Report Service Station), *Renmin Gongan Bao*,July 10, 1993, 1.
8. *Renmin Gongan Bao*, July 15, 1993, 3.
9. "Zhichi he baowei qiye zhuanbian jizhi" (Support and Protect Enterprises in the Change Process) in *Renmin Gongan Bao*, March 6, 1993, 1.
10. "Wei baohu qiye gaige jinli" (Work Hard to Protect Transformation of Enterprise), *Renmin Gongan Bao*, March 18, 1993, 3.
11. "Tielu gongan jiguan biaozhang xue Lei Feng xianjin jiti he ge ren" (The Railway Public Security Organs Cite Groups and Individuals for Being Advanced Study of Lei Feng), *Renmin Gongan Bao*, March 9, 1993, 1.
12. "An Shan zhong jiang huo Lei Feng" (An Shan Heavily Reward "Lei Feng in Real Life."), *Renmin Gongan Bao*, January 21, 1993, 1.
13. "Yinzhou gongan fenju ganjing, renren yongyao 'santaijian' "(Yinzhou Public Security Police, Every One has "Three Big Items"), *Renmin Gongan Bao*, March 23, 1993, 1.
14. "Jilin quanmian qingli ganjing jingshang wenti" (Jilin Comprehensively Deal with Question of Police engagin in Commerce), *Renmin Gongan Bao*, August 7, 1993, 1.
15. "Zhaozhu 'pingheng' de zhidian" (Discover the Point of "Balance"), *Renmin Gongan Bao*, March 9,1993, 2.
16. "Jingcha qu-qi de kulei ren sheng" (The Joy and Bitterness Life of Police's Wives), *Renmin Gongan Bao*, March 9, 1993, 2.
17. "Baijin zhuyi dui dongnan yanhai dequ, bianfang, xiaofang guangbing de sixiang yingxiang buke digu" (The Effect of Money Worship on Fire Officers in the South-eastern Coastal Region and Border Areas Should Not be Underestimated), *Renmin Gongan Bao*, July 29, 1993, 1.
18. "Officials turned entrepreneurs centre of disputes," *China Daily*, January, 27, 1993, 4.
19. Wen Lang Li and Hsin-yi Ou-yang, "Marxian vs. Confucian Effects on Elite Mobility: An Analysis of Turnover in the NPC Standing Committee, 1953–83," *Issues & Studies* 27 (11): 57-78 (1991).
20. *China Daily*, 17 February 1993, 1.

21. "Qiantan xian(shi) gongan jigou cunzai de wenti he gaige yijian" (A Brief Discussion of the Problems Existing in County (city) Public Security Organs and Some Reform Suggestions), *Renmin Gongan Bao*, July 13, 1993, 3.
22. "Renmin jingcha you kunnan zhua shei" (Who Can the Police Turn to When They Have Difficulties), *Renmin Gongan Bao*, July 10, 1993, 2.
23. Lei Jingtian, "Gaizao sifa gongzuo de yijian" (December 18, 1943).
24. James Brady, *Justice and Politics in People's China* (London: Academic Press, 1982), especially chapter 4: "Popular Revolution and the Creation of People's Justice," 55–69.
25. "Ministry of Public Security" in *The Directory of Chinese Government Organs, 1989–1990* (Hong Kong: New China News Ltd., 1990), 48–52.
26. *Zhonghua renmin gongheguo xianfa* (1982) (PRC Constitution, 1982) (Passed by the 5th NPC at the 5th session on December 4, 1982, promulgated by the NPC on December 4, 1982) in *The Constitution of The People's Republic of China* (Beijing: Publishing House of Law, 1986).
27. *Zhonghua renmin gongheguo renmin jingcha tiaoli* (PRC People's Police Regulation) (hereinafter *Police Act*). (Passed at the 76th meeting of the Standing Committee of the NPC on June 25, 1957; promulgated by the Chairman of the PRC, June 25, 1957.)
28. *Zhonghua renmin gongheguo daibu juliu tiaoli.* (Arrest and Detention Act of the People's Republic of China. (Passed by the 6th Meeting of the Standing Committee of the 5th NPC, February 23, 1979. Promulgated by the Standing Committee of the NPC on February 23, 1979.)
29. *Zhonghua renmin gongheguo xingfa* (PRC Criminal Law) and *Zhonghua renmin gongheguo zhian guanli chufa tiaoli* (PRC Public Security Regulations).
30. *Zhonghua renmin gongheguo xingshi susong fa* (PRC Criminal Procedure Code) and *Zhonghua renmin gongheguo xingzheng fuyi tiaoli* (PRC Administrative Hearing Regulations).
31. "Gangan bu zheng jiajin xiuga renmin jingcha fa caoan" (The MPS is Intensifying sffortz to Amend the People's Police Law Draft Proposal.), *Renmin Gongan Bao*, March 27, 1993, 1.
32. "Ministry of Supervision" in *The Directory of Chinese Government Organs (1989–1990)*, 57.
33. "Renmin jingcha zhiye daode guifan" (gao) in *Renmin Gongan Bao*, July 6, 1931.
34. "Zhenggong ganbu de sandai suzhi" (Three Important Qualities of Political Leaders), *Renmin Gongan Bao*, February 23, 1993, 3.
35. "Tao Siju tan shehui zhian he gongan duiwu jianshe" (Tao Siju Discussed about Social Security Situation and Public Security Force Organization) in *Renmin Gongan Bao*, March 27, 1993, 1.
36. "Jiasu gongan gongzuo zhuangui bufa" (Speed Up Public Security Work Transformation Process), *Renmin Gongan Bao*, February 23, 1993, 2.
37. "Jianli fangcha jizhi" (Establish Visit and Inspection System),*Renmin Gongan Bao*, July 24, 1993, 1.

38. "Kai hao 'chuangkou' na meijing" (Open Up the "Window" and Admit the Ceautiful Views), *Renmin Gongan Bao*, February 23, 1993, 2.
39. "Lun 'gongguan qigai' shiye" (A Discussion on "Public Relations Beggars" Unemployed), *Renmin Gongan Bao*, August 21, 1993, 3.
40. "Jingcha guanli kexue yanjiu hui zai jing juxing" (Police Administration Science Held Conference in the Capital), *Renmin Gongan Bao*, March 9, 1993, 1.
41. Ibid.
42. Ibid.
43. "Lishan fenju quanmian shixing jizhi gaige" (Lishan Sub-Station Implement Comprehensive Organization/Process reform),*Renmin Gongan Bao*, March 6, 1993, 2.
44. Long Zhao Heng (Guizhou qiandong nanzhou gonganju), "Gongan gongzuo yu shichang jingji jiegui de ji dian jice" (A Few Strategic Points on Connecting Public Security Work with the Market Economy), *Renmin Gongan Bao*, March 9, 1993, 2.
45. *Renmin Gongan Bao*, March 6, 1993, 2, op. cit., note 43, *supra*. .
46. "Gongan gongzuo ying lunyan zhian xiaoyi" (Public Scurity Work Should Investigate and Discuss about Public Security Utility), *Renmin Gongan Bao,* March 23, 1993, 2.
47. "Guoqu: 'duizhang paihuo' xianzai: 'dadang jifen" (In the past: "team leader flexible assignment," Now: "Partnership Point System."), *Renmin Gongan Bao*, January 2, 1993, 1.
48. "Tuixing beidong peichang zhi" (Implement Burglary Compensation System), *Renmin Gongan Bao*, July 1, 1993, 3.
49. "Shangdong shixing anjian fangfan zeren chajiu zhi" (Shangdong Implemented Criminal Prevention Responsibility Accounting Aystem), *Renmin Gongan Bao*, July 13, 1993, 1
50. "Paichusuo guifanghua jiangshe sikao" (Reflection on Standardization of Police Post), *Renmin Gongan Bao*, August 5, 1993, 1.
51. "Jia, zaodao gongan toushang" (Fakery, on the Head of the Public Security), *Renmin Gongan Bao*, July 20, 1993, 1.
52. "Fujian gongan ganjing, tongyi zhuozhuang bangong" (Fujian Public Security Police Wear Uniform on Duty), *Renmin Gongan Bao*, January 2, 1993, 1.
53. "Jingxianzhi qianghua le jingrong fengji" (Police Ranking System Strengthens Police Appearance, Conduct and Discipline), *Renmin Gongan Bao*, July 8, 1993, 3.
54. "Jingxianzhi cujin duiwu zhenggui hua" (Police Ranking System Advances Troop Regularization), *Renmin Gongan Bao*, July 8, 1993, 3.
55. See interview with Vice-Minister of Public Security in "Jingcha tiaoli yizhousui" (Anniversity of Police Law), *Renmin Gongan Bao*, July 1, 1993, 1 & 2, esp. 2.
56. "Beijing xunjing shang jie" (Beijing Patrol Pfficer in the Street), *Renmin Gongan Bao*, January 2, 1993, 1.
57. Ibid.
58. "Jianli chengshi xunjing tizhi shi gaige de zhongyao tupokou" (Establishing an Urban Police Foot Patrol System is a Breakthrough in Reform), *Renmin Gongan Bao*, July 1, 1993, 1.

59. Ibid.
60. Ibid.
61. "Zhongguo xunjing kaishi qibu" (China's Foot Patrol is Beginning), *Renmin Gongan Bao*, July 1, 1993, 1.
62. "Zouxiang kexuehua zhian guanli" (Move Towards Scientific Public Security Control), *Renmin Gongan Bao*, July 6, 1993, 2.
63. "Kaifeng jianli liangji, sancengci wangluo" (Kaifeng Established Two Levels and Three Layers of Network), i*Renmin Gongan Bao*, July 8, 1993, 1.
64. "Kaichu zhaoshou baojingche" (Kaichu Police Report Vehicle with Waving Arms), *Renmin Gongan Bao*, July 13, 1993, 1.

## Chapter Eight

1. Edward Muir andGuido Ruggiero, *History from Crime* (Baltimore: John Hopkins University Press, 1994).
2. Egon Bittner, *The Functions of Police in Modern Society* (Bethesda, Md.: National Institute of Mental Health, 1970), 36–47; Door Malcolm Gaskill, *Crime and Mentalities in Early Modern England* (Cambridge: Cambridge University Press, 2002).
3. *Hansard*, CCCXXVII, June 19, 1888, cols 605–6.
4. Zhu Qilu and Wang Dawei, "A comparison between Western Community Policing and China Social Security Comprehensive Management" (Sifang shequ jingwu yu zhongguo de shehui zhian zonghe zhili zhi bijiao), *Journal of Chinese Public Security University* (*PSUJ*) 57: 10–14 (1995).
5. David L. Carter, *Reflections on the Move to Community Policing*, Policy Paper, Regional Community Policing Institute at Wichita State University (2000).
6. G.L. Kelling, T. Pate, D. Dieckman and C.E. Brown, *The Kansas City Preventive Patrol Experiment: Tactical Report* (Washington, DC: Police Foundation, 1974).
7. Kansas City, Missouri Police Department. *Response Time Analysis: Executive Summary* (Kansas City, Mo.: Board of Police Commissioners, 1977).
8. W. B. Sanders, *Detective Work: A Study of Criminal Investigations* (New York: The Free Press, 1977).
9. Philip Gutis, "Long Island Interview: Daniel P. Guido; New Head of Police Speaks Out," *New York Times* April 10, 1988.
10. J. Q. Wilson, *Varieties of Police Behaviour* (Cambridge, Mass.: Harvard University Press, 1968).
11. Mark Bevir and Ben Krupicka, "Chapter 6: Police Reform, Governance, and Democracy," in M. O'Neill, M. Marks, /A-M Singh, Anne-Marie (Editors), *Police Occupational Culture* (United Kingdom: Emerald Group Publishing 2007).
12. Robert W. Benson, "Changing Police Culture: The *Sine Qua Non* of Reform," *Loyola of Los Angeles Law Review* 34: 681–690 (2001); P. Waddington, "Dying in a Ditch: The Use of Police Powers in Public Order," *International Journal of the Sociology of Law* 21: 335–53 (1993).

13. David Bjerk, "Racial Profiling, Statistical Discrimination, and the Effect of a Colorblind Policy on the Crime Rate," *Journal of Public Economic Theory* 9 (3):521–545 (2007).
14. George L. Kelling, Anthony Pate, Amy Ferrara, Mary Utne, and Charles E. Brown, "The Newark Foot Patrol Experiment," Research Brief (Washington, D.C.: Police Foundation,1981).
15. Wesley G. Skogan, *Police and Community in Chicago: A Tale of Three Cities* (Oxford, U.K.: Oxford University Press, 2006).
16. Herman Goldstein, *Problem-Oriented Policing* (New York: McGraw-Hill 1990).
17. R. Trojanowicz and B. Bucqueroux, *Community Policing: A Contemporary Perspective* (Cincinnati, Ohio: Anderson Publishing 1990), 5.
18. Trojanowicz et al., *Community Policing: A Survey of Police Departments In The United States* (Lansing, MI: National Center for *Community Policing*, 1994).
19. National Ministry of Safety and Security: Draft policy document on the philosophy of community policing, 1996.
20. Bureau of Justice Assistance, *A Police Guide to Surveying Citizens and Their Environment* (Washington, D.C.: Bureau of Justice Assistance, 1994).
21. National Ministry of Safety and Security, op cit., note 19, *supra*.
22. Ruiqing Luo, *Lun Renmin Gongan Gongzuo* (A Treatise on People's Police Work) (Beijing: Qunzhong chubanshe, 1994), 57.
23. Kam C. Wong, "Black's Theory on the Behavior of Law Revisited II: A Restatement of Black's Concept of Law," *International Journal of the Sociology of Law* 26 (1): 75–119 (1998).
24. Chung-li Chang, *The Chinese Gentry: Studies on Their Role in Nineteenth Century Chinese Society*. (Seattle: University of Washington Press, 1955).
25. See Chapter Three, *supra*.
26. Kang Damin, *Treatise on the Broad Definition of Public Security* ("Guangyi gongan lun") (Beijing: Qunzhong chubanshe 2001), 200–205.
27. James R. Townsend, "Chinese Populism and the Legacy of Mao Tse-tung," *Asian Survey* 17 (11):1003–1015 (1977).
28. Stuart Schram, *The Thought of Mao Tse-Tung* (Cambridge: Cambridge University Press, 1989).
29. Mao Zedong, "Where Do Correct Ideas Come From?" In *Selected Readings from the Works of Mao* Zedong Beijing: Foreign Languages Press, 1967), 406.
30. Mao Zedong, "On Coalition Government" (April 24, 1945), *Selected Works of Mao Zedong* (Beijing: Foreign Languages Press, 1977), vol. 3, 25.
31. Mao Zedong, "Introductory Note to "This Township Went Co-operative in Two Years" (1955).
32. Mao Zedong, "On The Correct Handling of Contradictions among the People," *Selected Works of Mao Zedong* (Beijing: Foreign Languages Press, 1977), vol. 5, 384–421.
33. Donald C. Clarke and James V. Feinerman, "Antagonistic Contradictions: Criminal Law and Human Rights in China," *The China Quarterly* 141: 135–154 (1995).

34. Mao Zedong, "Get Organized!" (November 29, 1943), *Selected Works of* Mao Zedong (Beijing: Foreign Languages Press, 1977), vol. 3, 158.
35. Inscription for a production exhibition sponsored by organizations directly under the Central Committee of the Party and the General Headquarters of the Eighth Route Army, *Liberation Daily* of Yenan, November 24, 1943.
36. Mao Zedong, "A Talk to the Editorial Staff of the *Shansi-Suiyuan Daily*" (April 2, 1948), *Selected Works of Mao Tse-tung* (Beijing: Foreign Languages Press, 1977), vol. 4, 243.
37. Zhu Qilu and Wang Dawei, op. cit., note 4, *supra*.
38. Cyril D. Robinson and Richard Scaglion, "The Origin and Evolution of the Police Function in Society: Notes toward a Theory," *Law & Society* 21(1):109-153(1987).
39. John Austin, *The Province of Jurisprudence Determined*, W. Rumble (ed.), (Cambridge, U.K.: Cambridge University Press, 1995) (first published, 1832).
40. Peter K. Manning, "Organizational Constrains and Semiotics," In M. Punch (edit.), *Control in the Police Organization* (Cambridge, Mass.: MIT Press, 1983), 169–194.
41. Lisa L. Miller, "Rethinking Bureaucrats in the Policy Process: Criminal Justice Agents and the National Crime Agenda," *Policy Studies Journal* 32(4): 569-588 (2004).
42. Laura Nader, *Law in Culture and Society* (Berkeley: University of California Press, 1969), 337–348.
43. James L. Gibbs, "Law and Personality: Signpost for a New Direction." Ibid., 176-207.
44. Richard Madsen, "The Public Sphere, Civil Society and Moral Community: A Research Agenda for Contemporary China Studies," *Modern China*, 19 (2): 183–198 (1993).
45. Elizabeth E. Joh, "The Paradox of Private Policing," *Journal of Criminal Law and Criminology* 95 (1):49–131 (2004).
46. J. Gross, "Introduction to Alternative Dispute Resolution," *Alberta Law Review* 34(1):1–33 (1995).
47. Kam C. Wong, "A Matter of Life and Death: A Very Personal Discourse," *Georgetown Journal of Law and Public Policy* 1 (2): 339–361 (2003).
48. Kam C. Wong, "A Preliminary Assessment of Hong Kong Interception of Communications and Surveillance Ordinance." *Commonwealth Law Bulletin* 34(3): 607-621 (2008).
49. Jeremy Bentham, *An Introduction to the Principles of Morals and Legislation* (1781).
50. Birthe Jorgensen, "Transferring Trouble—The Initiation of Reactive Policing," *Canadian Journal of Criminology* 20: 257–279, 276 (1980).
51. Daniel Klerman, "Settlement and the Decline of Private Prosecution in Thirteenth-Century England," Independent Institute Working Paper #19, January 2000.
52. "The self-policing society," in 19–24 Charles Leadbeater, *The Self-policing Society* (London: Demos, 1995); Neal Katyal, "Community Self-help," *J. L. Econ. & Pol'y* 1: 33-67(2005).
53. Donald Black, *The Social Structure of Right and Wrong*, rev. ed. (San Diego: Academic Press, 1968).

54. Elaine Cumming, Ian Cumming, and Laura Edell, "Policeman as Philosopher, Guide and Friend," *Social Problems* 12 (3): 276–286 (1965).
55. Herman Goldstein, op. cit., note 16, *supra*.
56. PPSRT is being put into practice in two communities in Cincinnati, Ohio, that of Bond Hill and North Avondale since September 2007. The initiative is called CDCC (Community Driven Crime Control).
57. I am indebted to Professor Goldstein for reading and commenting on an earlier version of this paper.
58. Herman Goldstein, "The New Policing," *Research in Brief* (Washington, D.C.: Department of Justice, Dec. 1993).
59. *The Functions of Police in Modern Society* (National Institute of Mental Health, 1970), 36–47. Reprinted in Richard J. Lundman, *Police Behavior* (New York: Oxford University Press, 1980), 28–41, 38.
60. Ibid., 41.
61. David Matza, *Delinquent and Drift* (New York: John Wiley & Son, 1964), 111–126.
62. "Guan Zhong" (Chinese: 管仲, Wade-Giles: Kuan Chung) (born 725 B.C., died in 645 B.C.) was a politician in the Spring and Autumn Period.
63. "Guan Zi. Mumin" (管子. 牧民) is a chapter on herding ("mu") the people ("min").
64. Mark Findlay, *Alternative Policing Styles* (Boston: Kluwer Law and Taxation Publishers, 1993), 6.
65. Charles Reith, *The Blind Eye of History* (Montclair, N.J.: Patterson Smith, 1952), 177–252.
66. Brian Chapman, *Police State* (London: Macmillan, 1970).
67. ` John Austin, *The Province of Jurisprudence Determined*, W. Rumble (ed.), (Cambridge, U.K.: Cambridge University Press, 1995) (first published, 1832).
68. Colin Sumner, "Censure, Crime, and State," in Mike Maguire, Rod Morgan, and Robert Reiner, *The Oxford Handbook of Criminology*, 2d ed. (London: Oxford University Press, 1997), 4499–4510.
69. Karl Marx, *A Contribution to the Critique of Political Economy* (Moscow: Progress Publishers, 1977) (first published, 1859)..
70. Peter Manning, *Police Contingencies* (Chicago: University of Chicago, 2003), ix.
71. Arthur I. Waskow, "Community Control of the Police," *Transaction*, 7 (December 1969), 4.
72. Todd R. Clear and David R. Karp, "The Community Justice Movement," in David R. Karp (ed.), *Community Justice* (Lanham: Rowman & Littlefield Publishers, 1998), 3–31.
73. Ibid.
74. Sir Henry Sumner Maine, *Popular Government* (Indianapolis, Ind.: Liberty Class, 1976) (First published 1885), 34.
75. Brian Chapman, op. cit., note 66, *supra*, 55.
76. Andrew W. Lintott, *Violence in Republican Rome* (Oxford: Clarendon Press,1968).

77. Donald Black, "The Social Organization of Arrest," *Stanford Law Review*, 23:1104–1110 (1972).
78. V.A.C. Gatrell, *The Hanging Tree: Execution and the English People 1770–1987* (New York: Oxford University Press, 1994), 29–30.
79. Carolyn Hoyle and Andrew Sanders, "Police Response to Domestic Violence: From Victim Choice to Victim Empowerment," *The British Journal of Criminology* 40(1): 14–36 (2000), esp., "The Decision to Call the Police," 22–23.
80. F.A. Hayek, *The Road to Serfdom* (London: Routledge & Kegan Paul, 1944), 26.
81. Peter Manning, "The Police: Mandate, Strategies, and Appearances," in Manning and J. van Maneen (eds.), *Policing: A View from the Street* (Santa Monica, Calif.: Goodyear, 1978), 7–38.
82. T. Flanagan, "Consumer Perspectives on Police Organizational Strategy," *Journal of Police Science and Administration* 13:10–21 (1985).
83. F.K. von Savigny, *Of the Vocation of Our Age for Legislation and Jurisprudence* (1831), transl. by A. Hayward (New York: Arno Press, 1975).
84. H. Ley-Bruhl, *Sociolgie du droit,* 6th ed. (Paris: Presses Universitaires de france, 1961). As cited in Roger Cotterrell, *The Sociology of Law*, 2d ed. (Butterworth, 1922).
85. L.W. Doo, "Dispute Settlement in Chinese-American Communities," *American Journal of Comparative Law* 21:627–663 (1973).
86. Robert Ardrey, *Social Contract* (New York: Athebeum, 1970), 11.
87. Ibid.
88. W.G. Sumner, *Folkways* (N.Y.: New American Library, 1960), 17–18.
89. Robert Ardrey, *The Social Contract* (NewYork: Atheneum, 1970), Chapter 3 "Order and Disorder."
90. Clive Grace and Philip Wilkinson, *Negotiating the Law: Social Work and Legal Services* (London and Boston: Routledge & Kegan Paul, 1975), 30.
91. Richard D. Alexander, *The Biology of Moral Systems* (N.Y.: Aldine de Gruyter, 1987).
92. F.E. McDermott (ed.), *Self-Determination in Social Work* (London and Boston: Routledge & Kegan Paul, 1975).
93. Clive Emsley, *The English Police: A Political and Social History*, 2d ed. (London and New York, 1991), 80–81.
94. Ibid.
95. Mao Zedong, "On Coalition Government" (April 24, 1945). *Selected Works of Mao Tse-tung* (Beijing: Foreign Languages Press, 1977), vol. 3, 257.
96. Sun Yean, "Shehui zhian de zhengzhi bixu da renmin zanzheng" (The Reorganization of Public Security Must be Through the Waging of a People's War), *Gongan Lilun yu Shijian* (Theory and Practice of Public Security) 6 (3):1–4 (1997).
97. "Baozheng zhengfan yundong jiangkang fazhan" (Guaranteeing the Healthy Progression of Movement to Suppress Counterrevolutionaries) (May 10, 1951, Third National Public Security Meeting, May 10 to 15, 1951, Beijing), *Lun Renmin Gongan Gongzuo*, 75–85.

98. "Gongu, jiaqiang he tigao renmin gongan gongzuo" (Consolidate, Improve Upon, and Strengthen Public Security Work) (May 28, 1953 at the Central Public Security College), *Lun Renmin Gongan Gongzuo*, 180–193.
99. Ibid.
100. Rob Gurwit, "Communitarianism: You Can Try It at Home," *Governing*: 6 33-39 (August 1933).
101. *Selected Works of Mao Tse-Tung* vol. 1 (Beijing: Foreign Languages Press, 1977), 28.
102. James Q. Wilson, *Varieties of Police Behavior* (Cambridge, Mass.: Harvard, 1968), 287.
103. "Guanyu yunnan zhengfen yu tugai qingkung de kaocha baogao" (Inspection Report Concerning Conditions of Suppression of Counter-revolutionaries and Law Reform Circumstances in Yuannan) (March 18, 1951), *Lun Renmin Gongan Gongzuo*, 57.
104. Malcolm K. Sparrow, "Information Systems and the Development of Policing" U.S. Department of Justice, National Institute of Justice, Perspectives on Policing (Washington, D.C.: March 1993), 4.
105. "Gonganjun bixu miche lianxi renmin qunzhong" (Military Police Force Must Work Closely With the People-Mass) (November 11, 1956), *Lun Renmin Gongan Gongzuo*, 317–322.
106. "Renmin jingcha shi renmin de qinwuyuan" (People's Police Is the People's Servant) (Dec. 12–14, 1957), *Lun Renmin Gongan Gongzuo*, 347–352.
107. In November 2007 I visited with some Chinese People's Public Security graduate students at their dorm. They frankly admitted to me that they have little knowledge of, and still less interest in, studying Mao.

# INDEX

Jeffrey Ian Ross, *General Editor*

This book series is a forum for cutting-edge work that pushes the boundaries of the disciplines of criminology and criminal justice, with the aim of exploring eclectic, un- and under-explored issues, and imaginative approaches in terms of theory and methods. Although primarily designed for criminology and criminal justice audiences—including scholars, instructors, and students—books in the series function across disciplines, appealing to those with an interest in anthropology, cultural studies, sociology, political science, and law.

Books in the series include:

*Hawking Hits on the Information Highway,* by Laura Finley
*Blood, Power and Bedlam: State Crimes and Crimes Against Humanity in Post-Colonial Africa,* by Christopher W. Mullins and Dawn L. Rothe
*Chinese Policing: History and Reform,* by Kam C. Wong
*Arrest Decisions: What Works for the Officer?* by Edith Linn
*Drug Court Justice: Experiences in a Juvenile Drug Court,* by Kevin Whiteacre

Authors who would like to submit a proposal for a volume in the series, or a completed book manuscript please direct all inquiries to:

Chris Myers, Peter Lang Publishing, 29 Broadway, New York, NY, 10006
ChrisM@plang.com

To order other books in this series, please contact our Customer Service Department:

800-770-LANG (within the U.S.)
212-647-7706 (outside the U.S.)
212-647-7707 FAX

Or browse online by series at:
www.peterlang.com